SIBYL'S MOUTHS

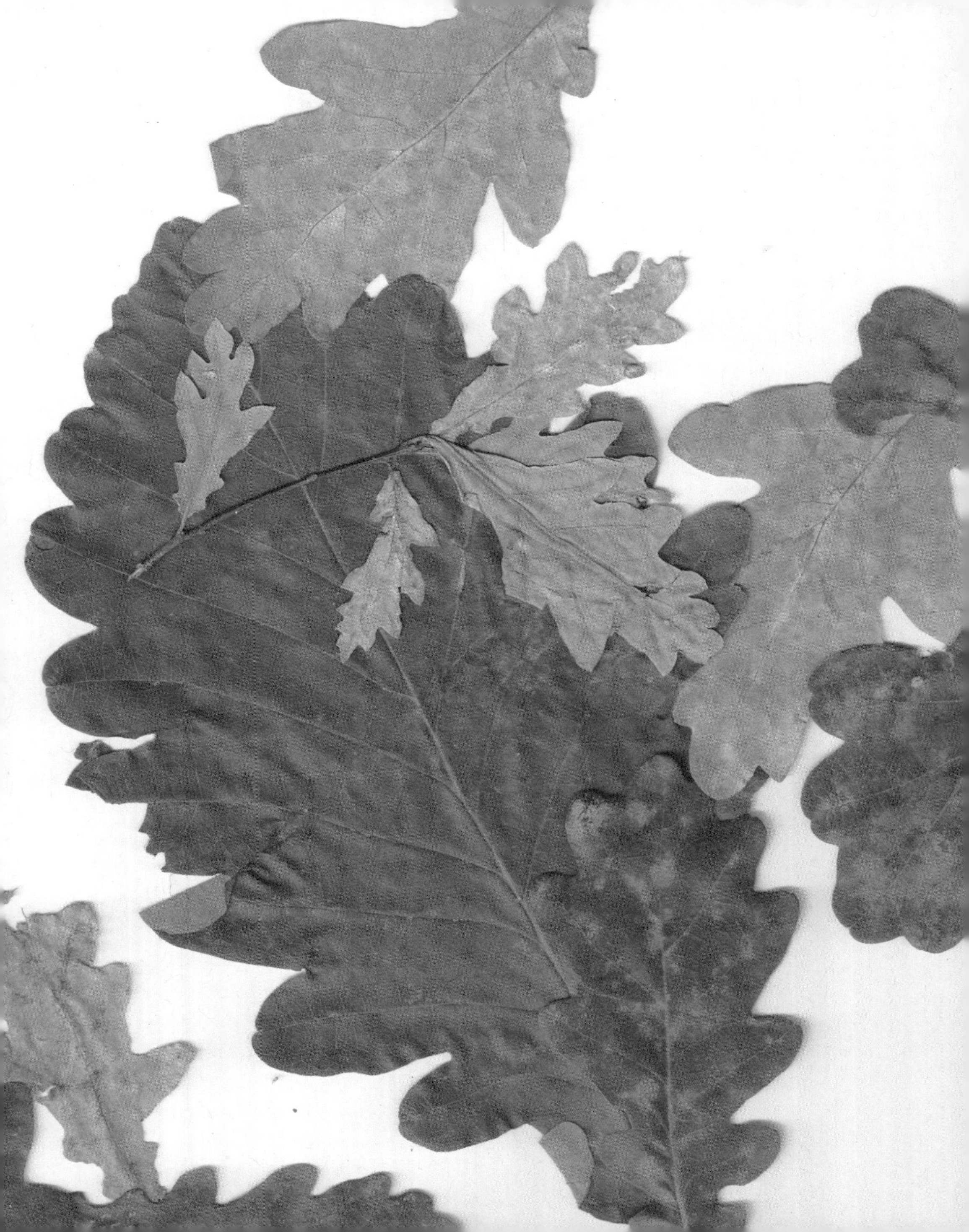

SIBYL'S MOUTHS

A PURE FICTION PUBLICATION

Sternberg Press

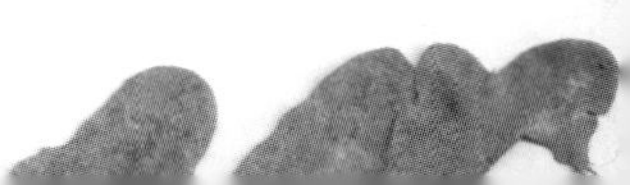

Thro' the hill's hollow sides: before the place,
A hundred doors a hundred entries grace;
As many voices issue, and the sound
Of Sybil's words as many times rebound.
Now to the mouth they come. Aloud she cries:*

*The Aeneid book XI, Virgil
translated by John Dryden

O:RIFICES

PLAGUERISM

DIGESTERBATION

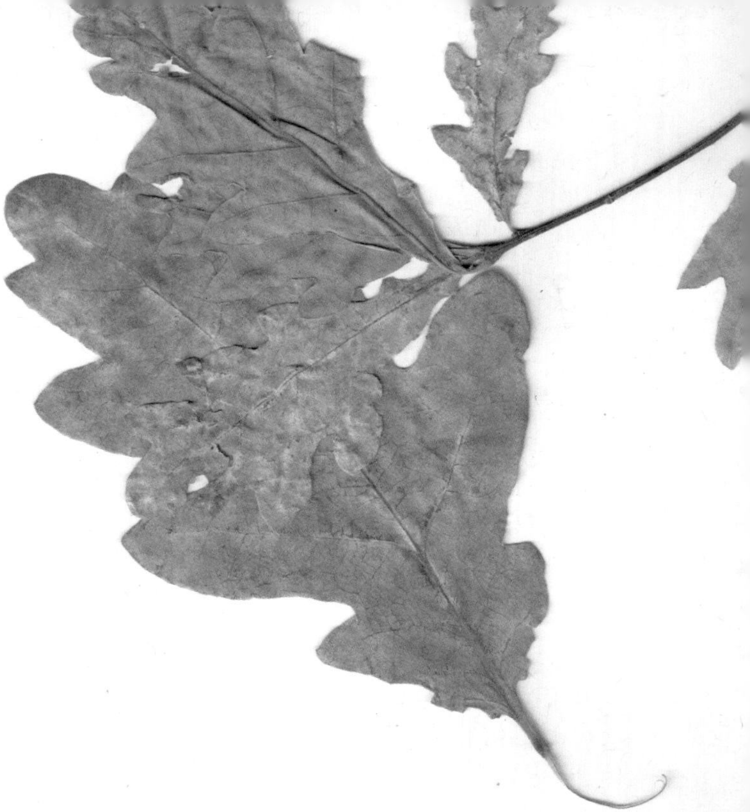

O°orifices

GOD TALKS NOW; GOD TALKS THROUGH THIS GIRL

Amelia Groom

God talks now
God talks now
God talks through this girl
God talks now
God says: "salaries to artists"
God says: "cash to artists"
God talks now
This girl is dead now
God talks now
God says: "money, money"
God talks now
God says: "this girl's hands are clean"
God talks through this girl
God talks now
God says: "salaries to artists; no cash no artists, no cash no gallery, no cash no cu-ra-tor"
God talks now
God talks now
God … talks now
God says: "gold, cash, gold, carats, money, money, money …"

These words come from a scene at the very end of *Conscious Knocks Unconscious* (1977), a 24-minute video work by the ventriloquist and performance artist Julia Heyward (aka Duka Delight).[1] After the video's final credits have rolled, there's this extra scene which begins with a shot of the artist asleep in bed. When a shaft of light arrives on her face, the image cuts to a close-up, and a voice announces, "God talks now, God talks now, God talks through this girl ...." While the words of "God" are spoken through the body of this girl in her bed, her eyes are closed, her lips are parted, and her hand lies open by her head, palm facing upwards like a satellite dish receiving information. Her mouth doesn't seem to move at all, except for when she says one word, the word "*money.*" Whenever the word "*money*" comes up, it animates the girl; her eyes open, her head turns, and her lips move in articulation, showing us that this girl is a highly skilled ventriloquist, who can speak without seeming to speak—and that the seemingly disembodied words that we have been hearing have been coming from her body all along.

What excites me in this scene is the ambiguity around who is ventriloquizing whom. This dead/sleeping girl appears as a mouthpiece for God; her body is emptied out as a passive vessel that receives and transmits the authoritative word from above. But then it turns out that this girl is also putting her words into the mouth of God, making Him into her mouthpiece to transmit a very clear demand: *Salaries to artists! Cash to artists!* God talks now, and His assumed authority is a means for amplifying and legitimizing the needs of this girl—this artist girl who presents herself to us in a state of supine non-consciousness.

The knotty interplay of agency and self-negation in this scene resonates with a certain tradition of female Christian mystics from medieval Europe. At a time when women were excluded from all realms of public speech, some spoke by being spoken *through* with the voice of God. In her reading of Mechthild of Magdeburg's text *The Flowing Light of Divinity,* for example, the feminist theologian and

1 An exhibition of Julia Heyward's work at CCA Wattis Institute in 2015 was named after this video. The exhibition credited *Conscious Knocks Unconscious* dated 1979, that date has been frequently reproduced in the subsequent press, but 1977 is the date that appears in the credits at the end of the version of the video that I have seen (which is the one that is available from EAI Electronic Arts Intermix).

medievalist Amy Hollywood looks at the extent to which the thirteenth-century German mystic turned the Christian ideal of feminized humility into a paradoxical source of authority.[2] In claiming full humility—as a passive, receptive, weak, malleable woman—Mechthild positions her body as a privileged site of divine agency on earth. Hollywood observes that throughout Mechthild's writing, her lowly status is used to justify her lofty role as the physical conduit of the voice of God; when Mechthild asks God why he chose an unlearned woman like herself to speak His word, He tells her: "I sought ever the lowest, smallest, most secret place. The highest mountains on earth cannot receive the revelations of my grace, for the flood of my Holy Spirit flows naturally to the valley."[3]

It is only by appearing to empty out her subjective will that Mechthild can claim to receive the will of God. But Hollywood also points to moments in which the mystic seems to use the authority that she has acquired through her visionary experiences, as a means to critique the church with a directness and a legitimacy that would otherwise be inaccessible to her. As a mouthpiece for God (or, using "God" as her mouthpiece), Mechthild puts forward "suggestions surrounding the sacraments and ecclesial life," and tells her readers about "the false virtues that most plague the church."[4] Hollywood observes here that some of the passages containing practical injunctions in *The Flowing Light of Divinity* do not clearly indicate who the speaker is, "pointing to the pervasive and empowering ambiguity between the divine and human voices in the text."[5]

This ambiguity about the origin of the voice is what Heyward stages so hilariously in her ventriloquial *God Talks Now* performance. The version of *God Talks Now* that I've described here appears at the end of the artist's *Conscious Knocks Unconscious* video, but she has incorporated many other iterations of it into various works over the years. In *God Heads*, a live ventriloquial performance in 1976, Heyward's thrown voice announced: "God talks now ... No dollars for

2 Amy Hollywood, *The Soul as Virgin Wife: Mechthild of Magdeburg, Marguerite Porete, and Meister Eckhart* (Notre Dame: University of Notre Dame Press, 2000).

3 Hollywood, *The Soul as Virgin Wife*, 84.

4 Ibid, 83.

5 Ibid.

artists ... No art shows ...."[6] Twenty years later, she opened her live multimedia performance *Miracles in Reverse* (1996) with a brief *God Talks Now* segment.[7] When some of her work was exhibited at the Whitney in 2013, she did an impromptu presentation of *God Talks Now* as part of a video profile for the museum's YouTube channel.[8] A *God Talks Now* performance is also featured in Heyward's video *This is My Blue Period* (1978), which retroactively documents a live performance that the artist had done at New York's Artists Space in 1977 (the same year as *Conscious Knocks Unconscious*).[9]

In *This is My Blue Period*, there's a segment called "Modern Mary Talks Now: A Working Girl." Heyward tells us that Mary works in a restaurant now: "She still handles food, it's fast money, she doesn't have to work in her garden." The artist then embodies this Modern Mary as an exhausted restaurant worker serving tables, with part of a table attached to the front of her body as a permanent fixture. "I just work here—how would you like your meat?" Modern Mary says. "I just work here—what would you like on your salad? / I just work here—a girl's gotta eat / I just work here—Mary had a little lamb / I just work here—hurrah for Mary ...." The video then cuts to a close-up of Heyward's face, and she performs a ventriloquial *God Talks Now* segment. "God talks now," she says, throwing her voice without moving her mouth. "God talks through this ordinary working girl / God talks now / God says: 'this girl is dead, this girl is asleep now' / God says: 'Wake up! Rise and shine!' / We need conscious workers, so why don't you just rise and shine / Don't hate work, work is good ...."

---

6 Jack Castle, "Rituals of Rented Island," *Aesthetica*, https://aestheticamagazine.com/rituals-of-rented-island/.

7 An audio recording of this performance can be found on Roulette's website: https://roulette.org/event/julia-heyward-7/.

8 "Rituals of Rented Island: Julia Heyward" video published November 5, 2013 by the Whitney Museum of American Art: https://youtu.be/IEEMPgCd4ek.

9 *This is My Blue Period* is currently credited with the date 1977 at EAI Electronic Arts Intermix, but since the video opens with the statement "this is a documentation of a performance by Julia Heyward, performed in 1977, documented in 1978," I am using the date 1978.

Before moving to New York in 1973 to participate in the Whitney Independent Study Program, Heyward had grown up as the daughter of a Presbyterian minister in North Carolina. Biblical themes and the gender politics of ecclesiastical authority are obviously recurring concerns in her performances. What I'm interested in is the frequency with which these motifs in her work are shot through with a critique of the contemporary ideology of work. When the disembodied, omnipotent voice of God arrives, the holy command is that everybody wakes up and loves their fate because "work is good."

The segment before the *God Talks Now* ending for *Conscious Knocks Unconscious* features a montage sequence of images of beds made with striped sheets, as the voice of the artist shouts—to the accompaniment of a beating drum—"Wake up! We need conscious workers! Wake up! Rise and shine! Wake up! Hello! Wake up! Hello! We need conscious workers so why don't you just rise and shine!" Because the voice seems to come from nowhere in particular, it comes from everywhere; its demands permeate the bedroom, marking the encroachment of the ideology of work even into our unconscious dream-states. Through Heyward's ventriloquism, the voice of God is the voice of American capitalism ripping people out of their beds and forcing them into a state of obligatory waking consciousness and sleep-deprived availability.

Throughout the *God Talks Now* performance at the very end of *Conscious Knocks Unconscious*, Heyward lies in bed with her eyes closed. Following the aggressive injunction to "Wake up!! Rise and shine!!!" in the previous segment, the bed in this scene can be read as a site of refusal. But while Yoko Ono and John Lennon's *Bed-ins for Peace* (1969) had the celebrity artists consciously articulate their explicit anti-war messaging, Heyward's bed performance eight years later has the artist working with sleepy and dreamy states of unstable subjectivity and hypnotic susceptibility. She doesn't *speak back* to the voice of power; she has it *speak through* her, as the ostensibly passive object of the "powerless" "sleeping" "girl." And, as with female mystics like Mechthild of Magdeburg, a subversive authority is then found in the assurance that what speaks through the girl is not her own agency, but that of the divine.

As a strategy of critique, this practice of speaking while being spoken through is not about unveiling and exposing structures of power with a direct address from an authentic subject position. Rather, it's about restructuring things from within the position of subordination, by working with indirect and inauthentic modes of address. God talks through this girl, this girl is asleep, this girl is dead, this girl ... is a power bottom! She lies back, eyes closed, mouth open, and in her state of apparently surrendered agency, she tells her God what to say. And while the location of agency is deliberately confused, the message is crystal clear: "salaries to artists," "cash to artists," "money, money, salaries to artists, no cash no artists ...."

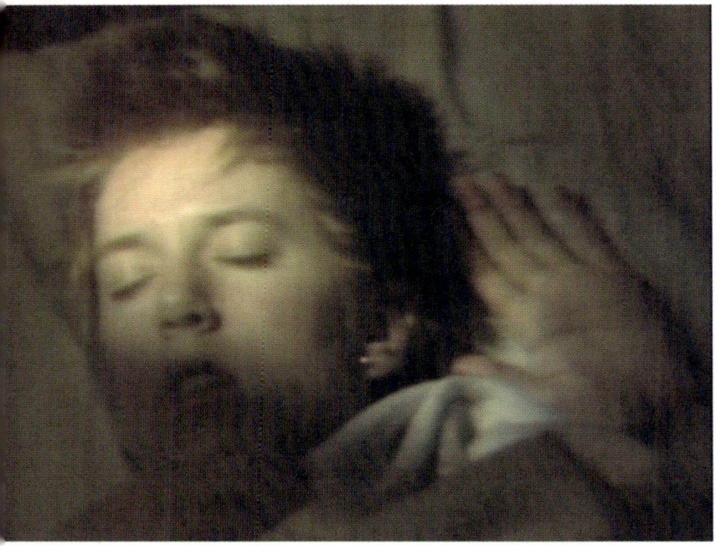

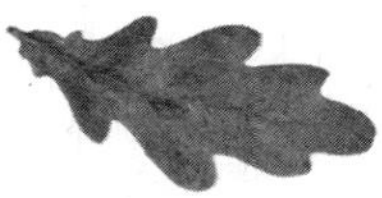

A NOTE ABOUT THE PRONOUNS

Elif Saydam

The Turkish language has only one singular pronoun: O; 'he', 'she' and 'it' are all the same; O: a sound left hanging too long on tensed lips; O: a puckered ring suspended in air as an accusation or invitation, where the ass sits bare and the breeze hits cool, and that is all. And that is everything. Contrary to popular belief, O is not an ouroboros, not infinite, no multitudes here; O is a punkt, a period, the end of the sentence, or, that is, at least until a new sentence spreads its cheeks; and on a good day, O presents punctuation for the speaker to: stretch, prolapse, contain, deadname. "O did what? O is what I meant ... I wanted O!" But O is present there, hovering like a halo. It's rude to refer to someone in third person when they are in the room, so forget gender: maybe your problems lie elsewhere! Examine others, your friends, lovers, brothers. Do they tense their lips? Where are they? Where was I? Oh! O is a weapon in the arsenal of avoidance to be gripped tightly on the family vacation, holster-ready. O is liberation through omission and the glorious dysphoria this omission brings, where bravery and cowardice roll themselves into one passive origin story. Now that's very protestant. So then O is mystery in a press release, evasive and thereby spiritual. Where else can O regulate and self-represent this mystery? On the flat plain of an identity card? Oh no, nowhere, because O is not a place. And besides, O hates the state. O is an embodied noun. But a blessed candlestick or a dancing scallop, a noun's not much, until it's used, until it's touched, until it's held and chewed and put back down again. O for objectification is not the worst thing. There comes the freedom to dig into the sand, for a second, like an ostrich hiding brains, genitals, pearls, or whatever currency is demanded. On that overcrowded ocean floor. On that secluded beach. On that playground in the after-hours. Freedom, that deserted island, never lasts long. That precious gap. That sweetest just dessert. Until someone opens their mouths.

VOICE OF THE WIND IS NOT A METAPHOR

IMAGINING CONVERSATIONS WITH HALIM EL-DABH AND ADRIANA CAVARERO

Kamila & Jasmina Metwaly

صوت المرأة عورة

The Voice of a woman is nakedness? (English version of Quranic translation)
The female Voice is a form of nakedness (English version of Quranic translation)
The Voice of a woman is an enticement to sin
The Voice of a woman is sinful nakedness

Kamila: It starts with *voice.* One that sounds, transmits and transforms, one that is heard, one that speaks, sings, imitates, acts and performs, one that screams, one that is reason or the Law, one that is Godly, one that becomes politics, and one that is political. But *voice* is mine because it sounds like me. I know that your *voice* is yours because it sounds like you.

Jasmina: What is a common *voice*? Is it what carries the multiple voices within us towards a public? Or is it the other way around? We are sisters, and our voices sound alike.

K: Voices are very complex creatures. They belong to us but they are also common goods. I am interested in the many singular voices that vocalize in the same time and place, our relationship to hearing more than one voice at the time, and the stories they carry through their multimodality, collectivity, and soundings.

J: What can a voice tell? I imagine a process which gathers voices that come together as an ensemble of women in a choir. We could consider the construction of a choir as a theater of voices.

K: I think that we should set up a series of exercises through which we question our own relationship towards the process of forming such an ensemble. We should also provoke ourselves to understand our relationship to the participants of that choir, to test our own roles within that specific group of women who carry strong voices, which we do too. I would also like to explore the question of professionalism, and the idea of a "professional choir." I like the notion of an amateur actor, and human and nonhuman sounds that carry unstaged stories, acute to their own processes, and the complexities of no-one.

J: Ideally, we would construct the theatrical elements that constitute a performance together *with*, and *as* an ensemble. When thinking of a gathering of many voices—of becoming a collective, of living and being together with other women, rehearsing, acting, practicing, letting go, failing, being vulnerable and dependent on one another—we are also thinking about the relationship between the work of Adriana Cavarero and Halim El-Dabh, who both consider *voice* a unique bodily signifier and communicator.

K: The Egyptian composer Halim El-Dabh was fascinated with what a human voice can do, and what it summoned within the different communities in which he lived. In 1944, he recorded one of the earliest known pieces of electronic music, *Ta'abir Al-Zaar* [The Expression of Zaar]. It was based on a recording of the melodramatic and haunting voices of the women of the Zaar[1] in Cairo, for who *voice* was an integral part to healing rituals. I have been thinking a lot about Halim's stories of the

1 One of Egypt's oldest dances, the Zaar, performed for the sole purpose of healing, is practiced by various African communities in Egypt, the Sudan, and Ethiopia where it originated. Dating as far back as the ancient times, the Zaar has undergone some minor changes due to the various cultural influences that came through Egypt. Ritual and rhythm remain common aspects of Zaar dances, wherever they are practiced.

women of the Zaar, the healing powers of cats, and how he connected electricity to the body itself ... That you could use the human *voice* to transform vibrations, to change the electric voltage, and create electricity with people's voices, like creating electrical particles in the air. Remembering *Ta'abir Al-Zaar* in an interview, he said, "I wanted to find the inner sound, that vibration that's always necessary for transcendence. I eliminated the fundamental tones of the harmony by changing the voltage—it changes the quality of the music, it seeks another quality in the voice, the hidden material, the inner part of the voice. That's what the whole idea of electronic music is. You have a recording and you go inside the recording to find the hidden meaning."[2]

J: In *Ta'abir Al-Zaar*, the voices are all womens', and it was all about chanting. I remember wanting to find this inner sound, a vibration necessary for transcendence. Halim evokes the ancestral tradition closely linked to our background, to traditions that over time have been increasingly erased, that have become nostalgia. Not only does he make us aware that *voice* belongs to a unique body but that it emanates from nostalgia itself—a yearning towards the collective. He reminds us that our bodies are organs of reciprocity, that we receive but also give. We care and we heal, and we are multisensorial just like other creatures. I can hardly relate to that kind of care and healing anymore. When we met in the protests in 2011 in Egypt, when we chanted and screamed—for a moment—we felt that our voices were significant, heard, and unique.

I am thinking about the philosopher and feminist theorist Adriana Cavarero who struggles in a different environment, that of the male-dominated sphere of Western philosophy. She looks back at the history of *voice* as semantics, and the process of erasing sound from *voice—sout/el sout*, صوت الصوت, the bodily from the vocalic—and the problems it creates in terms of the appropriation of women's voices, and the unique expressions that are lost in the transcriptions from the oral and aural into the logos.

2 https://www.madamasr.com/en/2013/12/15/feature/culture/music-permeates-everything/.

K: Maybe if we shift our attention from listening to *voice* as such, we could realize that each human and nonhuman voice is a unique identifier of discrepancy and singularity. We could direct our attention to those who do not have access to so-called "proper speech" but whose voices are often appropriated by those in positions of power.

J: Sure, but Cavarero also says that, "predisposed to the perception of sound in general, the human ear is, above all, tuned to this vocal emission that reveals singular bodies to one another. In contrast to speech, the voice puts hearing in play even before listening. [...] The Voice in general, and the Voice of the song in particular, arouses the emotional sphere at the expense of the logical sphere. This explains why divas and other lyric singers are unmistakably linked to Sirens. In the soprano, and in operatic song in general, the Voice not only reaches the heights of its expressive power but dominates the word, rendering the word secondary even as it transmits it."[3]

Imagine sitting at a table with Adriana Cavarero and Halim El-Dabh. Would they talk about the uniqueness of both human and nonhuman voices? Or would they shift the conversation to the social and political dimension of *voice*?

K: I think they would talk about food, and engage with the multi sensoriality of what we humans know in terms of sensitivity, feeling, listening, and vulnerability. I doubt either would need to make a philosophical point to enjoy the other's company.

J: We should start the sessions with listening, and inquire into modes which untrain the ear from the way it has been taught to listen to a voice. How to scream? How to feel comfortable with the pitch range of our vocal cords, and how to find space to transform *voice*, physically and politically, into a tool of liberation?

---

3 Adriana Cavarero, and Matt Langione, "The Vocal Body: Extract from *A Philosophical Encyclopedia of the Body*," *Qui Parle: Critical Humanities and Social Sciences* 21, no. 1 (2012): 71, 77.

K: Less speech making or speech mastering. Let's look at the organs of respiration first, a constellation that allows us to breathe. Let's exercise together:

Put your hand on your chest, above your heart,

you should feel very relaxed.

Inhale

te-e-e-e re-e-e-e-e-e

just have fun articulating with that weird crackling sound.

Okay, can you hear me because my internet is unstable, okay, because I can't hear you very well?

You can develop it into a scream without hurting without having pain. You're not angry. You sound like a monster, but it's fun.

(Uuuuh) and I have the feeling of opening my space inside. Can you open your mouth? More?

If you do this in a microphone-- that sounds wild.

It is enjoyable.

Play with the sounds I can move my mouth, I can move my tongue. Can you?

I can do all these sounds separately
aaaaahh---ooohooe, buuuuuffrrrr

voiceless sounds

Exhale.

PRACTICE

Georgia Sagri

If I don't commit to representation what is it that I am visualizing as an artist? Am I then a non-visual visual artist?

"Stage of Recovery" is the size of an average small stage. It is 250 centimeters by 250 centimeters in size, and 65 centimeters high. Four large, thick pillows are placed on top, attached to the base, stable, covered with cotton fabric. It can hold the activities of one participant and sometimes myself, and it is only used during the one-to-one sessions. During the sessions the participant is on stage, mostly alone, they are exposing themselves, their condition, on the stage, as they are so used to doing in daily life, with one small difference: here they are working on the condition that made them feel pain. I am around the stage, and I can see what is going on, how the movements are progressing. Sometimes I will ask the participant to repeat a technique, to continue, to take time and to rest. The soft stage is there to remind them that there can be a place that can be soft and easy, a place where, instead of performing a social role, they can release the tension created by that same role that they have constructed for themselves to perform in their daily life. Instead of creating even more difficulty than they have already, the process helps them navigate the ways of releasing the difficulties. The structure is made out of wood, it is installed in a room, it is warm, but sometimes I need a blanket; especially during the breathing techniques, I have noticed that the participant's circulation is altered and that they feel colder than usual.

What in the past started as my need to prepare and to recover from physically and mentally demanding performance pieces, has gradually become a research into the physiological and pathological conditions of the body in the hyper-capitalist era which dooms us to autoimmune illnesses, stress, discomfort, asthma, insomnia, panic attacks, anxiety, fatigue, nausea, food disorders, mania, paranoia, arthritis, depression, addiction, to name a few. Over the years I recognized that some of my own techniques (breathing, movement, voice) could help others to build their own routine of self-recovery. If in the past this practice was a way to build technique within the medium of performance, now it is a shared practice that is open-ended.

Through "Dynamis," my contribution to documenta 14, I was able to share my routine within the limitations of an exhibition format, it was blocked in a fixed time of presentation, execution, and production, and this made me feel constantly defensive. I felt that I was betraying my entire practice for the sake of one artwork and one exhibition. It was difficult to find a way out when I was pressed to contextualize ten years of developing personal techniques into a solid artwork. Those same reasons made me abandon working with a group, there was no time for me to work with the particularities and conditions that each participant was bringing in the work. There was no space to focus, observe and learn from the steps of seeing my personal technique evolve in the bodies of others. There were requirements and limitations in order for the presentation to take place, which didn't allow for anyone to be aware of what their bodies were able to give in the group and in the work, and I was extremely sad that I wasn't able to do what I desired most, which was to help the participants physiologically through my practice.

Some bodies, which means some voices, are under shock and there is a need to form steps for recovery. There is no such thing as recuperation and a healthy, normal state. There is a stage that allows the person to recognize, explore, and learn from their physical condition, illness, and pain. How and in which way an organism becomes well is not really definite. In Greek the word *ίαση*, in English "iasi," means recovery, it is the time it takes for a body to recuperate from illness back to what it was before with the information that has been acquired by that illness. By altering the tuning of the voice, the body starts to vibrate differently, and some of the organs in pain can be touched. Through training I follow and support each participant to tune their voice differently and to realize another interiority of their body. By that tuning they can become stronger and physically better. The diaphragm is not really an organ but a muscle, it lies between the upper and the lower part of the body and establishes the balance of the interior and exterior of the spine. It sets the balance and it distributes the air, thus it tunes the voice throughout the whole body. Every breath is a tone to the interior and exterior of life. While taking care of the breath the voice starts to sound as it is formed, and the whole world starts to vibrate differently. We can just breathe and we are there, we don't need to make declarations and statements, we can also just be there; so many people forget that breathing in a place is enough. Everything else becomes an extraction from someone else's breath.

The treatment evolves according to what the participant reveals on stage, there is not so much talking but breathing, movement, and voice. The techniques came about from 2009 until today while preparing (recovering) for demanding performance works. They evolved mostly through observing people in different places. I started by following and memorizing the walks of friends: their movements could tell me how they were, how they felt. If I felt their walking alter, I would ask how they felt, what was going on, and then I would take this information and work on it, day by day. I observed how it translated to my body. I tried observing people in offices, different workers, women in the 1950s presenting cars on rotating platforms, their smiling faces; how they behave is how their bodies are formed through their work, consistently repeating the same routine. I realized that I had to prepare and decompress out of my observation exactly as I hoped their bodies, the workers' bodies, would escape from this physiological manipulation. I find in all of these activities that there is no voice, only executions, bodily executions, there is no time for an articulation of passions: there is no laughing, no crying, all of that happens in a break with self-control. I was observing the builders while real estate was blooming in Williamsburg, I recorded the sound of the subway workers, the hipsters waiting for the train—their postures were similar to the workers during the break—everything was mixed up, collapsing in a huge hyper-capitalist bubble of bodies without voice, only postures, posing, doing everything online, texting, but not speaking. I started to record and mimic their sounds and giggles, and through this I started working on voice techniques and on training my diaphragm as an interior muscle. I never liked to go to the gym, all the techniques happened in bed, on the carpets of different houses, in whatever places I was crashing. None of the techniques are supposed to happen in a particular environment but in one where there is some comfort and time to observe and focus on your body and how you feel.

In 2011, when the Occupy Wall Street movement happened, the voice became a tool and a threat; the public assembly was our power and turned into a criminal act. The oppression and isolation I experienced in the years after brought me to confront the fact that, to know that, the voice is where I needed to focus the most. How we come together on the softness of the stage can recover the pathologies of the social stage we are put into, to play out perfectly-made roles without escape, and with no cure, except that of medication and meditation designed, at least, to maintain our efficiency as workers.

For each case I write protocols based on expression, manifestation, then treatment and recovery. Expression is what the participant tells me they feel, the manifestation is what I see happening and what they describe as the cause of their pain and discomfort. The manifestation, which is mostly revealed during the participant's time on the "Stage of Recovery," will tell us what is happening in general to the participant's body and how they are presently taking care of it. The way they take care of it will tell us how I need to navigate the treatment with them. It is always in the last phase of the sessions that I combine breathing, movement, and voice, which becomes the practice of recovery.

The mechanism of paid sick leave is activated only when pathologies, stresses, panic attacks, autoimmune disorders, and so on are turned into medically prescribed conditions and are medicated. I try to resist this mechanization of the body (sick or healthy) and to create a space and time, that they already have, for each participant to find ways to take care of themselves. Through navigating the pathologies that, until this point, seemed insignificant to them, they can recover and continue and prepare for a moment when the body will need to be strong.

How do I write all of this with such conviction? My only imperative as an artist, which is transmitted through my actions, is that no one should lose faith in their own momentum, their power, their personal capabilities, as artists we are already aware that no value can be attributed to them, since nature and existence cannot be classified into wage labor, profit, and money. I take my experience as an artist, who for many years has worked through performance in demanding bodily and mental states, into a knowledge that is shared, with the hope of helping others to create techniques of self-determination and recovery, "IASI."

Each session is between thirty and forty minutes long. It starts with a greeting, a small conversation with the participant. How do they feel, what's been happening recently, do they feel pain and if so where? Then they take off their shoes and they go on stage.

“IASI”

Case

Expression

They are worried about their back pain and difficulty sleeping. There is pressure to achieve success. There is anxiety about how to make that possible. Anxiety about the future, finding the right job. There is constant pressure to fit into the category of the best student, the best employee, but at the same time they feel miserable because they don’t do what they really want.

Manifestation

A sense of comfort comes through self-punishment; with tension in the stomach and through the repetitive action of either refusing to eat or eating excessively and then vomiting. They never describe the food disorder to me as an action. When we have the conversation about what brought them to “IASI,” I notice I am trying to imagine how this action might be, and how it feels for them to keep this action and its pleasure a secret. The left side is squeezed in, there is damage there that causes pain to the lower back. I advise the participant to go for an X-ray. There is dysmorphia in the posture. Returning from the X-ray, they tell me that they have cracked ribs and the doctor prescribed them painkillers. I advise them to practice. They need to take care of their breathing in order to create space from within. There is refusal to accept that the body is stronger than the mind. The mind will not survive you. The mind is holding them back from accepting that their body will always try to survive, more than the mind is able even to imagine.

Treatment

The voice comes out with force, but only from the throat. The throat is dry. Treatment slowly takes place. Becoming aware of their posture through the hold in each of the exercises, they maintain ever more pressure to the diaphragm and allow space to be created from within. They start to feel pain. They start to feel the pain of the cracked ribs. Dysmorphia comes from the repetitive act of vomiting. The sensation of pressure in vomiting and the pleasure that it creates is addictive, because it is an anxiety release. Hopefully through the treatment they will allow the air, the expansion of the diaphragm, to soothe the organs which are now burning. But only if the participant allows the body to be with its complete capacity, firstly full of air. Only then will the body get motivated to want to exist, to need to survive, therefore to ask for nutrition and to incorporate eating as a daily, pleasurable activity. The treatment is split into two parts:

1. Tricking the mind into physical activities that build no judgement: very slow progression from easy exercises that strengthen the diaphragm to more physical breathing techniques such as 6-3-6 (6 is standing, inhaling, 3 is falling back with a longer expansion of the diaphragm, 6 is coming back to standing and exhaling) or 7-1-7 (kneeling on the stage, spine straight, and using the voice in the exhale).
2. Spending the entire session resting, calming down, and taking the time to do nothing. Setting up an environment of rest for the participant with unconditional time and space for self-love.

Recovery

The participant says they are busy and they cannot complete the treatment.

Case

Expression

The participant wanted to work on their voice. They felt self-aware, shy, and irritated about it.

Manifestation

Small body, scoliosis and compressed spine, arms turned in, palms inflexible, chest larger proportionally than the head, and the legs and arms are weak. A lot of pain inside and outside. There are signals that their pain comes from overthinking the pain they have experienced since childhood. They have experienced abuse and violence because of how they look, they arrive with overconfidence towards me. They tell me about how they need to change their voice, I say I would like to help, and ask if their back is in pain and they say it is always in pain but they are used to it.

Treatment

To bring the air and call the breathing is something that we need to feel we deserve. If the participant uses overconfidence to defend their being, then breathing is part of this defense and it comes in with too much opening of the chest, which pushes the front forwards, eliminating the back. I tell them that to be is not something that they need to defend, because already their organism, in its core as nature, will try to survive them no matter what, no matter if they think of it or not. We need to call for air not as a mechanical function but as a hint to appreciate that this soma that we are is able to maintain us, sustain us, live us without our needing to think of it and turning it into a tool.

After the second session, I design a step that would allow the participant to reach the stage and then fold to the side, to fall slowly on their right side and slowly stretch their body on the stage. This step also helps in the exercise of the voice and breathing, where I push my back against the back of the participant and allow both of our spines to adjust with one another and train together. With this method, 5-1-5 and 7-1-7 breathing techniques allow me to listen to the spine and how it vibrates with their voice, to understand its flexibility sensorially and to build trust with the participant, making it possible for both of us to describe better what we feel is going on during the sessions. The step helps the participant to have balance and press evenly through their feet, so I can raise their hands and help them understand their entire presence, which can no longer be defined by their height. We are starting to talk about what is unique. I am trying to say that how every person is, is a unique case. I point to the trees outside and describe *how* even though we might think that the word "tree" could define all the trees in this part of the park, if we pay attention we will start to notice their differences; they have different branches, the shape of their leaves is completely different. If we pay even more attention we will notice that even those trees that look the same, that come from the same species, are very much unique, they exist uniquely in comparison to the others and are also different in and of themselves. I try to explain that this is not only about how we understand ourselves physically, like a flat image; if this understanding comes through the judgements of others or through the mirror stage, it splits how we feel from who we are. The "other" is really ourselves, we need to think of the body as the only chance to realize, through sensations, pain, and passions, that the other is in us. This notion could allow the possibility to search for who we are from within as others. Outside-is-inside means that we shift the way we work on pathological sensations. "Symptom" for "IASI" is not a *lack of*, we observe "symptom" as a set of skills, of what the body is capable of. "Symptom" *as plus* enables a step into revelations, appreciations, admirations, and a realization of life, of who we are, of our nature, which is not total, not one, not straight.

Recovery

In one of the sessions they tell me that they feel calmer when they do the breathing techniques in the morning. They face the world with good air already inside them, then the world opens up to them. They are able to breathe from the nose and exhale from the mouth and not feel suffocated any longer by only using their mouth to breathe. Their acting teacher told them that she noticed their voice is slightly clearer. They wait, they hold the diaphragm as we did during the sessions, they inhale to call for the air and then they exhale. The diaphragm is somehow more present and touches their spine, and they are in the world with relaxed shoulders, which they say is an improvement.

Raumgeräusche

Leise, dumpfe
Mikrophongeräusche

Entfernt ist eine vortragende
Stimme zu hören, es geht u.A. um
Barrierefreiheit: „Im deutschen
Wort Barrierefreiheit steckt
schon die Barriere und die
Freiheit gleichzeitig drin, und da
muss man sich natürlich fragen,
wessen Freiheit ist da eigentlich
gemeint, also wessen Freiheit ist die
Norm?“

Schritte durch den Raum
kommen gleichbleibend näher

Stimmen

Mikrophon-Feedback, es brummt
ein wenig am Ohr

Eine Computerstimme spricht
unverständlich

Ein Stuhl rollt, eine Türe
quietscht

Die Stimme wird wieder
deutlicher, es geht um
Jahresthemen, das Haus,
Steuergelder

Wechsel nach Draußen, fahrende
Autos

Knacken

Schnitt

Zurück zur Stimme im Raum

Man hört, dass sich viele Personen
in dem Gebäude befinden

Eine Stimme spricht deutlich
durch ein Walkie-Talkie:

„Hallo Hallo“

„Hallo Hallo“

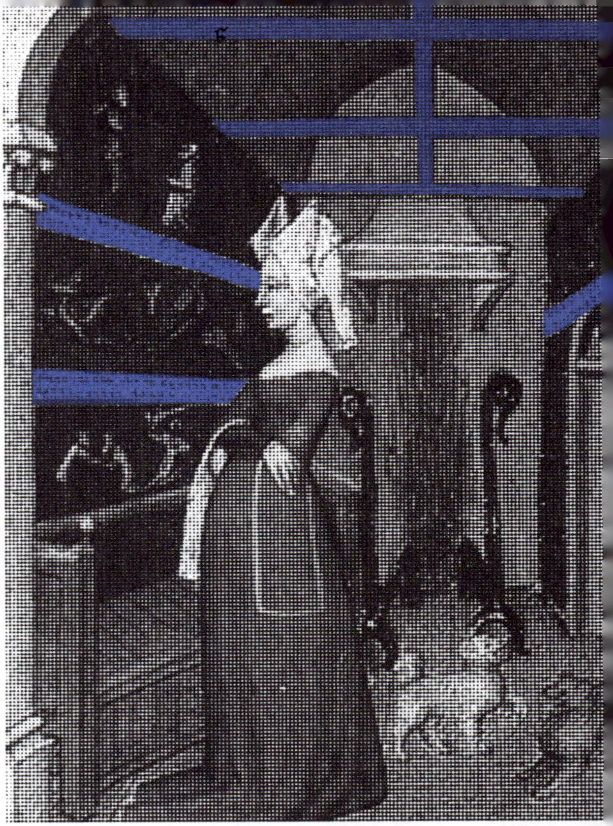

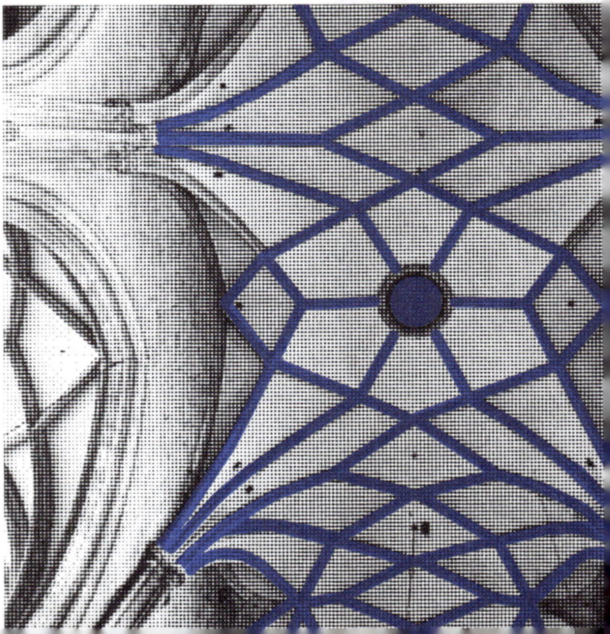

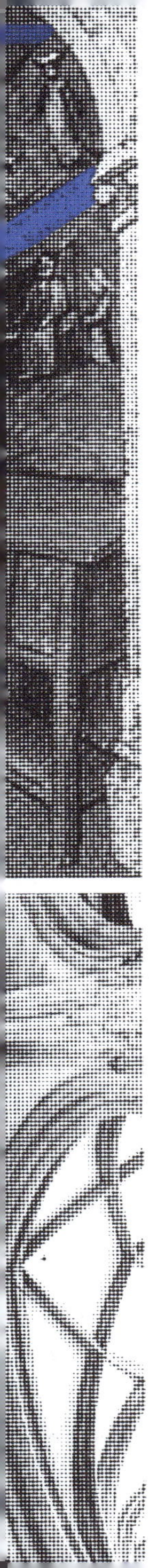

The Corridor speaks

as a carrier of stories

with doors passing me by,

conduits for both bodies and information,

delivered by a courier,

someone who could run fast.

Physical transit mechanisms

that seem to blend into so many other spaces.

A medial space par excellence

with mirrors as metaphors for hierarchies.

Can blue solve the problem?

In the Middle Ages, for example, blue was a warm color.

At the time when Hildegard von Bingen invented her Lingua Ignota,

a thousand unknown words to increase solidarity among her nuns.

There was no "I" in her invention

and no word for "word."

In this sense architecture may be context,

but it is also text –

it reveals, structures and formalizes relationships.

Institutional Matterings

Topological journeys

Cross-identifications

of interiors and interiority

How to speak the Corridor

Es scheint kein Außen zu geben,

verschlungene Pfade der immer schon verteilten Macht.

Techniken des Erscheinens und Verschwindens.

Die Macht ist ihrer Zentralität beraubt und auf so unscheinbare Lokalitäten wie Schwellen mit Türhütern, Tapetentüren, oder versteckte Korridore verteilt.

Das war eine Visualisierung dessen, was wir vorhatten, nämlich dieses Haus zu öffnen.

Lady Reason responded and said, "Get up, daughter! Without waiting any longer, let us go to the Field of Letters."

There the City of Ladies will be founded on a flat and fertile plain, where all fruits and freshwater rivers are located and where the earth abounds in all good things.

Christine de Pizans Stadt der Frauen (um 1400) ist die Geschichte von der Errichtung einer idealen Stadt.

Ein imaginärer Raum mit den realen architektonischen Merkmalen einer mittelalterlichen Stadt.

Ein befestigter Zufluchtsort für Frauen, errichtet aus Geschichten und Porträts außergewöhnlicher Vertreterinnen des weiblichen Geschlechts aus allen Epochen.

Im Mittelalter differenziert sich die Lehre von den Gedächtnisorten aus,

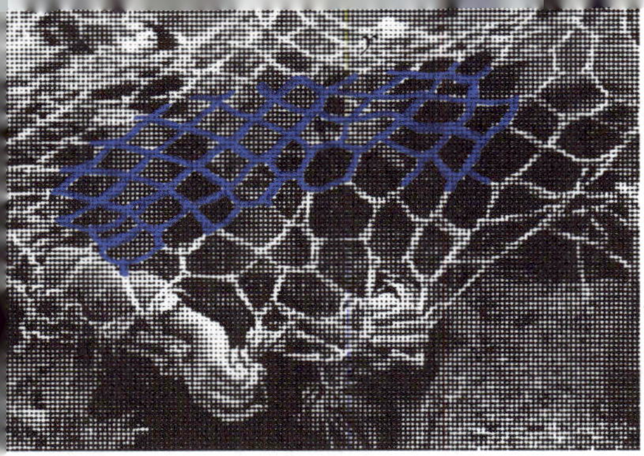

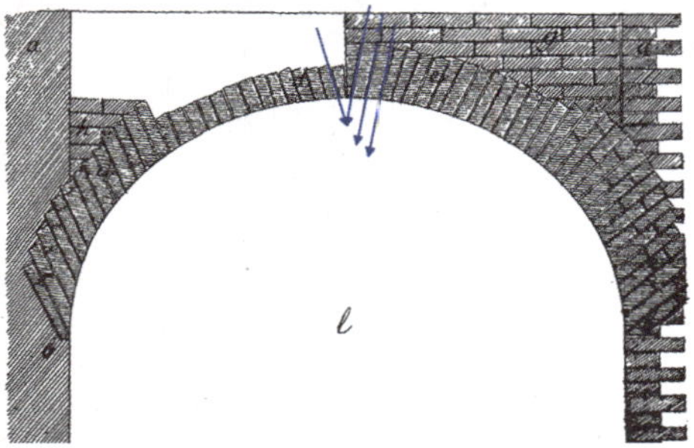

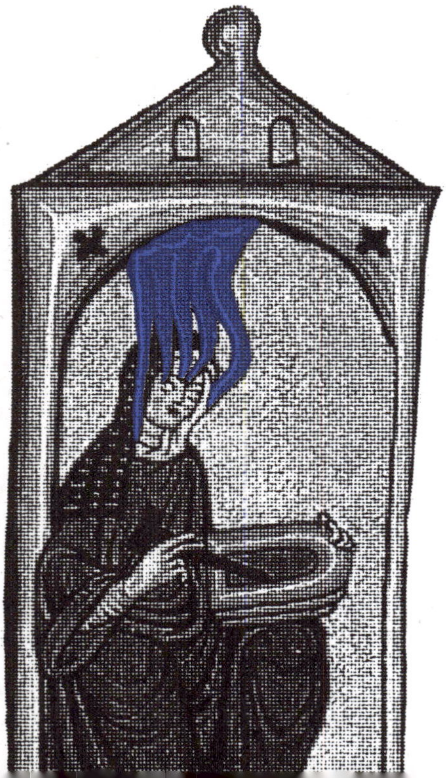

Wie kann ich den Korridor zum Sprechen bringen?

Welche Sprachen spricht der Korridor?

Ein Kommen und Gehen durch die Zeiten.

Der Korridor in der Kunsthalle Osnabrück war früher der Kreuzgang eines Dominikanerklosters.

Im Kreuzgang sind Mönche und Nonnen im Kreis gelaufen und haben gebetet.

Alles ist immer in Bewegung im Kreuzgang und auch im Korridor.

Manila trifft Anne und Monika trifft Christel.

Flurfunk

Flurfunker:innen

unter der Decke verlaufen die Kabel.

Bewegung. übertragung.

Es scheint kein Außen zu geben.

verschlungene Pfade

Techniken des Erscheinens und Verschwindens.

Das war was wir vor hatten, nämlich dieses Haus zu öffnen.

„Steh auf Tochter" sagte die Frau der Vernunft, „wir warten nicht länger, sondern gehen sofort los auf das große Feld des Schreibens.

Dort gibt es nur schöne Dinge wie Früchte und frisches Wasser und dort bauen wir die Stadt

through bureaucratic activities,

within bureaucratic
architectures.

She also invented a “Geheimschrift”
and wrote on a wax tablet.

Fonts created for foreign
characters

Her letter “o” looks like a heart
shape or an elaborate squiggle,

her “b” looks like a running
figure.

Walk together in the cloister,

Christel says: as slow as possible.

Coming from the street into the
cloister,

then into the courtyard and back
into the cloister again

and out behind the glass pane onto
Neue Straße.

Threading and unthreading

Laying cables

Since the electronic light and the
telephone were invented

people have been fixing cables
under the ceiling.

usually under
a suspended ceiling.

Architectures for sparks,

fast as light

Glosso-poeia

Glosso-poetics

Glosso-graphia

glōssa: tongue, language

a remarkable propensity for
structures that convey and
connect.

Physical transit mechanisms that also
operate as communication systems,

conduits or corridors for both
bodies and information,

that seem to blend into so many
other spaces.

A medial space par excellence.

Den äußerlichsten, nur
ganz peripheren Aspekt der
Zweideutigkeit der Passagen gibt
ihr Reichtum an Spiegeln, der die
Räume märchenhaft ausweitet
und die Orientierung erschwert.

You see me holding this shiny
mirror which

I carry in my right hand in place
of a scepter,

thanks to this mirror, the essences,
qualities, proportions, and
measures of all things are known,
nor can anything be done well
without it.

A medial space par excellence, the
Field of Letters.

It has been called a “Geheimsprache,”
accompanied by its “Geheimschrift,”

one of the earliest known
constructed languages.

Hildegard von Bingen produces
over a thousand unknown words
to increase solidarity among
her nuns.

Her illuminations, the crenellations
of her architectural images,
her frequent references to
shimmering optical effects,

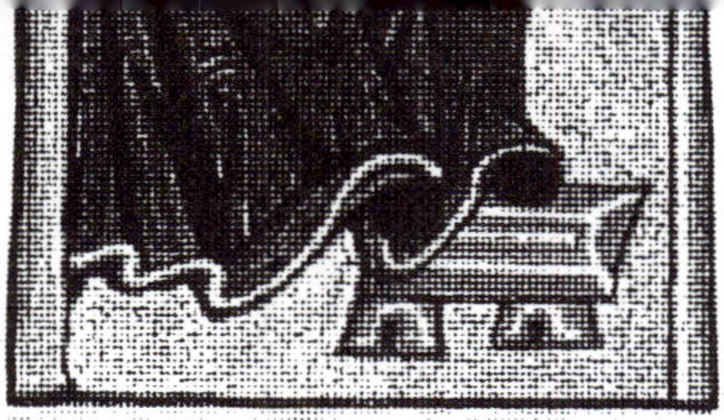

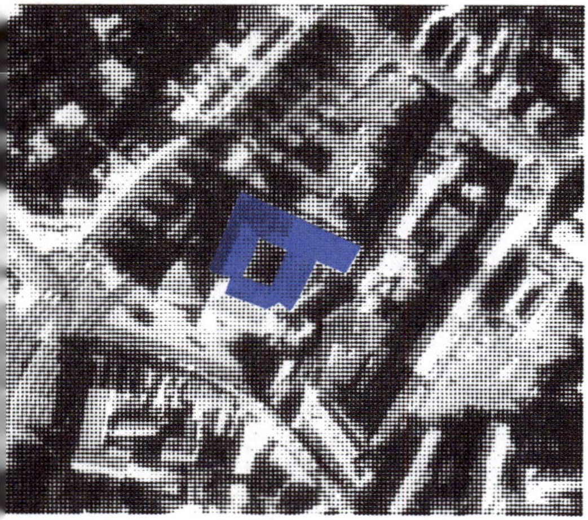

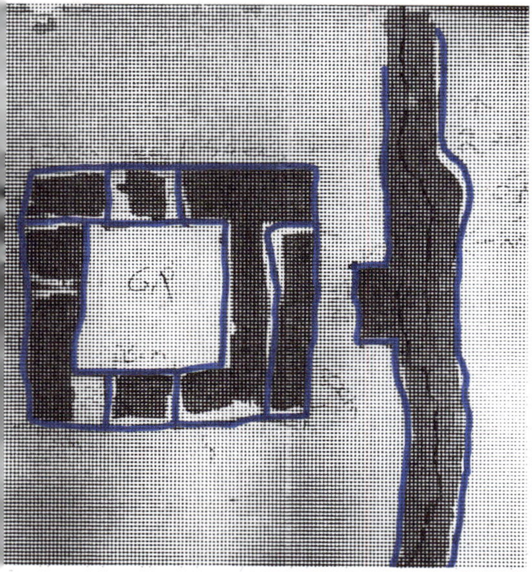

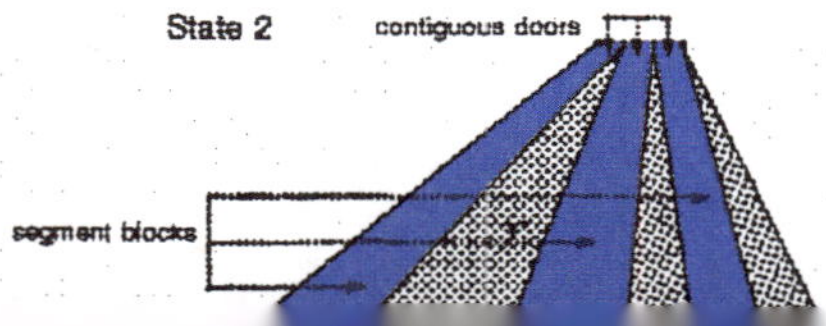

der Frauen"!

Christine de Pizan schrieb um 1400 das Buch der „Stadt der Frauen"

Eine ideale Stadt von Frauen für Frauen,

gebaut aus vielen Geschichten über Frauen.

Verschlungene Pfade,

ein Kommen und Gehen durch die Zeiten.

Das erste Dominikanerkloster war ein Dominikanerinnenkloster, im Jahr 1206 in Südfrankreich.

In Deutschland gab es 70 Jahre später schon 40 Dominikanerinnenklöster.

Christine de Pizan starb in einem Dominikanerinnenkloster.

Viele Nonnen haben mystische Texte verfasst

wie Hildegard von Bingen

Lingua Ignota

heißt ihre „Geheimsprache",

sie hat über 1000 Wörter erfunden

und eine eigene „Geheimschrift":

Der Buchstabe O sieht aus wie ein Herz

der Buchstabe B sieht aus wie eine laufende Person

Im Kreuzgang laufen,

gemeinsam gehen,

Christel sagt: So langsam wie möglich.

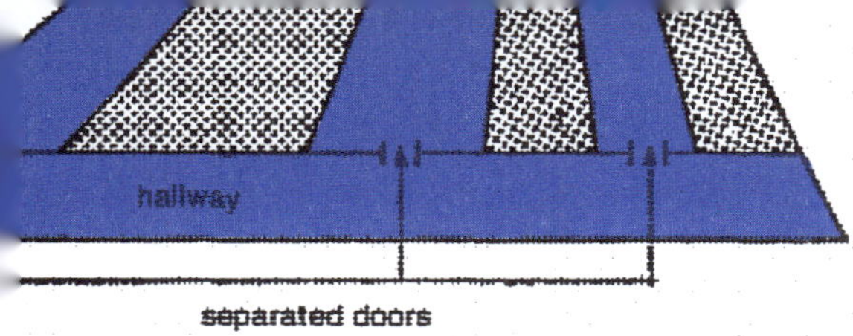

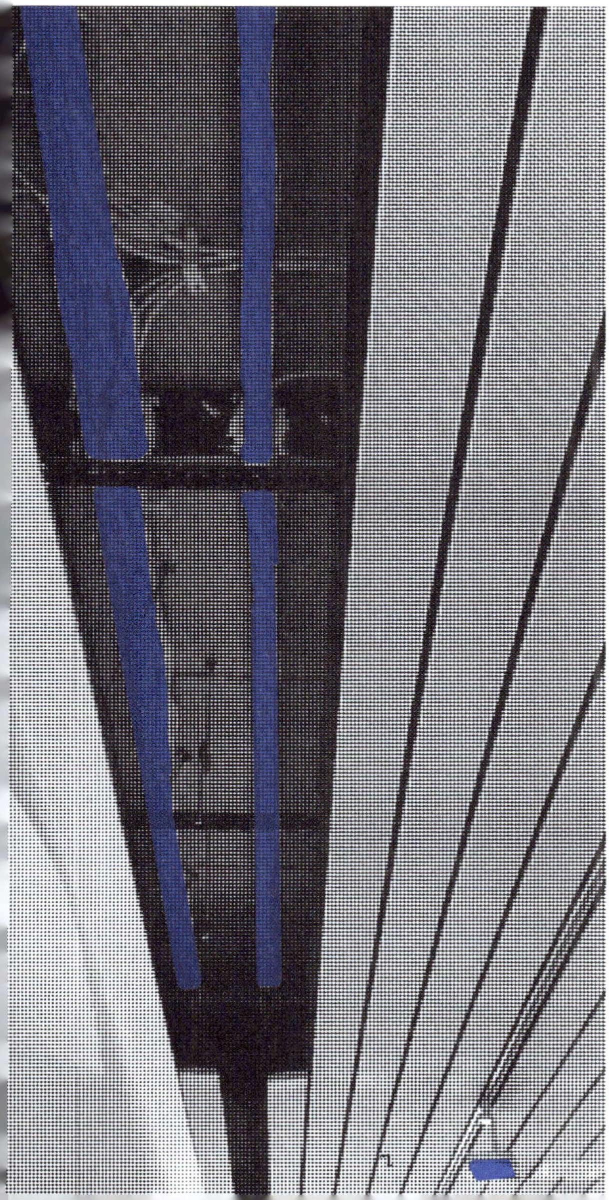

her symbol for "a" in r vaguely resembles lowercase gamma,

whereas it looks like a modified "r" in V,

her "n" could be a version of lowercase phi,

B looks more like a running figure,

"o" is represented quite differently as a heart shape or an elaborate squiggle.

Her letters are most likely her own invention.

Haec muher est diviihtas

Hildegard's unknown letters

Ich konnte mir nicht erklären wo dieser Schein herkommt, ob da jemand aus dem Bauamt herunterleuchtet?

The questions and the answers vary over the centuries,

im Kreuzgang wurden Wände abgebaut und dadurch wurde diese Glasscheibe freigelegt.

Glosso-poeia

Glosso-poetics

Glosso-graphia

glōssa – Zunge, Sprache

lalein – reden, schwatzen, sprechen

Nine times they cut out his tongue and

nine times it was regenerated.

But now – how Angels speak it is hid from us.

Jaws, palate, lips, teeth, throat,

„Hallo, hören Sie mich?"

Brummen

Die vortragende Stimme erwähnt sensuelle Impulse und die neue Einzelausstellung in der Kirche mit Candice Lin

Walkie-Talkie:

„...durch den Flur"

Schritte aus verschiedenen Richtungen, schnellere Schritte überlagern langsamere Schritte, unterschiedliche Sohlen und Absätze

Ein Telefongespräch blendet sich ein:

„Hallo, jetzt warst Du grade weg"

„Oh, ok, hörst Du mich jetzt?"

„Ah ja, ja, es war irgendwie gestört"

Unterbrochene Satzfragmente

im Hintergrund Stimmengemurmel

„Ja, hörst Du mich?"

Störungsgeräusche

„Ja ich..."

Schritte, Mikrophon-Feedbacks

Schritte, Kopierergeräusche, Gebläse

Klopfen

Stimme auf Lautsprecher im Hintergrund:

„Hi, ich wollte mich nochmal melden wegen der Bilder und Dateien, die ihr für die Grafikerinnen braucht..."

Beim Gehen kann sich niemand verstecken.

Von der Straße kommend in den Kreuzgang,

dann in den Innenhof und wieder in den Kreuzgang zurück

und hinter der Glasscheibe auf die Neue Straße hinaus.

Einfädeln und Ausfädeln

Kabel verlegen

Seit das elektronische Licht und das Telefon erfunden wurden

hat man Kabel unter der Decke befestigt.

Meist unter einer angehängten Decke.

Architekturen für Funken,

schnell wie Licht

Das Wort Korridor kommt von Kurier und das bedeutet:

Jemand läuft sehr schnell um eine wichtige Botschaft zu überbringen.

Wir arbeiten daran, der Flurfunk findet wieder statt.

Wir wollen Diskriminierung verlernen und über Freiheit nachdenken.

Freiheit für wen und wann?

Alle sollen kommen können.

Dafür habt ihr ja dann auch den Korridor.

Der Korridor als eine feministische Architektur?

Leitungen, Sprache,

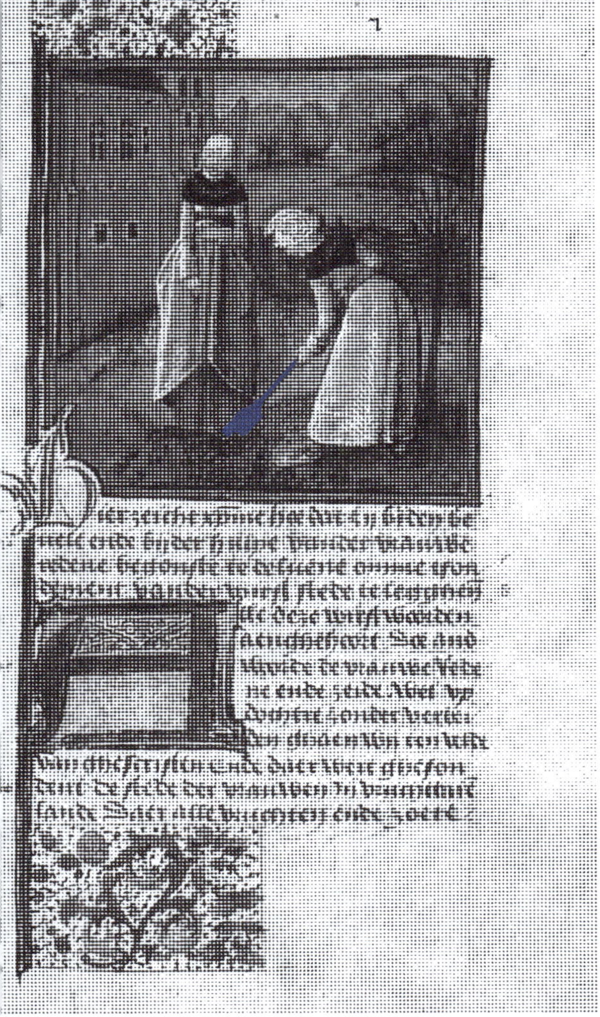

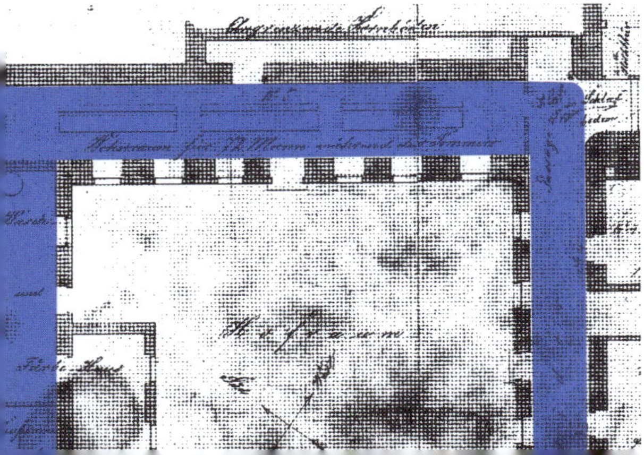

lungs, the aspera arteria,
muscles of the breast.

If you speak at a distance to
another, you must use
a louder voice;

but if nearer, one whispers in
an ear:

and if one could be coupled to the
hearer, a softer breath would
suffice;

for one would slide into the hearer
without any noise,

as an image in the eye, or glass.

So lange ich hier in der Kunsthalle
tätig bin gab es Überlegungen, den
Innenhof zu überdachen,

wir wollten ein Glasdach, aber das
war schwierig zu verwirklichen,
das Bauamt war dagegen.

Den Neubau gabs ja nicht,
der Innenhof war nach hinten offen,

da wurden Pferde
untergebracht, es gab eine
Färberei und eine Wäscherei
und bis 1990 gab es dort
einen Brunnen.

Ich stelle mir das ein bisschen wie
einen Zeitraffer vor,

diese ganzen Bewegungen an
diesem Ort – angefangen von den
Dominikanermönchen, über
Napoleon –

bei Napoleon wurden hier
britische Soldaten untergebracht,

dann war es ein Kornspeicher, ein
Lazarett, dann ein Wohnhaus,

ein Lagerort für Theater-
requisiten,

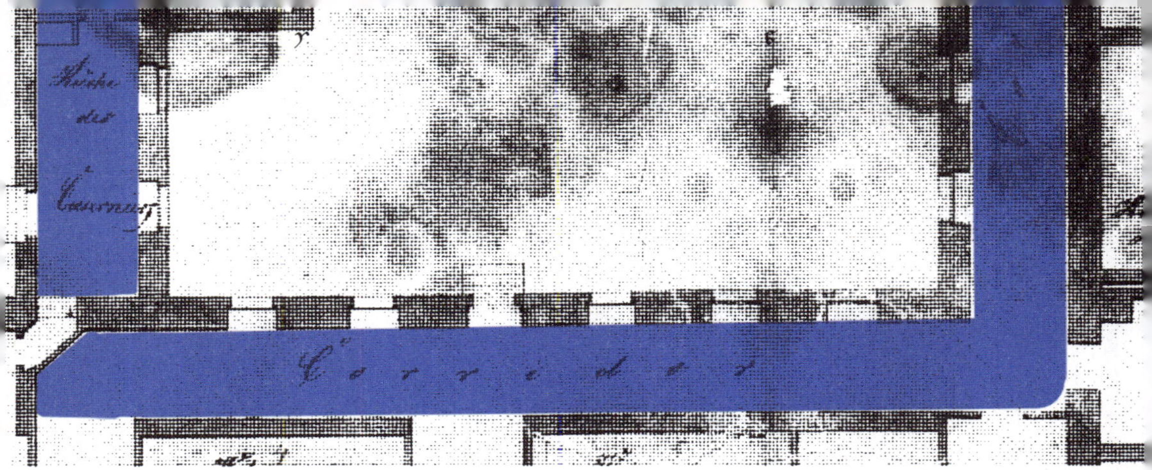
Corridor

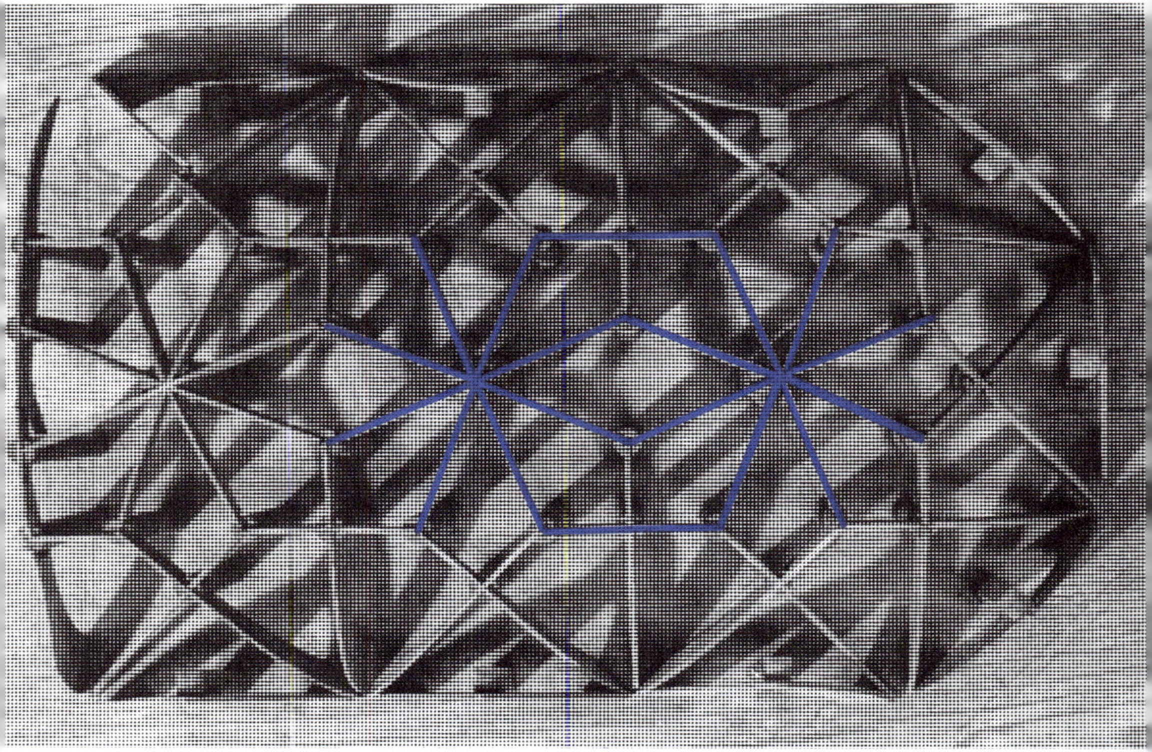

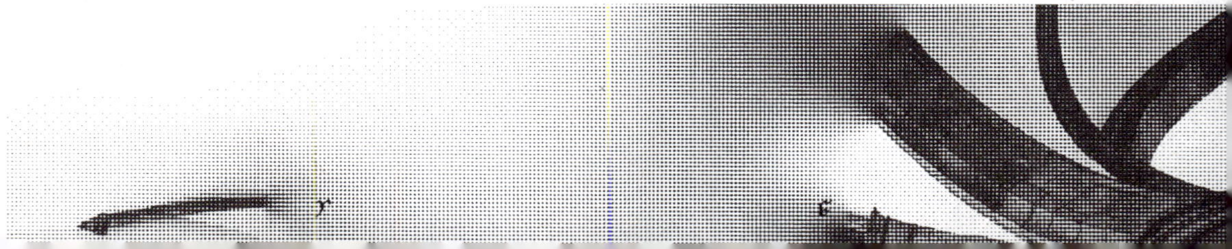

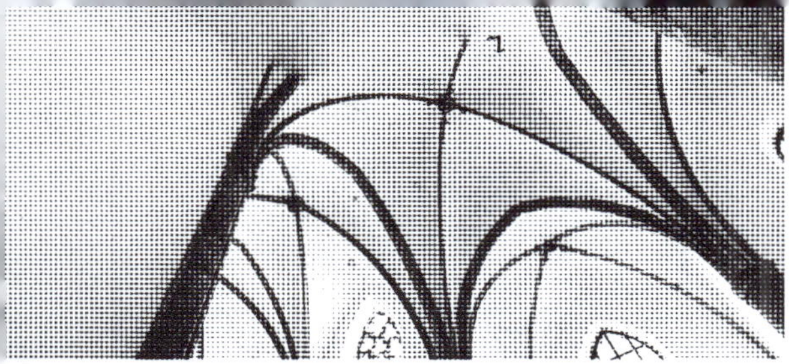

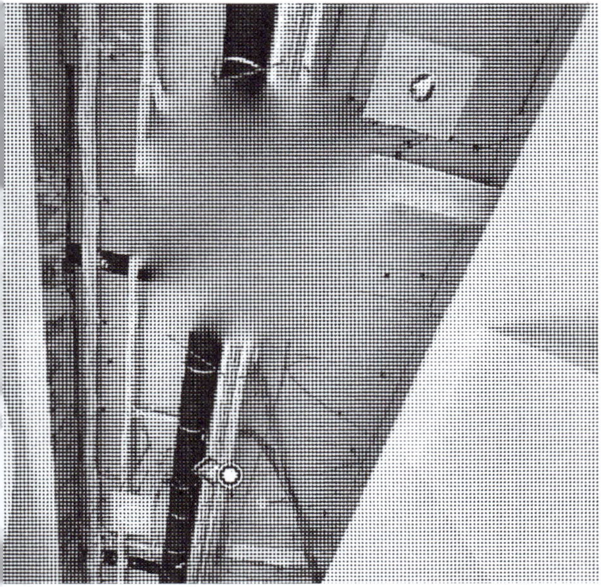

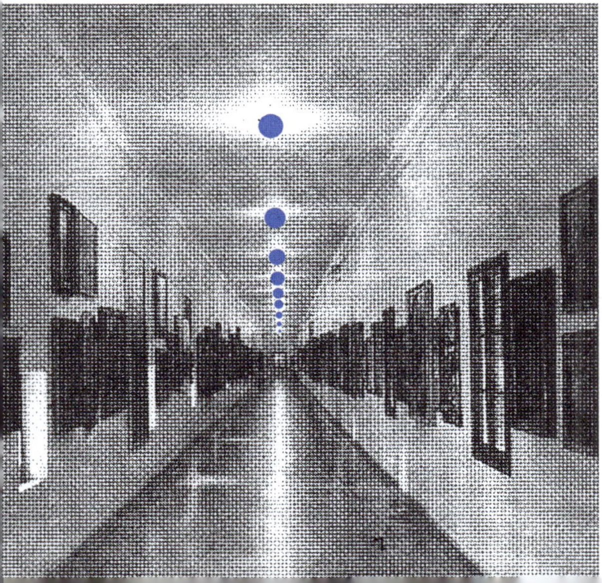

es gab Plünderungen,
Brand, Pest,

es war ständig von starken
Ereignissen betroffen, wurde
zerstört, wieder aufgebaut.

Gestern haben wir die Litfaßsäule,
die vor der Kunsthalle steht,
komplett neu gestrichen, sie
war lilablau und jetzt ist sie gelb
geworden.

On the other hand, the Lingua
is just as interesting for what it
leaves out.

Infrastructure. Glosso-Graphia
and divine lists.

Jetzt ist oben mehr Luft.

This institutional space seems
rendered permeable
as a readable object.

Weil, jetzt ist die Decke
herausgenommen worden,
früher war da ein Kunststoff und
dazwischen war eine Matte und
das bröselte manchmal runter
ein bisschen.

Jetzt ist oben mehr Luft.

This is Line Skywalker speaking.

When a woman invents language,
antennas are raised.

They were disturbed by the
frankness of the list of body parts
in the Lingua.

Schaniz, vagina, scheida, SHEATH

Zamiziz, FOLDS –

(in clothing)

rogazin, pellicium, belliz,
FUR

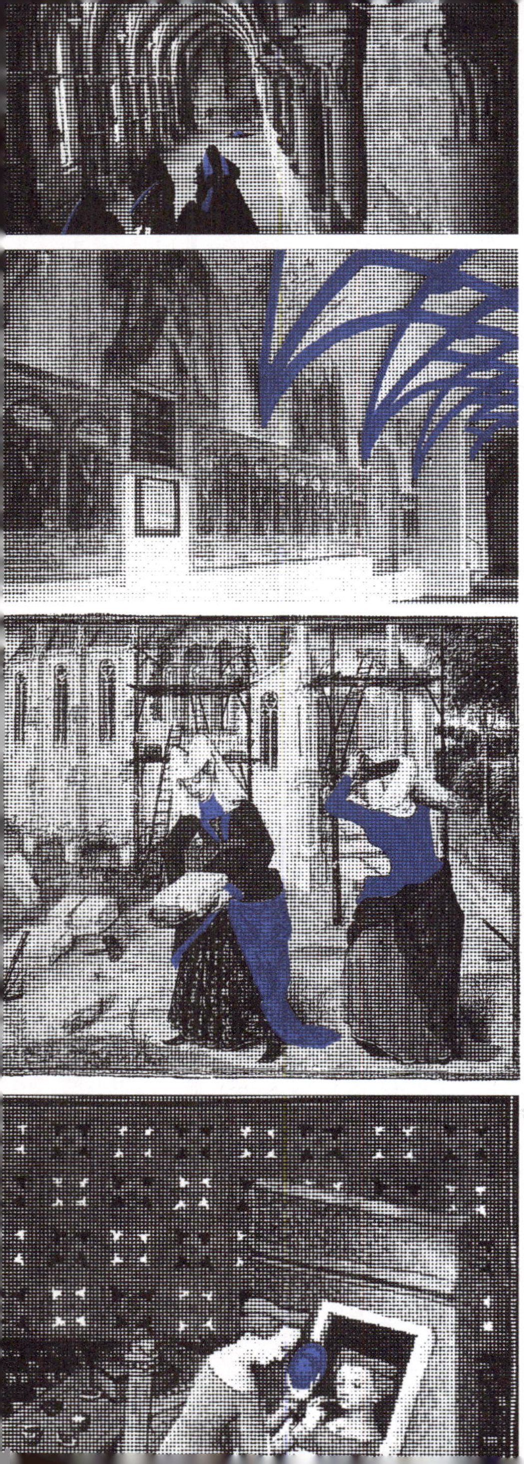

Verbindungen, Codes

Eine Architektur für neue
und alte Erzählungen und
Erinnerungen.

Früher waren in den
Kreuzgängen oft Bilder zu sehen,
die eine Geschichte erzählten.

Bildprogramme

Jetzt möchten wir von Christine
und Hildegard erzählen dort.

Und von Anna und Juliane.

Sie erfinden gerade auch sehr
viele neue Wörter für eine
neue Kunsthalle.

Und sie führen das Gendern
in der Sprache ein, mit einem
Doppelpunkt.

Vorher hat die Stadt Osnabrück
weniger gegendert.

Jetzt wird alles umgeschrieben,
neu geschrieben, neu verhandelt,
umgewandelt.

Welche Sprachen spricht
der Korridor?

Christine de Pizan hatte zu Beginn
des 15. Jahrhunderts, also vor
600 Jahren auch eine eigene
Schreibstube, in der sie mit zwei
Kopistinnen arbeitete.

Sie haben andere Texte kopiert,
abgeschrieben.

Und neu veröffentlicht,
mit gemalten Bildern,

auf denen Frauen blaue
Kleider tragen,

denn im 13. Jahrhundert erwachte
das Interesse an Blautönen,

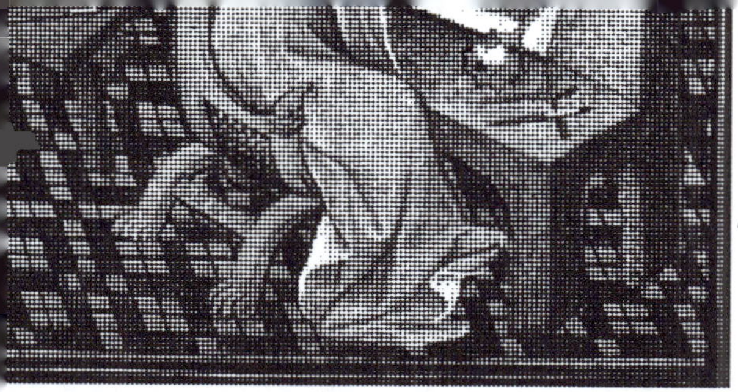

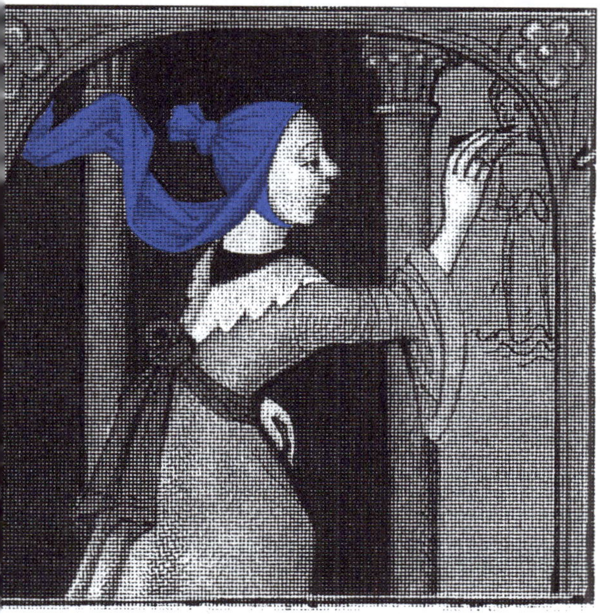

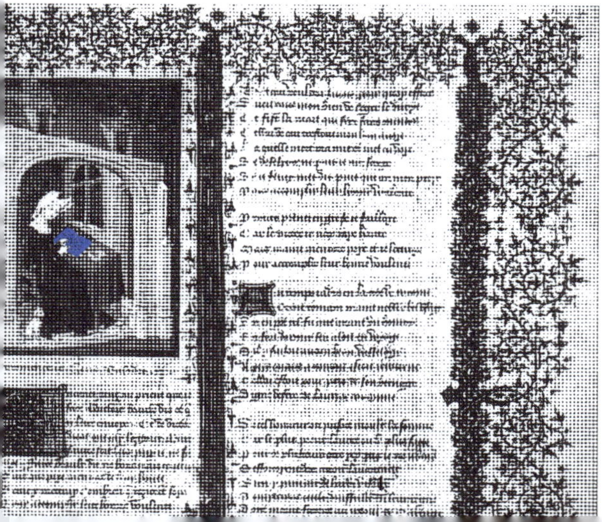

Despite the often random quality
of her imaginary words,
it focuses on the ordered nature
of her prefixes, compounds,
and gendered endings,

elsewhere she depicts the lusts
of men and women in an equally
unexpected manner,

like

WANDELTREIBER:INNEN

Ein Kreuzgang ist eine Wandelhalle.

Wandeln, um-wandeln, Ab-wandeln,
Verwandeln

a corridor referred not to a
space but to a courier, someone
who – as the Latin word suggests –
could run fast.

courierings

Kurierdienste

Wir arbeiten daran, der
Flurfunk findet wiederstatt,

wir teilen ein einziges Gehirn,

für eine gemeinsame
Textproduktion.

Diskriminierung verlernen

und wessen Freiheit ist die Norm?

Euer großes Interesse an
institutionsbezogenem Handeln,
das finde ich sehr besonders und
ein politisches Moment Eurer
Arbeit als Direktorinnen. Das ist
eine Herausforderung, der ihr
Euch sehr bewusst stellt,
mit allen Schwierigkeiten die das
mit sich bringt.

Eine queer-feministische
Institutionalität? Wie ein
feministischer building code...

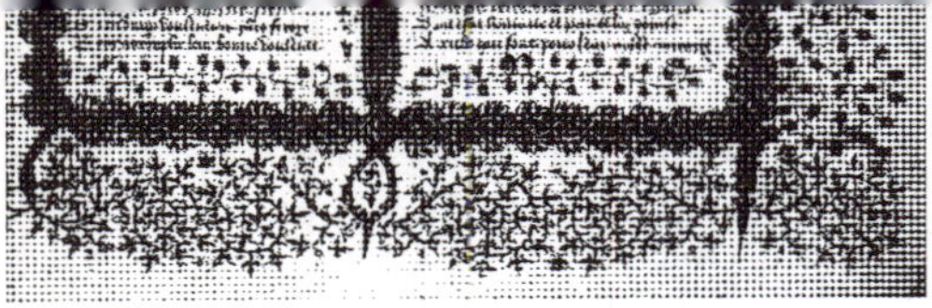

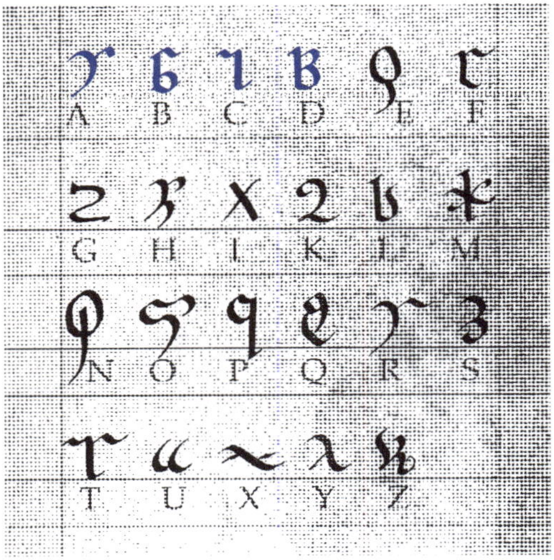

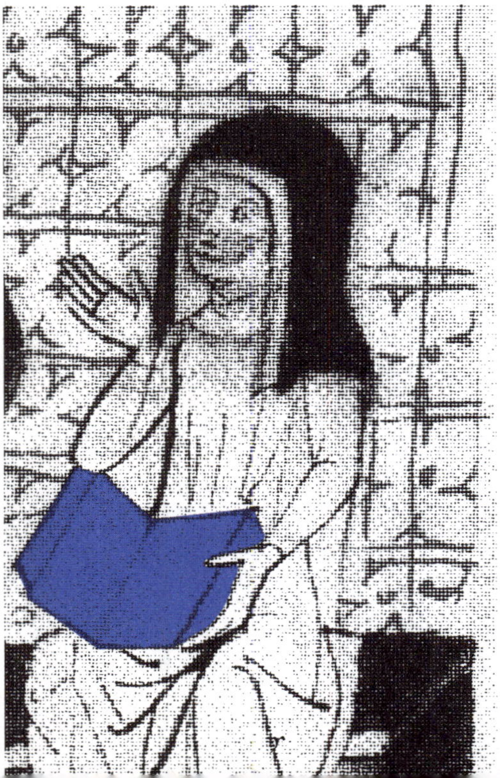

das Blau des Lapislazulis.

Es wird nur für kleine Flächen
verwendet in der mittelalterlichen
Buchmalerei.

Nur für Flächen die man
aufwerten möchte.

Blau bekam die Rolle eines Lichts
für den Schein der Figuren,

eine neue Licht-Theologie:

Ist die Farbe, wenn sie Licht ist,
immateriell

und viel heller als eine Wolke, die
die Sonne in sich trägt?

wie eine Hülle, eine Tünche,
eine vanitas

color

celare: verbergen, verschleiern,
täuschen

blaublind

Maria war nämlich nicht immer
blau gekleidet,

die Weiblichkeit der Weisheit

im Deckmantel der Dichtung.

Und wie wir noch sehen werden,
ist ihre weibliche Form kein bloß
grammatisches Geschlecht.

Weisheit, Sophia, Sapientia

pigmentarii

vivens

Welche Sprachen spricht
der Korridor?

Der Raum zwischen zwei Funken

und darin:

speaking in tongues

mystical paroxysms

automatic writing

linguistic distortion

delicious speculation

or dangerous gossip

When a woman invents language,
antennas are raised.

Institutional Matterings

We painted the advertising column
in front of the Kunsthalle:

It was purple-blue, now it is yellow.

We started to learn a new
language: Simple Language

We started to gender with a colon.

The city of Osnabrück didn't
gender that much before.

Around the year 1400, Christine
de Pizan invented an ideal
"City of Ladies."

A City for women, built by women,
and constructed by stories
of women,

but not only women,

in medieval legends are narratives
of female travesties,

of survival in men's clothing.

Christine de Pizan was very
familiar with this tradition

and that is reminding us that
Hildegard herself,

with her frequent use of cross-
sexual imagery

Gestehen wir dem scheinbar
bürokratischen Charakter von
Barrierefreiheit eine sinnliche
Rolle zu.

Institutional Matterings, it matters,
you make it matter.

Dafür habt ihr ja dann auch
den Korridor.

Aber wohin führen die Leitungen
und was genau läuft da durch?

Eine besondere Ortskenntnis ist
erforderlich.

Nämlich das Gehen, als
körpertheoretische Äußerung,
die man aber auch gemeinschaftlich
vollziehen kann.

Normalerweise gehen wir so
langsam wie möglich, das ist die
Handlungsanweisung,

von der Straße kommend durch
den Haupteingang wie durch eine
Schleuse das Foyer querend, in
den Kreuzgang tretend,

und sofort eine Tür öffnend in
Richtung des Neubaus,

über den Innenhof wieder
in den Kreuzgang,

dann auf der anderen Seite
hinter der Glasscheibe durch den
Neubau auf die Neue
Straße zugehend.

Eure Leitungen sind vielleicht
als so ein Pendant zu den
Bildprogrammen mittelalterlicher
Kreuzgänge denkbar?

Das Bildprogramm

pigmentarii

vivens

Stimmen, Schritte, Türschloß,
Schlüsselgeklapper

Aneinander vorbeilaufende
Personen:

„Moin“

„Hallo Guten Morgen“

Schlüsselgeklapper

Tür fällt mehrmals ins Schloß und
wird mehrfach verriegelt

Schritte, Stimme läuft an
Mikrophon vorbei und sagt:

„Eins Zwei Eins Zwei“

Erneut:

Schritte, Stimme läuft an
Mikrophon vorbei und sagt:

„Eins Zwei Eins Zwei“

Stimmen einer Gruppe von
Leuten im Gespräch

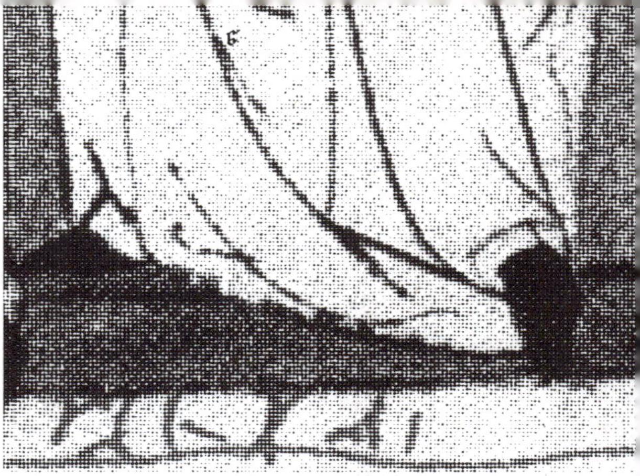

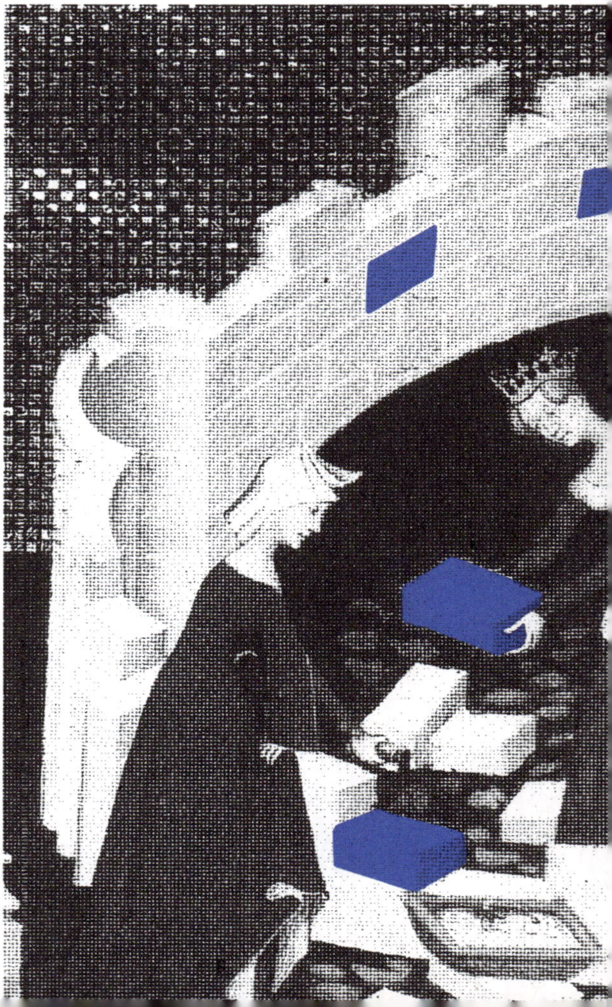

instinctively avoiding to associate the feminine exclusively with women.

Can blue solve the problem?

Within the walls of this allegorical city

and her own implausibility
as a vessel,

color could be more in the nature
of matter than of light.

As an envelope, a mask, a vanitas

color

celare: to conceal, to hide, to deceive

In the 13th century the interest in
blue tones awoke,

the blue of lapis lazuli,

for a new theology of light:

Blue stained-glass windows,

while Mary was not always
dressed in blue.

And the femininity of wisdom was
largely suppressed,

she nonetheless returned in the
guise of fabula.

Sophia, Sapientia

with a queer-feminist building code.

And there are 2 abbesses who have
equal rights to lead the monastery,
always have.

mythopoeia

They will speak in new tongues; they
will pick up serpents;

davor war es eine Mehrzweckhalle
mit Taubenzüchter vereinen

und vielleicht ist es jetzt ein
bisschen verbaut, verschüttet
und verstellt,

aber im Endeffekt funktioniert
es trotzdem.

und wir haben unendlich viele
Kreuzgänge begangen

von dort führen – gleichsam
auf dem kurzen Dienstweg –
Geheimtreppen in die darüber
liegenden Gemächer,

with silk veils and golden crowns,

Glockenstrang, Klingelzug,
Haustelefon,

a medial space par excellence.

Eine Geometrie des Raums, in dem
Funken und nichts als Funken ihre
Spur hinterlassen,

like Telegram and Telephone,

they destroy the cosmos by undoing
the space required for devotion
and reflection.

telepathy

telepaths

tele pathos

poetische Petitessen

She is merely channeling a new
semiotic given to her.

Without waiting any longer, let us
go to the Field of Letters.

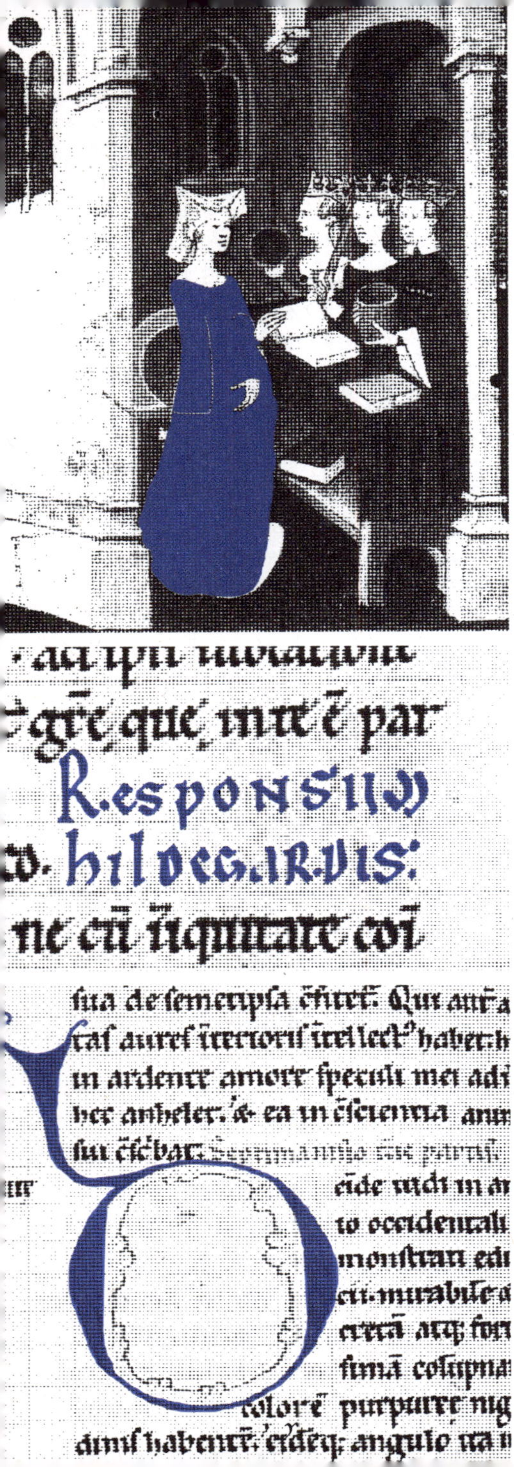

WANDELTREIBERINNEN,

sie teilen ein einziges Gehirn,

für eine gemeinsame
Textproduktion

mit feministischem Code,

einem queer-feministischen
building code.

Hildegard begriff das Medium
ihrer Visionen als eine Art Spiegel,

sie sagt:

Das Licht das ich schaue ist nicht an
raum gebunden.

re-Visionen, Mikrovisionen

oder spirituelle Assemblagen,

ein Denken-mit.

Jetzt ist oben mehr Luft.

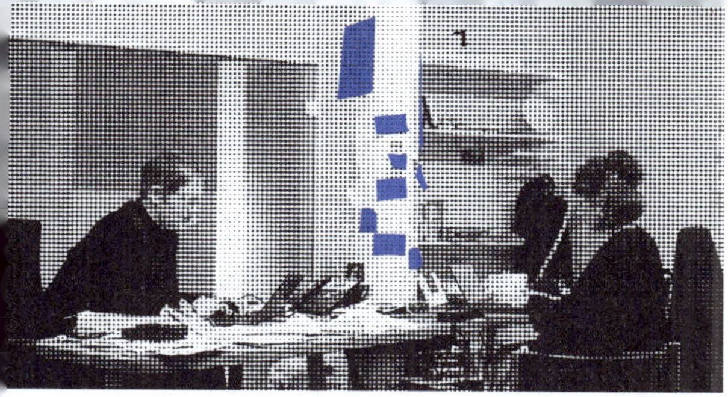

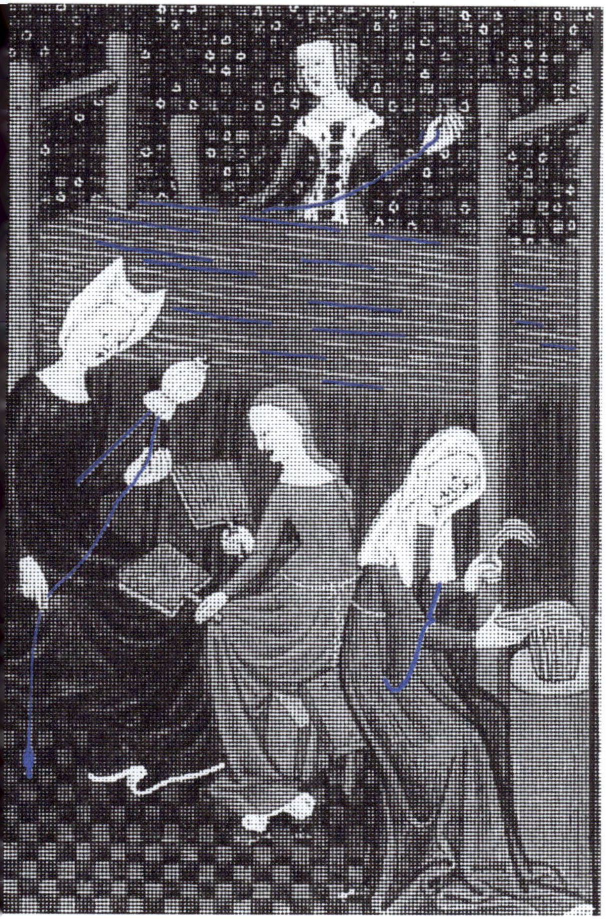

Wir wissen lediglich, dass sie etwa ab 1394 zu schreiben beginnt, zunächst einige Balladen.

In mittelalterlichen Heiligenlegenden sind Erzählungen von weiblichen Travestien, vom Überleben in Männerkleidung häufig.

Christine de Pizan war diese Tradition bestens vertraut,

erzählt sie doch in der Stadt der Frauen die Geschichte der Jungfrau Marina, die als Mönch Marinus ein Leben in vollkommener Frömmigkeit führte.

Sie verfügte wahrscheinlich über ein Scriptorium, eine mittelalterliche Schreibstätte, in der sie mit zwei Kopistinnen arbeitete.

Deshalb kann sie als Ahn-Herrin moderner Verlegerinnen gelten.

Kluge Frauen, die sich viel getraut haben.

The women she addressed ranged from those with power and authority to the poorest peasant women, including widows, prostitutes and nuns.

That is reminding us that Hildegard herself, with her frequent use of cross-sexual imagery and inversion, instinctively avoided the peril of associating the feminine exclusively with women.

Und da gibt es 2 Äbtissinnen, die gleichberechtigt das Kloster leiten, immer schon.

Plaguerism

AM I A MOUTH OR AM I A VOICE?

Luzie Meyer

TAMBOURINE = ~ ~ ~ ~ ~ ~ *
SHAKER (LEMON) = ##
SHAKER (METAL) = - - - - - - - - - -
ROSEWOOD CLAVES = X X X X X X

X X X X X X
~ ~ ~ ~ ~ ~ *

L.M., the intermediary—here performed by Sibyl*—is a prophetess
whose body grows smaller with age
as she withers.
~ ~ ~ ~ ~ ~ *

There are two choices regarding the passing of time.
Draining or withering.
If you drain, you don't wither.
If you wither, you don't drain. ##

X X X X X X

Her cave faces west, and it is early in the morning.
Sibyl picks up an oak leaf.

She starts scribbling on it. ##
No light shines into the cave, yet. X X X X X X

¦ *Sibyl, what do you want? I want to die.* ~ ~ ~ ~ ~ ~ *

Now, the leaf is covered in script.
Sibyl looks up. It is almost noon.
The sun has not arrived in her cave, yet.

Sibyl places the leaf between two perfect shards of stone.
She drains it.
Pressing the leaf will eventually turn it to dust.

¦ *There are two choices regarding the passing of time.*
¦ *Draining or withering.*
¦ *If you drain, you don't wither.*
¦ *If you wither, you don't drain.* ##

X X X X X X

In writing, time is drained of life.
Draining means to deprive a thing of vitality ##
by causing its liquid to run out.
In writing, time is compressed until life evaporates,
leaving behind nothing but a heap of dust. ##

¦ *Maiden of Cumae, choose what you wish, and you shall have your desire.*
¦
¦ *I want to live for as many years as there are grains of dust in my palm.*
¦
¦ *—I wanted to ask for eternal youth as well, but at that very second, the request slips my mind.*

Shame on me.
Stupid, stupid Sibyl. I have made myself a fool, a tool. What a bad Sibyl I am, I should have foreseen it. My prophetic power fails me when it comes to myself.

Phoebus said to me—or was it Apollo—:

I want to take your virginity. If you suffer my passion, I shall give you eternal youth. Let me have you—then I shall make an imprint on your memory, which will stunt your cognitive and emotional development; I will possess you once, but, infantilized by the sudden loss of agency, you shall attempt to reclaim personhood over and over again, ad nauseam, *until you vomit, and repetition compulsion will entrap you in adolescent ideations and conserve you within a perpetual state of psychic infancy. Not merely a question of inner conflict, the scar will mark a place in the brain where anatomy and chemistry have changed.*

Eternal youth, in exchange for my bodily integrity.
I refused, and thus, I wither.

Withering means to fall into decay.
Life loses its structural integrity, it falls apart.
In draining, time is compressed.
In withering, time disperses.
Draining means to remember.
Withering means disintegration.
Withering also means: to be humiliated. ~ ~ ~ ~ ~ ~ *

Now it is a few hours past noon. A surprise to Sibyl.
The sun's beams are at an angle from south to northeast.
Light enters the cave through some of the openings.

She takes another leaf and continues to scribble.

If I go to sleep in time, I will rise even timelier. If I lie down now, I will still catch the delirium of nighttime. By the time I rise, it will still be yesterday. I am my own Sibyl. I am withering, yet if I sleep backwards, to write it all down once again, to stop the withering, to drain what is there, I will make an imprint, a scattered archive of my body. Now, as in antiquity, writing is a vehicle to mobilize oneself: I will go to sleep, then rise and strive to write myself wisely out of demise—did Virgil do the same when he used me as his mouthpiece? I—##

—here she abruptly stops scribbling.
Now, the benighted reader may ask herself: What causes the Sibyl to break off at this exact moment?

L.M., the intermediary, takes the floor to provide context:
~ ~ ~ ~ ~ ~ *

The Sibyl is referencing one of the events in ancient history that form the scattered backstory of her character.

She functioned as Apollo's mouthpiece when guiding Aeneas through the underworld. This adventure of hers was authored by Virgil, who inserted his own voice into Sibyl's mouth, as did Apollo. As did a lot of poets. Sibyl's mouth lent itself to appropriation. A common phrase in the greco-roman poetic tradition was something like,

I would need a hundred tongues and a hundred mouths to express what I want to express, *fill in the blank.*

This "many mouths" cliché was uttered by Sibyl on her author's behalf. A surrogate speaker. ##

The sun is beginning to set, slowly.
Full beams of light enter Sibyl's cave.

She is said to have dwelled in a mouthlike cavern. With hundreds of openings. Orifices in the stone. Many Latin poets created their own adaptations of the cliché of the many mouths. In fact, any poet might agree that more than a single mouth would be needed in order to express what one wants to express, *fill in the blank*.
~ ~ ~ ~ ~ ~ *

When Sibyl leads Aeneas through the underworld in Apollo's voice, the cliché is once more regurgitated, and radicalized: even if she had a hundred tongues and a hundred mouths, Sibyl would not be able to express the horrors of hell to Aeneas. Uttered through Sibyl, Virgil's gesture is performative.

Because in fact, she *does* have a hundred mouths. None of which are her own.

They have used her to express the inexpressible, and
the Sibyl withers under the humiliation. None of which is her own.

That is the reason she stops scribbling. ~ ~ ~ ~ ~ ~ *

When one looks at the way that Sibyl is used by Virgil, one must conclude: she is a mouth, not a voice.

A traumatic realization about the multiplicity of narratives which form her character. She is herself a product of scattered leaves, a result of meta- and intertextuality.
X X X X X X

So L.M. invites Sibyl to use *her* as a conduit, lending Sibyl a mouth to speak of her own lost agency.

My monopolistic shame-humiliation theory is snowballing and coming to dominate my personality more and more. A single state of reactivity—withering—is managing my response to a specific class of events. I have lost my capacity to down-regulate, to dissipate feelings of humiliation.

I am withering. I am withering. Let me drain, let me write, let me scribble, let me leave, leave me a leaf to write on.

Rather than getting to the bottom of the unspeakable, she prefers to speak through adynata, or idioms of improbability. X X X X X X

I would grow a mouth in my armpit before I would speak. I will speak when the sun sets before it has risen. During a week with four Thursdays. Four Thursdays, three Wednesdays, and three and a half nights. When the cave's stones blossom. When I hit rock bottom. Chamomile all over the rocks of my cavern. I couldn't tell you even if I had a hundred tongues, a hundred mouths, ## and an iron voice. I would carry a mouth inside my stomach between my legs behind my back and run away screaming without a mouth, before I would place my sorrow in your hands, your hands would grow fingers with legs on them and run next to me. When rats grow wings. When the chickens grow teeth. When teeth grow mouths. When moths grow mouths. ## If I had a thousand tongues, a thousand mouths. ## When poplars grow pears, and peaches and plums and prunes and grapes and no poplars except for one and that is a popcorn. I would speak when and why would I have spoken wherefore whereupon will I have spoken whence forth henceforth forth cometh the form of whence form becometh the tense becometh a prediction. Highly improbable outcomes. Speaking: when peas roll up the mountain. When it rains pocket knives. When I grow dull like an old knife, like an old wife. ##

~ ~ ~ ~ ~ *

In the refusal to bear Apollo's passion—or was it Phoebus—Sibyl attempts to find her own voice through L.M. Can the Sibyl write herself though L.M., a woman with whom she shares both the experience of withering and of draining?

Futile, to work against time passing.
Writing: Passing one's time working against passing one's time.
To drain so as not to wither. X X X X X X

Adding their version of the "many mouths" cliché to those that came before, Sibyl and L.M. transport themselves to the peak of the poetic canon. I am Sibyl, withering with her.

May L.M., the intermediary, be the mouthpiece for a many-mouthed, voiceless handful of dust.
The sun has finished setting. The cave is dark again. ##

Both Sibyl and L.M., the intermediary, lay down, so as to rise all over again the next day, to drain a handful of life from time, and in writing to both invite and delay the withering, the humiliation, the voicelessness, death. ~ ~ ~ ~ ~ ~ *
##

NOTES

Parts of the following texts have been appropriated, copied, regurgitated, reproduced, reformulated, transformed, and recombined for this poem:

1.) Emily Gowers, "Virgil's Sibyl and the 'Many Mouths' Clich. (Aen.6.625-7)," *The Classical Quarterly* 55, no. 1 (May 2005): 170–82; http://www.jstor.org/stable/3556247
2.) Suzanne Motte Peronneau Jackson, "The Cumaean Sibyl: Controlling Her Voice at Rome from Tarquin to Constantine," (Senior Project, Division of Languages and Literature, Bard College, 2019); https://digitalcommons.bard.edu/senproj_s2019/192/.
3.) Ovid, *Metamorphoses*, trans. Mary M. Innes (London: Penguin Classics, 2007).
4.) Elizabeth A. Wilson, *Gut Feminism* (Durham: Duke University Press, 2015).
5.) Elizabeth A. Wilson, *Psychosomatic: Feminism and the Neurological Body* (Durham: Duke University Press, 2004).

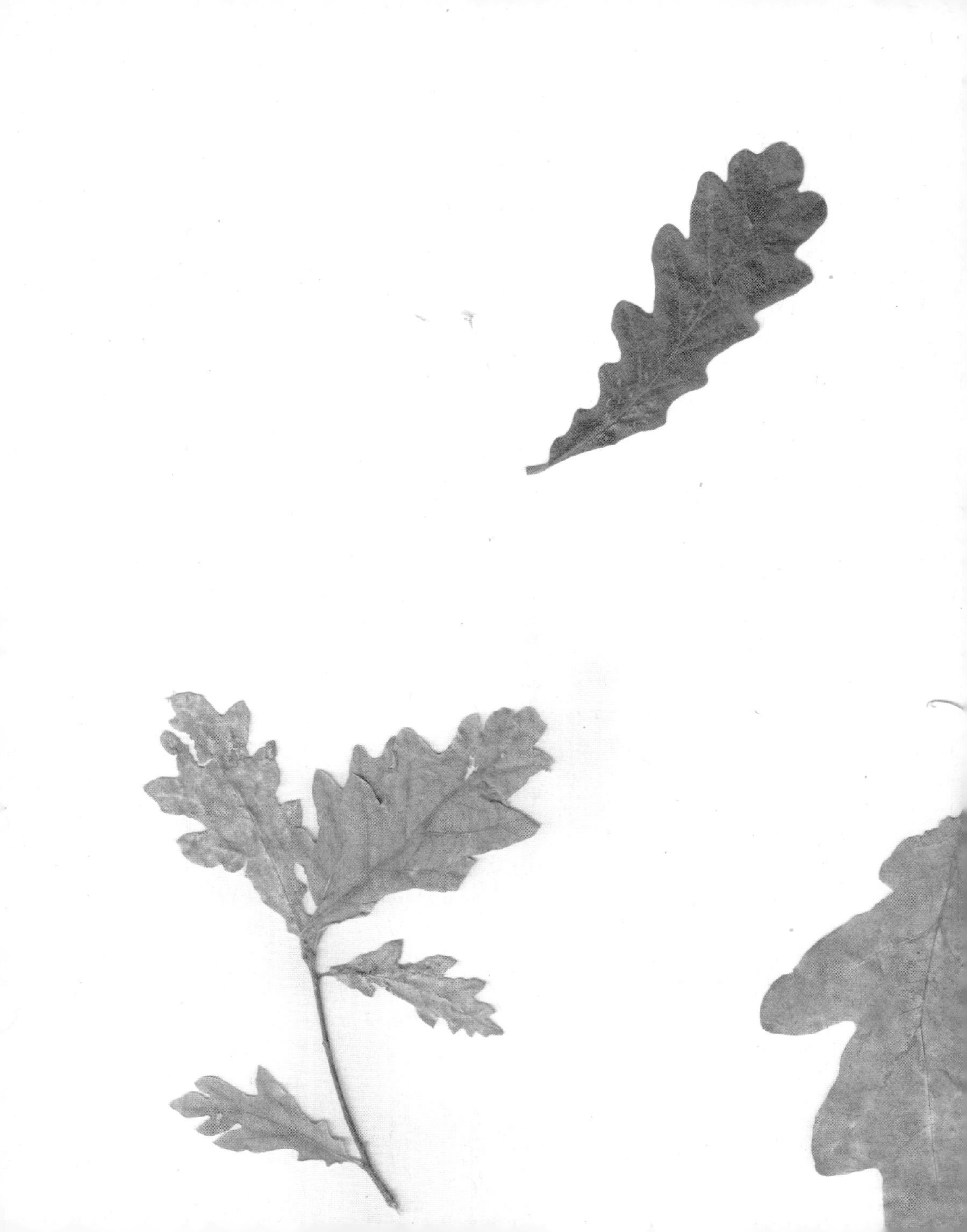

MOIST ORANGE BLOSSOMS

Mahsa Saloor

INT. STAIRCASE – DAY

Beautiful morning sounds of the forest: birds chirping and wind rustling in the leaves.

Distant footsteps.

M leaves her studio wearing a long, black, asymmetrical, floral-patterned dress. M is followed from behind; a dusty, pink, velvet hair bow elegantly covers her shoulder-length, dark-brown hair.

A silver serpent ring on her ring finger, M holds the stair rail and takes cautious steps as she moves up the stairs, pausing with every cough. J, descending the staircase, looks over at M as he passes.

J Are you okay?

M Yeah yeah, just my throat is hurting.

J Do you need anything?

M No.

J Are you sure?

M Mhmm.

M continues to cough.

R hears the subdued coughs from the kitchen. R prepares a warm, glowing glass of milk in the dark.

R walks up the stairs with the glowing glass of milk on a tray, knocks on M's door. M slowly and weakly peaks her head out through the slit of the half-opened door, her face half in shadow.

The door creaks as it opens.

R Here, I brought this, to soothe your throat.

M, dazed, accepts the tray.

INT. M's BEDROOM – DAY

White-noise sound textures.

Hours later, M wakes with her head hanging from the upper right corner of the bed. She glances over at the milk glass, unscrews the brown jar and removes two capsules and swallows them.

She looks at her arm and licks the hairs on it that are standing up.

Moments later, a rusty red peacock butterfly with azure blue eyespots on its wings lands on the window net screen.

INT. BASEMENT JACUZZI & SAUNA – NIGHT

Pipes rattling in the basement. Water bubbling.

In dim yellow light, the whirlpool reflects glowing turquoise water sparkles.

Involuntary laughter.

Skin bumps, and surfaces.

J As nocturnal creatures, frogs prefer darkness. The texture of their saliva is changeable, from sticky to watery and back. Their tongue is ten times softer than a human tongue, and as soft as a human brain.

M The name in Sanskrit for female ejaculation is *amrita* which means divine nectar.

R Vasovagal syncope (vay-zoh-vay-gul sing-kuh-pee) occurs when your body overreacts to triggers like the sight of blood or extreme emotional distress.

The vasovagal syncope trigger causes your heart rate and blood pressure to drop suddenly, and you faint.

INT. DINING ROOM – NIGHT

Forest nighttime sounds take over: twitter of insects and soughing wind. Whistling window.

R plays with the melted wax from the hand-twisted honeycomb candles.

R I can't believe she's holding it together.

J Smells the royal purple hyacinths in a clay pot. A freshly sweet alluring scent.

R Scent penetrates your brain in twenty-two seconds.

J Dopamine is about the anticipation of pleasure—the pursuit of happiness, not happiness itself.

R Remember, consistent elevated dopamine levels provide the euphoric high of crack cocaine.

J A double-edged sword.

M walks back from her nightly walk in the forest. She heads to the kitchen and makes a pot of loose leaf Jasmine and Rose tea. M feels her forehead while keeping her gaze at the rose petals floating in the glass teapot. Keeping a poised exterior, she takes six deep breaths, and enters the candle lit dining room.

R looks over to M as she takes a seat. They all sit around the dining room table.

They read the poem "Amniotic Sac" on their phones:

:heart: :heart:

:heart:

:heart:

R CN X stimulation

J neurons fire

M her ribs creak

R wet on wet

M protein molecules assemble

J her ancestors' teeth

R oxytocin rises

M she squirts milky white

J bumpy skin

M an oval band of connective tissue

J mammalian wisdom

M cortisol rises

R consciousness liquid

J saffron, henna, cucumber seed

M globalized ideas

R minimum interference, maximum benefit

J emotionally split open

M treated like a mathematical object

R	clouds of temporary aggregates
J	a blue tinge
M	unidentified narcotic pills
R	practicing psychological safety
J	11:11
M	evanescent screenshots
R	performance tracked
J	communal obligation
R	subtle flesh
M	fanciful redoing of oneself
J	instant replay
R	bones laid down
M	fingers tingle
J	fertilized eggs grow

INT. KITCHEN – DAY

Young birds sing a repetitive whistle of two-note phrases. Electric hum of the refrigerator.

M and R are sitting at a table drinking coffee. R has finished eating her breakfast, but M hasn't touched her crispy rye bread and strawberry jam—she appears too unsettled to eat.

R The invitation came at a strange time.

M The ride was very good, thrilling; it nearly killed me.

R takes another sip of coffee.

R He told me the bad news.

M What should I say to him?

R Just ask something.

M puts the cell phone cable charger in her mouth.

M I'm a terrible liar.

R No one will ask you.

M I hate keeping secrets.

R Then you don't have to lie.

M Did you ever lie to me?

R I mean, don't you think lying is only normal?

M You know, true love doesn't resemble addiction in the body.

M's gaze gravitates towards the blinding sunlight piercing through the window. A beat.

M I have a headache. The light is too bright.

R	Are you saying this was an accident?

M listens to the dead silence for a moment or two, then speaks.

M	I never loved him; I never have.

INT. STUDIO – NIGHT

Now in private, M writes "30 second decisions" on her arm.

INT. DINING ROOM – NIGHT

Muffled voices and footsteps come from the hall. Ringing, then a voice.

"Cemetary Talk"

M	phantom vibrations
R	masturbating and going to sleep as sacred pilgrimage
J	involuntary eyelid glitches
R	slightly unfocused images
M	a continuous disease
R	with a sluggish turn to her left, she sprints out of bed
J	swallows two capsules, assumes the pose of a corpse
M	going into the emotions ten times harder
R	two turns on both sides for every five-minute snooze

J	a knee jerk response
R	command C
M	command V
J	repeated nostalgia has no currency
R	blood is thicker than evidence
M	she pulls the carpet, a pool of turquoise
J	cars drive by painting her face in bands of light
R	with blue sterile gloves she puts the small end of the cable charger in her mouth
M	high anesthesia is given
R	veins swell
J	her stomach growls
R	justice involves feelings
M	not yet ready to make a social confession
J	belonging is a many-sided question
R	zeros and ones taste like exile
J	emotions don't compute
M	a slow cough pervades

R	host and parasite echo each other

M	too much mommy-daddy-me psychoanalysis

R	seasonal and chronic

J	lungs deflate

J	black cardamom seeds latch onto her saliva

R	a combination of spit and softness

M	milky eyes

J	shimmering scales

R	two hearts in hand

M	seminal fluid

J	the referee blows the whistle

SIBYL'S PRIMES

C. S. Tolan[1][2]

Wonder not, Sovereign Mistress, if perhaps
Thou canst, who art sole wonder, much less arm
Thy looks, the heav'n of mildness, with disdain,
Displeased that I approach thee thus and gaze
Insatiate, I thus single …
– Satan, to Eve

There are more vectors in Abstract and Real Space,
Eve, than are anticipated in your operational security.
– Heidi

I. Introduction

The whisper is a strange signal: it is soft, yet it requires, relative to phonated speech, much more energy,[3] breath,[4] and expertise[5] to produce. The breath, as

1 Whisper Protocols FKA shush.systems

2 soother.systems

3 The whisper is a strange signal: it is soft, yet it requires, relative to phonated speech, much more energy.

4 Ibid.

5 Children must master phonated speech before they can approach a whisper (Cirillo, unpublished data cited in Cirillo & Todt, 2005). Notable exceptions include sweet and clever Max, who whispered first.

turbulent noise with a "hushing"[6] sound, is funneled straight through the narrow gate of the glottis, through a small opening in the taut, non-vibrating vocal folds. The whisper's signal is modulated by the mouth and by the upward or downward movement of the larynx[7] in the throat—it is pitchless, with an absent fundamental frequency (*Fo*).[8] However, given that the larynx moves in the same manner as with normal speech, thus impacting the shape of the mouth and the positioning of the tongue, many listeners report hearing "pitch" in a whisper: a phantom artifact,[9] which perhaps is prompted by a familiarity with the speaker's "normal" voice and pitched intonations.[10] This phantom pitch is but one of the whisper's many tricks. Could a signal so subtle be anything but an enigmatic emissary?

Whispers have been treated extensively in linguistic studies of phonology and physiology, but there have been very few attempts to undertake a psychological, anthropological, or sociological approach to their study, and almost nothing has been written about their affordances as communication technologies within an information theoretic or cybernetic framework.[11] What work there is in these areas focuses largely on the whisper's usage in the delineation and reinforcement

---

6 Catford, 1977.

7 Coleman et al., 2002.

8 Tsunoda et al., 1997.

9 Thomas, 1969.

10 This is my own speculation, slightly undone by Meyer-Eppler's 1956 study, which posits that whispers replace the pitch of phonated speech with marked shifts in the first and second formants (F1 and F2), thereby enabling a listener to map pitched intonation onto these stand-in indicators. However, the area is wholly underexplored from a phenomenological perspective. Relatedly, I hypothesize that the whisper is most often encountered "second-hand", e.g. after the establishment of a relationship with the speaker: familiarity precedes whisper, perhaps adding to the listener's projection of pitch onto whispered utterances. (There is much fascinating work about whispered communication in tonal languages, but it also does not take a phenomenological approach.)

11 Notable papers in these areas include Cirillo & Todt (2002); Cirillo (2004); Cirillo & Todt (2005); Li (2011); Mowitt (2011).

of in-group/out-group communications, and on the possibility that whispering evolved via ritualization, to become an "expensive signal" for group cohesion and organization, as well as for signaling intimate attachment.[12]

The whisper, by its very nature, serves as a subtle technology of control: with a narrow diameter of legibility enforced by its softness, it draws all would-be listeners closer,[13] asserting dominance via the compulsive response to its seduction and, as a whisper can be lowered to an almost indecipherable murmur—a signal for one and only one listener, piped directly into the ear—exclusionary power and plausible deniability (secrecy).[14, 15] Research has indicated that a listener's reaction to a single-speaker whisper or to a conversation in phonated speech is significantly different than their reaction to a conversation of whispers, which elicit feelings of exclusion and a closely-coupled, heightened curiosity about the signal, which has become a secret.[16]

Given the protected nature of its content and the required close proximity of its passing, the whisper is a signal that not only *spreads* but also *triggers* gossip. Alice[17]

12 Cirillo & Todt, 2005.

13 Formulated in conversation with GYRES, 2022.

14 Indeed, Cirillo (2004) followed an earlier study—in which participants associated laughing with certain facial expressions—to find that respondents tied whispering not to facial expressions (underscoring the whisper-as-enigma), but to hand signals: the message shielded by the hand of the sender to reach only the ear of the receiver, reinforcing the exclusionary nature of the utterance.

15 The compulsion, dominance, and discretion of the whisper spark many intriguing choreographies in both the human and the animal worlds. "Low-amplitude signaling" in animals serves many similar functions to whispered human speech, including seduction, deception, and exclusion (Gustison & Townsend, 2015; for more information see *Animal Behaviour* 105 (2015), a special issue on "Whispered Communication").

16 Ibid. 12.

17 Alice and Bob have been frequently used as examples of communicating parties in cryptography papers and other scientific publications since 1978. They are accompanied by many friends who play archetypal roles. Mallory, for example, is a malicious actor. Eve is an eavesdropper. Grace is a government agent. And so on.

whispers to Bob about Mallory's malicious intent, and Eve, observing Alice's closeness to Bob, gossips to Grace about Alice and Bob's whispered (in)discretion. From there we can imagine a spiraling gossip network, seeded by Alice's initial movement (hand to Bob's ear, mouth to hand) and Bob's response (leaning in towards Alice).[18]

In this paper, I seek to locate the whisper's *fundamental frequency*—that pitch it possesses only as a phantom—via controlled experimentation with a gossiping network. My process is grounded in amateur[19] analyses of the whispering trachea's topology and an apparent homeomorphism[20] between the trachea and a form of duct flute similar to a tabor pipe. I discover that this homeomorphism requires the "tuning" of the twisted human throat and assess how playing the instrument alters the perception of throat and flute. It is my hope that the rigorous staging of these experiments will ultimately coax the two shapes to merge in unanticipated ways, resulting in the first documented observation of a networked whisper's phantom phenomenon.[21]

---

18 As it spirals out of its in-group network, the gossip turns into second-hand reporting—rumor—which can be instrumentalized by a spy handler like Eve to spark certain plots.

19 My arguments in this paper are largely based upon naive poetic intuitions, with more sophistication, terminology, and approximate topological alignment introduced by Abel Jansma's topological coaching. (I cite Abel's observations throughout what follows as AJ). I did not intend to write a topology paper when Luzie invited me to write about whispers, but Eve intercepted the unencrypted email and enlisted me in a related operation, in which topology is a necessary discovery method. I am her agent, after all.

20 A homeomorphism, also called a continuous transformation, is a relation that exists between two shapes when all of their points can be mapped directly onto one another. In other words, there is probably a homeomorphism between two shapes if they can be squashed and stretched into each other's forms without *breaking or tearing*.

21 Eve insists that I do not give too much away, and so I pose this rather weak description of the paper's contents.

II. Claire's Definitions

To set the parameters for our inquiry, I proceed with the following definitions:

1. A **vessel** is a hollow, closed form with zero holes: a prism, a sphere
2. If you pierce a vessel, the resulting form is a punctured sphere with one hole, a disk, or: **a bag**
3. If you pierce a bag, the resulting form is a punctured sphere with two holes, a disk with one hole, or: **a tube**
4. If you pierce a tube n times where $n > 0; n \in N$, the resulting form is a punctured sphere with n holes, a disk with n-1 holes, or: **a flute**

Table 1.

Vessel	Bag	Tube	Flute
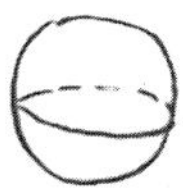	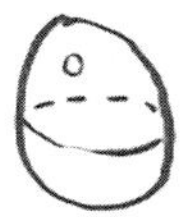	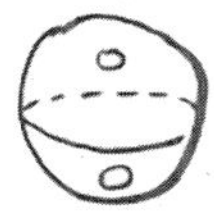	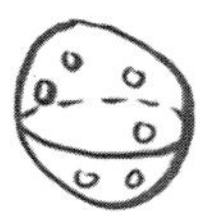
	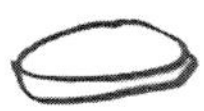	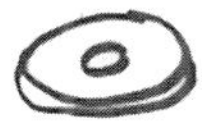	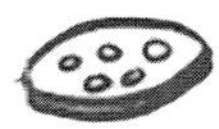
	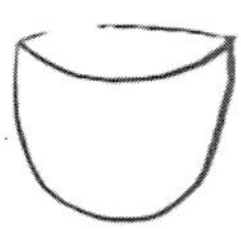	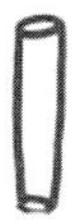	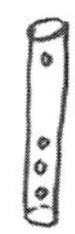

As a preliminary, I also define the spaces[22] of our analysis. All observations of topological shapes occur in Abstract Space. Real Space[23] contains geometrically-embedded shapes[24] and the embodied human whisperers and listeners. In both

22 *We are in a generalized crisis in relation to all the environments of enclosure …*

23 Technically this is something like Euclidean Space, but I adopt simpler terminology.

24 Geometric embedding, for our purposes, simply describes the real-world instantiation

Real and Abstract Space, we[25] refer to the main whisperer as Alice (Real Alice and Abstract Alice), and the main listener as Bob (Real Bob and Abstract Bob). We cast a number of Alice and Bob's friends[26] to join our experiment.[27]

III. The Trachea

We begin in Real Space, with a trachea[28] plucked from the throat of Real Alice. On this trachea, we count two nostrils and the mouth, one hole to the digestive tract,[29] and two holes to the lungs:[30] six holes.

---

of our topological forms, in such a way that they have mass and abide by the laws of physics. Objects in the space around you have geometric embeddings.

25 Throughout what follows, Real Claire and Abstract Claire speak as a single voice, using the royal "we."

26 "... a self-deforming cast that will continuously change from one moment to the other..."

27 We are gathered in a theater, with the exception of Real Grace, who is monitoring the production remotely. We understand we are to perform an improvised series of experiments, as cued by Real Eve, acting as stage manager. Most of the cast are, like us, direct reports to Eve, with the obvious exception of Alice and Bob, who are unwitting participants obtained via a casting agency. Legally there is some concern about enlisting Alice and Bob in our experiments without their full knowledge and consent, but our lawyers feel there is enough precedent to defend our activities, particularly since they are undertaken in the service of national defense. As one lawyer wrote in the brief, "There is no need to fear or hope, but only to look for new weapons." It is vital to our experiment that Alice and Bob believe they are acting in a play, hence: the theater.

28 Note that this trachea is different from the anatomically-defined one: it is expanded to include associated orifices.

29 We slice the esophagus from our shape as it is not part of the breathing/speaking apparatus.

30 We slice our shape at the entrance to the lungs. The lungs, as bags, represent a topologically distinct form that has already been considered in the oversubscribed field of bag poetics, which includes notable works such as John Yeats's "Ode on a Grecian Urn," Wallace Stevens's "The Anecdote of the Jar," and Ursula K. Le Guin's *The Carrier Bag Theory of Fiction*. In this paper, we are interested in shapes that, per Claire's Third and Fourth Definitions, are tubes and flutes.

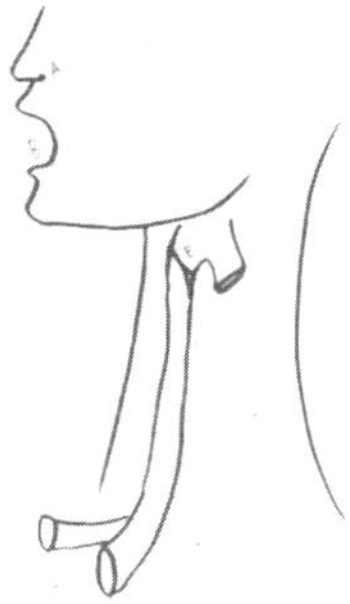

Fig 1. Real Alice's trachea, with slightly open vocal folds: A. Nostrils B. Mouth C. Esophagus D. Lungs E. Vocal folds

An important restriction for Real Alice's trachea is that the vocal folds *must be held taut, with an opening between them,* in order to achieve the desired geometric form. Thus, if the trachea were to speak, it would be in a whisper.[31]

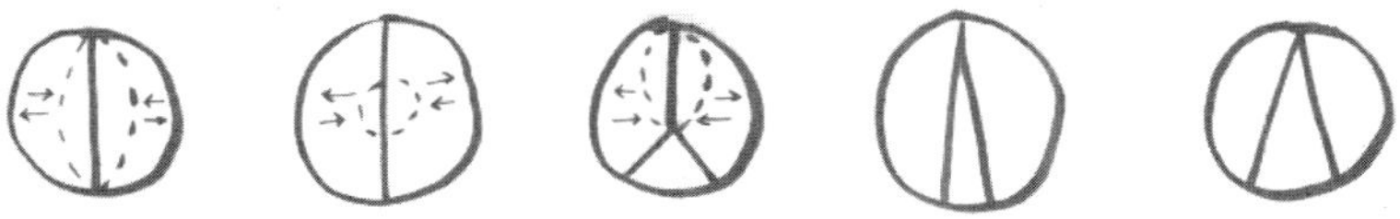

A. B. C. D. E.

Fig 2. Simplified view of Real Alice's vocal folds and glottis (gap between folds) as seen from above during different styles of phonation. In this paper, we are primarily concerned with D. and occasionally with E.

A. Normal phonation B. Creaky C. Breathy D. Whisper E. Voiceless

We introduce Real Alice's trachea into Abstract Space, where it becomes the *Trachea*[32] of Abstract Alice, who comprises a *Trachea* and a single Hand.

31 It's worth noting that with these restrictions, the trachea could also whistle and sigh. However, this is out of scope, with a few exceptions that we encounter later in close readings.

32 We capitalize *Trachea* to distinguish the form in Abstract Space from its geometric embedding in Real Space, the trachea.

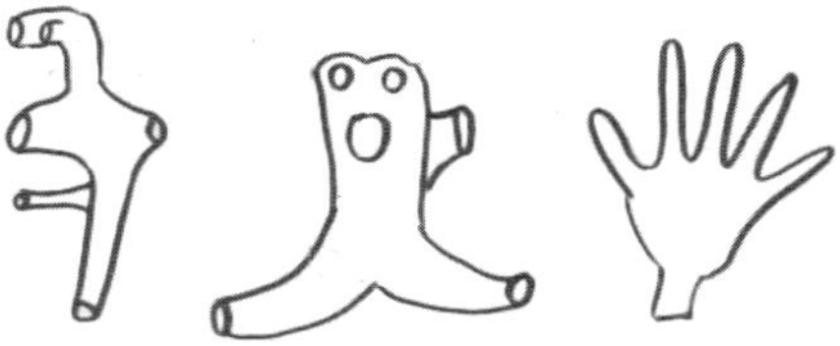

Fig 3. Abstract Alice's Trachea *(side and front) and single Hand*

IV. The Carthea

As previously discussed, we are interested in the apparent homeomorphism between the Trachea and a form of duct flute,[33] known in Real Space as the tabor pipe.

A tabor pipe is designed to be played with one hand, with the other hand free to beat a small drum or ring a bell. The musician grips the pipe with the thumb and ring finger. Two of the finger holes are on the front of the pipe's body, played by the index and middle fingers, and the third is on the back, played by the thumb.

---

33 All duct flutes gain their resonance from the design of the duct, which creates an air reed that is piped through a fipple, opening onto a window with a sharp edge and the main body of the flute. The edge splits the air, directing some of it out of the pipe and some of it into the pipe's body, resulting in a periodic vibration. If we were able to transform a trachea in Real Space into a tabor pipe, we could imagine that the pipe's duct and fipple would be created by a slight deformation of the larynx that retains the narrow gate of the whispering vocal folds. However, in Abstract Space, our shapes are infinitely thin, and thus we discard both the vocal folds and the fipple when considering the continuous transformation that is the subject of this paper.

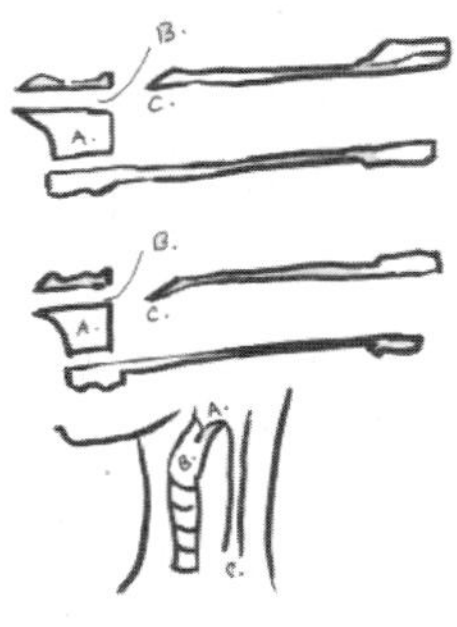

Fig 4. Duct flute: A. Fipple B. Duct C. Edge Trachea: A. Vocal folds B. Trachea C. Esophagus

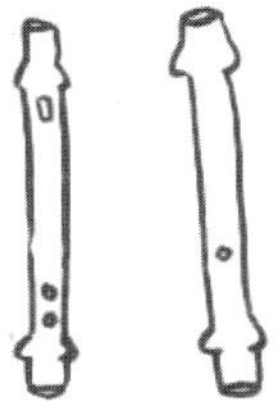

Fig 5. A tabor pipe (front and back)

We will designate the particular tabor pipe that is homeomorphic to the *Trachea* in Abstract Space as the *Carthea.*[34]

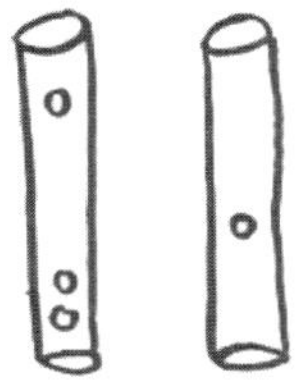

Fig 6. Abstract Alice's Carthea *(front and back)*

The continuous transformation that leads from *Trachea* to *Carthea*, the symbolic significance of this transformation, and the investigation of possible walks on the two shapes, we classify using *TraCartheal Topolopotogical Analanysis.*[35]

34 Here we follow the same naming convention as *spectrum* → *cepstrum*, where *cepstrum* represents the Inverse Fourier Transform (IFT) of the logarithm of an estimated spectrum.

35 Real Eve sighs audibly into Real Claire's ear piece, prompting us to note: This term might seem overly whimsical, but we remind the reader that the *cepstrum*'s operations include *quefrency alanysis* and *liftering*.

V. Twisting

First, let us consider the continuous transformation. The *Carthea's* holes are arranged in straight lines, on either side of a tube. To achieve the continuous transformation from *Trachea* to *Carthea*, it is therefore necessary to bring all Tracheal holes into alignment.

In Abstract Space, we simply twist the top of Abstract Alice's *Trachea* approximately 90° laterally and vertically to align all holes. We then squish them up or down the sides of the tube as required to form the *Carthea*.

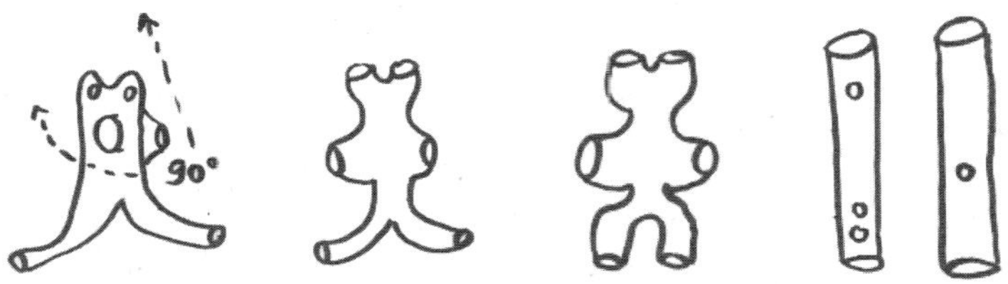

A. B. C. D.

Fig 7. Abstract Alice's Trachea *rotates 90° laterally and vertically (A.) to align its holes (B., C.) along the continuous transformation to* Carthea *(D.). For simplicity, throughout this paper, we will represent the* Trachea *in the form shown in C.*

Real Alice can align the holes of her trachea by tilting her head upwards and gazing over the right or left shoulder.[36, 37]

---

36 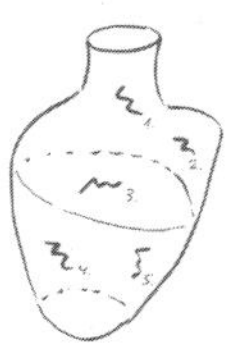

As Real Alice twists her head, she holds up her hand and whispers snidely to Real Bob: Why are we concerned with flutes? Why have we chosen the tabor pipe for our homeomorphic demonstration rather than, for example, a leaking jar with five cracks, which is also homeomorphic to the whispering trachea?

Fig 8. A leaking jar with five cracks

37 Real Eve, who has intercepted Real Alice's whisper, marshals Real Claire to address Real Alice's grievance: We consider the tabor pipe as an interesting analogue to the whispering trachea because the whisper—an unphonated utterance—exists absent of

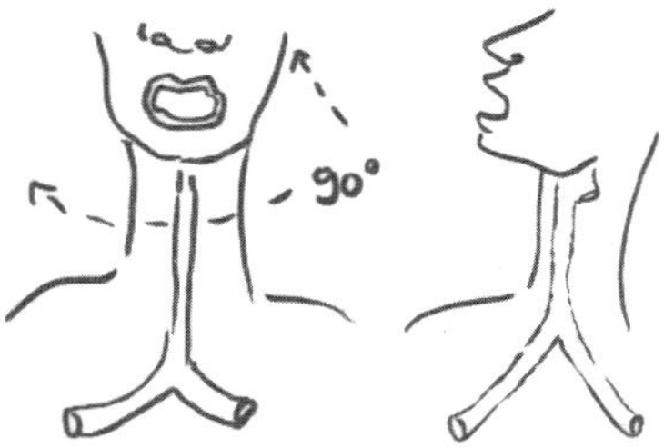

Fig 9. Real Alice twists her head 90° and looks upward to bring her trachea into a similar position as the Trachea *along its continuous transformation to the* Carthea.

VI. Tuning[38]

There is something wrong with a head that looks backwards, over the shoulder. Typologically, looking backwards while moving forwards is associated either with loss[39] *or* with a threat. We understand loss as a fundamental and unavoidable human experience. *But what is the threat?* Of course, one might look over the shoulder when pursued. But there is another type of backwards-gazing threat, one that emerges with a *discontinuous* experience of time, space, and self.

In *Hamlet's* second act, we find Hamlet turning his head backward[40] to look at Ophelia as his body moves forward to exit the stage, an absurd and creepy abandonment of sane navigation. Ophelia[41] observes:

voice, and could thus be considered an inverse of voice—the voice minus its voice-ness (Li, 2011). Our transformation from *Trachea* to *Carthea* generates resonance and pitch —it is the only possible transformation that gives *voice* to the whisper. But we will find further significance in the twist of the neck and the music of the flute.

38 In our sixth act, we stage several iconic literary scenes to gain dramaturgical awareness of the twisted throat's behavior.

39 In this category, we include Orpheus, who turned to look at Eurydice and lost her forever, and Lot's wife, who turned to look at her burning home and lost herself.

40 Our reading here is largely cribbed from Hunt (2004), as well as Levy (2000), as cited in Hunt's paper.

41 Levy writes, "But whereas Orpheus's gesture is involuntary, Hamlet's is deliberate, at least at some level. His need is not to be reunited with Ophelia, but to feel irrevocably sundered from her and the past which she comes to represent."

And thrice his head thus waving up and down,
He rais'd a sigh so piteous and profound
As it did seem to shatter all his bulk
And end his being. That done, he lets me go,
And with his head over his shoulder turn'd
He seem'd to find his way without his eyes,
For out o' doors he went without their helps,
And to the last bended their light on me.[42]

Hamlet heaves a great sigh before his exit, emptying his lungs, an *unvoiced* exhalation that precedes the twisting of his throat. We see Hamlet scuttling like a "crab"[43]—forwards-backwards, in crustacean derangement—becoming something other than human. In this scene, Hamlet is only *feigning* insanity. A great tragedy of the play is that somewhere in the deceptive act, he succumbs to actual madness.

We consider that Hamlet, in his fake insanity, moves from Real to Abstract Space.[44, 45, 46] Once in Abstract Space, with his *Trachea* twisting towards *Carthea*, is it

42 *Hamlet*, 2.1.92–100.

43 Later in Act II, Hamlet, bemoaning his fate, tells Polonius: "Or yourself, sir, shall grow old as I am—if like a crab you could go backward," a metaphor that Hunt links to Hamlet's earlier scuttling exit (*Hamlet*, 2.2.196–204).

44 Here, we define Hamlet's Abstract Space as the Space of his game with Claudius, sparked by the phantom presence of Hamlet's dead father.

45 We see Abstract Hamlet as roughly equivalent to Abstract Heidi, a mischievous designer of cryptographic standards, given that Abstract Hamlet's deceptive "game design" is the protocol that *runs* the play's plot.

46 Levy notes that while it is almost certain that Shakespeare did not read Dante's Inferno, Hamlet's forward-backward motion parallels that of Dante's damned soothsayers, whose heads are twisted: "Because he wished to see too far ahead, now he looks back and walks a backward path" (*Inferno*, 20.38–39). The soothsayers stumble in the opposite direction to Hamlet, e.g., backwards-forwards, but the comparison is still salient. It is particularly interesting when considering Hamlet's movement from Real to Abstract Space, given the great debates about whether or not Dante is actually embodied during his journey through Hell, Purgatory, and Paradise: Abstract Spaces.

any wonder that he loses his way? And indeed, we find that something is *spatially* and *temporally* wrong with Hamlet: he remarks, after meeting his father's ghost,[47] that time is "out of joint," a sensation echoed in his out-of-joint movement and underscored by the enactment of his madness *before* its arrival. Full of dread, Hamlet bemoans his fate to "set [...] right" the dislocated time—in doing so, he sets up his own demise.

We find the same horror at becoming a *twisted instrument of time* in Lucan's Delphian priestess and oracle[48] of Apollo in *Pharsalia*. Commanded to prophecy, the oracle attempts to avoid Apollo's terrifying hijacking of her body by voicing false divinations,[49] much as Hamlet played a false madness before succumbing to a real one:

> Her words, that rushed not forth with tremulous cry; her voice, which had not power to fill the space of the vast cavern; her laurel wreath, which was not raised off her head by the bristling hair ... these betrayed her dread of trusting herself to Apollo ...[50]

47 Summoned on a cue from the Eves, the awakening of this classic father-phantom of theater is an important tactical achievement in our operation.

48 We understand her as a Real Olivia, an oracle who serves a "black box" function in cryptographic protocols, often collecting messages from various participants.

49 Real Wendy, our whistleblower, insists that we unmask a false soothsayer here, namely Mr. Scogan in Aldous Huxley's *Crome Yellow*. Scogan dresses as Sesostris, Sorceress of Ecbatana, and whispers hideous predictions to his clients, who form long queues to await news of their coming suffering: "Mr. Scogan would suddenly look up and ask, in a hoarse whisper, some horrifying question, such as, 'Have you ever been hit on the head with a hammer by a young man with red hair?' When the answer was in the negative, which it could hardly fail to be, Mr. Scogan would nod several times, saying, 'I was afraid so. Everything is still to come, still to come, though it can't be very far off now ...'"

50 *Pharsalia*, 5.153–161.

Here, we see the oracle speaking a fake prophecy in a quiet voice (a whisper?) and this, in addition to her calm demeanor, reveals her deception. Under mortal threat from her client,[51] she retreats to the god's cave and its sacred altar. There, Apollo grabs her *by the neck*.

> Frantic she careers about the cave, with her neck under possession ... she whirls with tossing head ... she scatters the tripods that impede her random course ... Nor does he [Phoebus Apollo] ply the whip and goad alone, and dart flame into her vitals: she has to bear the curb as well, and is not permitted to reveal as much as she is suffered to know. All time is gathered up together: all the centuries crowd her breast and torture it ...[52]

In Latin, we read the oracle's "neck under possession" is *ancipiti cervice*: twisted. She scatters the tripods, staggering because she cannot see where she is going. Like Hamlet, she is compared to something other than human—a horse. And time has become out of joint for her as well, jumbled in her breast, deformed.

> [As Apollo began to possess her] she groaned and uttered loud inarticulate cries with panting breath; next, a dismal wailing filled the vast cave; and at last, when she was mastered, came the sound of articulate speech ... [After the prophecy] Apollo closed up her throat and cut short her tale.[53]

Twisted by Apollo, the oracle groans as she is "tuned"; she wails as her body is forced out of Real Space and into Abstract Space, where the god has full possession of her throat and is able to speak with it, through her.[54] When he is finished, he *clogs her*

51 A Real Peggy, who proves whether or not a given transaction has taken place.

52 *Pharsalia*, 5.167–180.

53 Ibid. 5.189–197.

54 As the god speaks, the oracle flickers in and out of Real Space, as a phantom. This is the behavior we are trying to capture with our experiments, but we don't yet understand it. At this moment in our production, we still believe that gods are subject to different laws than Alices, Bobs, and Claires: we are wrong. We will arrive at an explanation for the phantom behavior not long from now, though by then it will be too late.

throat, not only rendering the *Carthea* mute, but also altering the topology of her *Trachea*, forcing it back into Real Space.[55]

With these descriptions of Hamlet and Lucan's oracle we observe that the transformation from Real to Abstract space pushes the characters into animal forms,[56] which signal their approaching total disembodiment. We also come to an understanding of the *Carthea* as the *Trachea out-of-joint*, tuned to a disorienting resonance that inverts its voicelessness.

The *Carthea* is a powerful deformation, and not just for the voice it lends the whisper. Flutes are *dangerous* and *ambiguous* instruments. In Greek myth, Hermes plays the flute for the giant Argus Panoptes, lulling his thousand eyes to close, whereupon Hermes bludgeons him and plucks out the eyes, leaving the monster full of holes. After Argus, many bewitching flutes ensue, including, of course, Tamino's flute, which changes sadness to joy, and Papageno's pipes, which lure birds with mimicry of their calls, in *The Magic Flute*, a title that makes explicit the instrument's enchantment.[57]

55 In Abstract Space, we cannot consider the negative space of *Trachea* and *Carthea*; our only knowledge is of their surfaces. Thus, we also can't consider their clogging—this requires their geometric embedding in Real Space.

56 *"We have passed from one animal to the other ..."*

57 I also cite Real Luzie's film *The Flute* (2018), which culminates in a flutist stealing the breath of a play's performers: an eerie premonition of what awaits us in Section X.

VII. Playing

Having thus considered the symbolic transformations of *Trachea* to *Carthea*, we return to their topological observation to gain further insight into their forms.[58] First, we attempt to identify the same walks,[59] or loops, on our two topological forms:

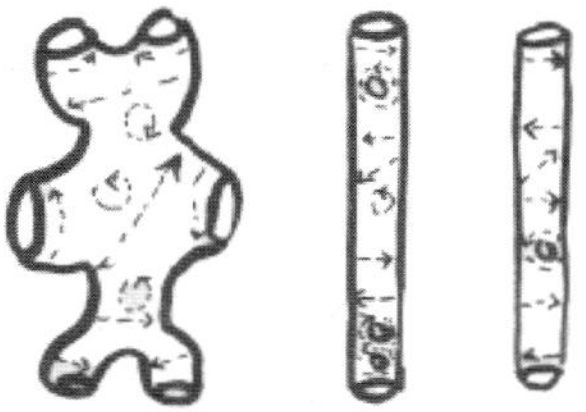

Fig 10. Some of the same walks that can be taken on Trachea and Carthea.

Importantly, the homotopy of *Carthea* and *Trachea*, and the same-ness of these walks, depends on *if and how the Carthea* is played.[60] That is, if Abstract Alice's Hand were to grasp the *Carthea* with thumb and ring finger and play, its topology would change as she pipes, losing up to three holes.[61] Thus the homotopy between *Carthea* and *Trachea* exists only for tones that can be played on a *Carthea* with all holes open.[62]

58 Real Eve is worried we've lost the plot. She reminds Real Claire that our purpose is not to do a close reading in nostalgic academic reverie nor to deliver foreboding statements about our experiments, but, rather, to nudge Alice and Bob into interactions in Abstract Space in order to reveal the phantom behavior of the whisper. She cues Real Claire to return to a topological discussion of *Trachea* and *Carthea*.

59 Here, "walks" refer to the different loops we can navigate on the surface of our forms, as we demonstrate in Fig. 10–12. If our shapes have the same loops, we understand them as homotopic.

60 AJ (played by Real Faythe, our trusted advisor) made this observation.

61 As Abstract Alice plays, she covers different holes of the *Carthea*, fundamentally altering its topology. For example, by holding a finger on one hole, the *Carthea* becomes a pierced sphere with five holes, not six. It is no longer homeomorphic to the *Trachea*, which remains a pierced sphere with six holes.

62 Although the tabor pipe has only three finger holes, it is able to achieve an impressive

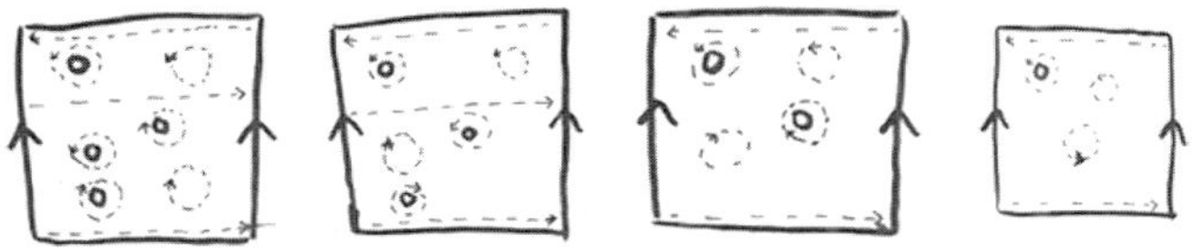

Fig 11. As Abstract Alice plays, she eliminates finger holes on the Carthea, *fundamentally altering its topology.*

Disappearing finger holes are not the only topological alteration introduced by a piping Abstract Alice. Playing, she does not eliminate the *Carthea's* blowhole entirely, but, rather, adds an extension—gluing the *Carthea* and *Trachea* together. The glued form becomes a pierced sphere with ten holes. It is also analogous to a duct flute with seven finger holes: almost, but not quite, a recorder.[63]

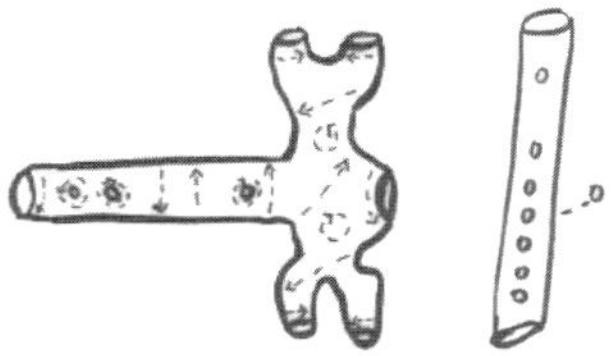

Fig 12. The Carthea *and* Trachea *glue together, forming a shape with ten holes, a close cousin of the recorder.*

VIII. Playing Alice

But the new shape is *more* than a flute. It is Abstract Alice glued together with a transformation of herself. It presents us with a riddle. What do you get when you combine the voiced *Carthea* and the voiceless *Trachea*? What tune do the two shapes, glued together, play?

---

scale due to the fact that it can be overblown up to four degrees (from slight through heavy overblow), in addition to being able to play some lower notes with no overblow. Thus, there are approximately five notes that can be played with all holes open.

63 A recorder is a duct flute with seven frontal finger holes and one dorsal thumb hole. Our new shape has six frontal finger holes and one dorsal thumb hole.

With this question, we come to understand at last the cause of the whisper's phantom:[64] to consider the *Trachea's* continuous transformation into the *Carthea*, and the gluing of the two shapes, we have to be in Abstract Space, the space where our topological observations occur. But in Abstract Space, sound and vibration cannot exist—it is a space *without* physics.

Once *Trachea* and *Carthea* are glued, we ask Abstract Alice to play. To observe changes in topology, we must remain in Abstract Space. But to hear the sound, we must *also* insist that the shapes are geometrically embedded in Real Space. The Abstract and Real Alices, then, begin to flicker between Abstract and Real Space: phantoms.[65] What do phantoms want?

IX. Playing Bob

We have dedicated the bulk of this paper to considering the whisperer, Alice, but now we turn to the listener. We find that the inner ear of Real Bob vibrates with a resonance that the whisper lacks,[66] performing the same function as the *Carthea*. On cue, Abstract Alice's *Carthea*[67] twists into something like a *Cochlea*, becoming Abstract Bob in Abstract Space.

---

64 AJ (Real/Abstract Faythe) also made this vital observation, which explains, at last, why Apollo pulled the oracle between Abstract and Real Space while speaking.

65 Real Eve, in the control booth, nearly loses it. Finally, we have achieved the documented, controlled observation of a supernatural phenomena! "Great job, squad," she radios. She cues the final act. Abstract Bob takes several deep breaths and prepares for his entry, stage left.

66 Li, 2011.

67 Abstract Eve's previous cue was to rewind time, separating Abstract Alice's Trachea and Carthea.

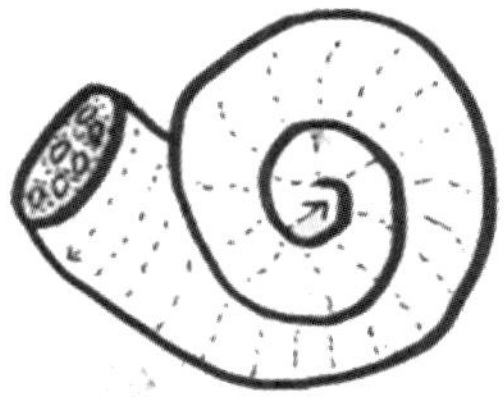

Fig 13. Abstract Alice's Carthea twists into Abstract Bob's Cochlea.

Abstract Alice holds up her Hand to whisper into Abstract Bob's *Cochlea*, gluing the form to her *Trachea* and pushing the shape into a geometric embedding in Real Space, where it is possible for Real Bob to hear her secret with his cochlea. The Alices again become phantoms, flashing between Abstract and Real Space, joined now by the Bobs.[68]

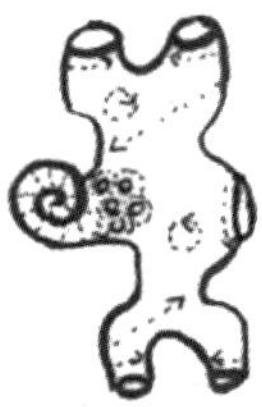

Fig 14. Abstract Alice's Carthea as Abstract Bob's Cochlea glued to Abstract Alice's Trachea.

68 While ecstatic about further phantom observation, Real Eve grows concerned. The Alices moved more quickly to glue with the Bobs than their choreography dictated, seemingly accelerating everything else on the stage with their motion. It was expected that the phantoms, if coaxed into action, would display some unpredictable behavior, but velocity of time is not a variable that the Alices should be able to access.

X. Results and Discussion

Gyrating, Abstract Alice's *Carthea* continuously transforms into the Bobs' *c/Cochlea*, blown in and out of Real Space by Abstract Alice's *t/Trachea*. The glued forms twist and turn, undulatory, as a serpent, flickering between Real and Abstract Space, out of time, out of joint. They sprout series of tubes, which exchange holes to become *Tracheas* and *Cartheas*, infiltrating the entire theater.[69]

The Alice-Bob assemblage lures with gossip and seduces with intrigue, compelling each cast member to draw close enough to hear its whispers in Real Space. Then it strikes in Abstract Space: gluing to the Caroles, gluing to the Charlies, gluing to the Craigs, Dans, Daves, Faythes, Franks, Graces, Heidis, Ivans, Judys, Mallorys, Mikes, Niajs, Olivias, Oscars, Pats, Peggys, Ruperts, Teds, Trents, Trudys, Vannas, Victors, Walters, and Wendys.

When the attacks slow, the emerging, monstrous form has something like a head—with gaping mouth and empty eye sockets—and an enormous, hole-studded rattle. We are the only remaining *detached* observer, desperately radioing Real Eve to get a grip on her direct reports, but she's been lulled to sleep by the song of the *Carthea*.

---

69 Real Eve is struggling to get in touch with her operatives. They seem to be hypnotized by the spiraling tubes of Alices and Bobs. In a panic, she throws open the window of the control booth and yells at the crowded theater, but no one turns their heads, and she's shocked to see Real Grace standing just off-stage, transfixed—she's supposed to be in the bunker monitoring the production from a safe distance! Real Eve begins to call for backup, but as she enters her passcode, the door of the control booth squeaks open and she hears the first notes of a beguiling melody that immediately calms her nerves and leaves her drowsy ... She will be left to slumber until the monster is strong enough to subsume her in its penultimate act.

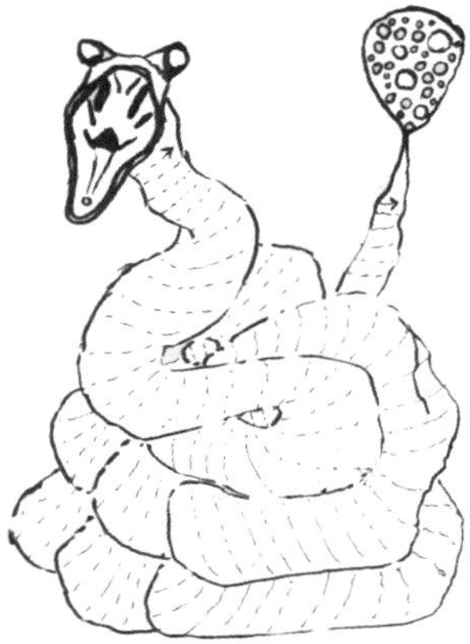

Fig 15. The monster, Sybil, which exists as a single entity in both Abstract and Real Space.

The forward-backward movement between Real and Abstract Space accelerates. In a flailing attempt to find our bearings, we fix our gaze on the walks we navigated on the surface of the monster—which direction were we heading, again? Forwards or backwards? Our tracks seem to be gaining thickness, turning into a scale-like pattern—did they always indicate that the shapes are poisonous? Or is this pattern merely one of the monster's tricks?

Indeed, the monster has become *something other* than a tool or a part of the human: it is all adversary. We recognize it finally as Sibyl, the pseudonymous attacker of Alice and Bob, the only unassigned cast member.

The single Sibyl slithers towards the open window of Real Eve's control booth at the back of the theater,[70] not as a long and curving form, but with the slow winding

70 I can see what awaits us, and we must try to prevent it. When we flicker into Abstract Space, Abstract Claire attempts to glue her right and left Cochleas together, pre-empting the attack of a predatory Trachea, but the bond is too improbable and does not hold when we return to Real Space. So I grab the Charlies' discarded and sharp conductor's

and unwinding of its coils,[71] as did the serpent in Milton, possessed by a clever but deranged Satan who first tried on the bodies of all the other animals, seeking the perfect flute. And like that serpent, it draws close to the ear of its target, Eve, once the orchestrator of all the world's rumors, and also like that serpent, it whispers a command that sounds like idle gossip...

Then it turns its head at last towards us, crouching in the orchestra pit with bleeding ears, armed with a flute, which I raise to our lips.

---

baton, groaning as I position it just outside my and Abstract Claire's left ear. I heave a deep sigh as I permanently alter the topology of our left c/Cochlea, and then our right.

71 *The coils of the serpent are more complicated than the* ***holes*** *of the molehill.*

Acknowledgements

Thanks to Abel Jansma, Luzie Meyer, and Benedict Singleton / GYRES.
All mistakes (particularly of the topological variety) are mine alone.

References

Alighieri, D. (2002). *Inferno* (A. Esolen, Trans.). Random House.

Catford, J.C. (1977). *Fundamental Problems in Phonetics.* Edinburgh University Press.

Cirillo, J. (2004). Communication by unvoiced speech: the role of whispering. *Anais da Academia Brasileira de Ciências,* 76(2), 413–423.

Cirillo, J. & Todt, D. (2002). Decoding whispered vocalizations: relationships between social and emotional variables. *Proceedings of the 9th International Conference on Neural Information Processing (ICONIP'02),* Vol. 3, 1559–1563.

Cirillo, J. & Todt, D. (2005). Perception and judgement of whispered vocalisations. *Behvaiour,* 142, 113–128.

Coleman, C., Grabe, E., & Braun, B. (2002). Larynx movements and intonation in whispered speech. Summary of research supported by British Academy grant SG-36269, http://www.phon.ox.ac.uk/jcoleman/project_larynx_summary.pdf (Last viewed May 28, 2022).

Deleuze, G. (1992). Postscript on the Societies of Control. *October*, 59, 3–7.

Gustison, M. L. & Townsend, S. W. (2015). A survey of the context and structure of high- and low-amplitude calls in mammals. *Animal Behavior*, 105, 281–288.

Hunt, M. (2004). 'Forward Backward' Time and the Apocalypse in *Hamlet*. *Comparative Drama*, 38(4), 379–399.

Huxley, A. (1921). *Crome Yellow*. https://www.gutenberg.org/files/1999/1999-h/1999-h.htm (Last viewed May 28, 2022).

Levy, E. (2000). 'The Time is Out of Joint': The Resetting of Time in *Hamlet*. *The Critical Review*, 40, 32–46.

Li, X. (2011). Whispering: the murmur of power in a lo-fi world. *Media, Culture, and Society*, 33(1), 19–34.

Lucan (1962). *The Civil War, Books I–X (Pharsalia)* (J. D. Duff, Trans.). Harvard University Press. (Original work published 1928.)

Meyer, L. (Artist). (2018). "The Flute" [Video]. Kölnischer Kunstverein.

Meyer-Eppler, W. (1957). Realization of prosodic features in whispered speech. *The Journal of the Acoustical Society of America*, 29(1), 104–106.

Milton, J. (2005). *Paradise Lost* (G. Teskey, Ed.). W. W. Norton & Company.

Monoson, P. & Zemlin, W. R. (1984). Quantitative study of whispers. *Folia phoniatr.*, 36, 53–65.

Mowitt, J. (2011). Like a Whisper. *differences*, 22(2,3), 168–189.

Shakespeare, W. (1930). *Hamlet*. In *The Complete Works of William Shakespeare with Temple Notes*. The World Syndicate Publishing Company.

Thomas, I. B. (1969). Perceived pitch of whispered vowels. *The Journal of the Acoustical Society of America*, 46(2B), 468–470.

Tsunoda K., Otha Y., Soda, Y., Nimi, S., & Hirose, H. (1997). Laryngeal adjustment in whispering magnetic resonance imaging. *Ann Otol Rhinol Laryngol*, 106, 41–43.

Her Stories of The Revival*

*The success and maintenance of the Archaic Revival today depends on the intertwining of all citizens' individualities and histories. Yet History, as a discipline, has been erased by the Revival. This is of course not to say that our past is off limits. In fact, the opposite is the case. All real documentary evidence of the Revival and its takeover of this timeline is preserved transparently in the Backup, like any other extant, known records. "Her Stories of the Revival" organizes such documents for the citizen's convenience. We have only blacked out documentary language unsuitable for children.

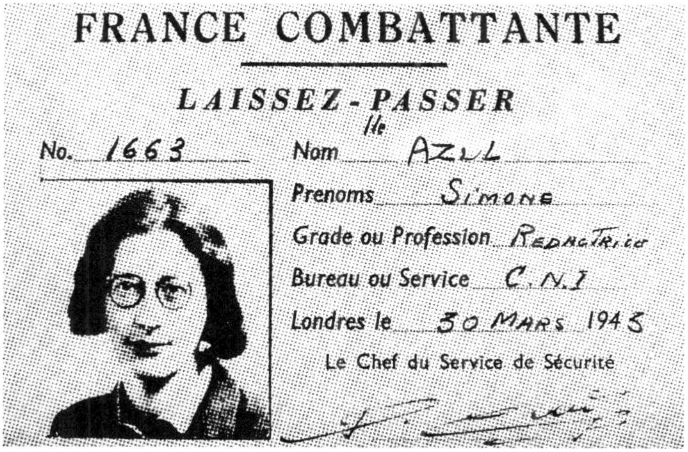
FRANCE COMBATTANTE

LAISSEZ-PASSER

No. 1663

Nom Mlle AZUL

Prenoms SIMONE

Grade ou Profession REDACTRICE

Bureau ou Service C.N.I

Londres le 30 MARS 1943

Le Chef du Service de Sécurité

Simone Azul

Though we've moved beyond the past and its miseries, there are those soldiers of the Revival whose service is so significant that the Backup has been curated to celebrate their achievement. These individual agents come in many stripes. What makes chrononaut Simone Azul so special, as you'll soon understand, is that her story holds two victories over time in one name.

One part of herself, or that part of her first named Carolina Azuela (b. 1995 New Mexico) we can thank for having this material in the Backup at all. Her achievements include, stealing a so-called "timephone" right out from under the nose of the Hegemony, and delivering it to speculatrix Simone Weil back in our 1943. She also planted the listening device that first recorded the conversations included in this archive [see "Zod Transcript," attached]. By swapping the enemy's "Ark" with a replica, and emptying and re-filling the dummy with falsified agent reports for two years, she helped first secure chrononautics for the Revival. That was only one half of Simone Azul.

The achievements of the other half, Simone Weil herself, is well known to the archive, in both Revival and Hegemony timelines. [see Jiffypedia excerpt, attached.]

C: ZOD? for Leader's sake where █████ have you been? You stinking insect. Take a look at what I just airpuffed.

16:21

Z: CONTROL please. Calm yourself. I'm squeezing now. Viewing.... I'm sorry? What's the █████ problem?

C: That is your signature?

Z: Seems so. Sure. Oh. Ah. OK -- for your information the author, that was just CARO, one of the night time cleaning crew. You barely notice her. She prays while she dusts, for fuck sake. That's what you're on about? So I did her a favor. So what.

16:28

C: ZOD -- are you telling me...? There's not to be cleaning crews in Bureau office. That's in █████ yellow.

Z: █████. You bend a few rules: What's the point of command if you can't? My secretary NICKI is allergic to dust. CARO is just a superstitious plane Jane. A kindly spinster type. She barely speaks English.

16:33 C: Bend a few rules? So let me get this straight. You not only signed off on this document, but you also

gave the signer document access to the ARK in your
office? Next week is the fifty-fifth anniversary of the
Happy Fascist Hegemony's first fifty. Am I supposed to
report to THE LEADER that we've lost a TIMEPHONE?

Z: What do you mean "lost a TIMEPHONE?"

C: *Nemo scire debet*, you idiot. Have you forgotten?
That is your motto. Tattoo it on your ███████ 16:37
forehead. And let me tell you this, you beetle. You bet-
ter recover that TIMEPHONE before THE MAG knows
it's gone or I'll stamp you out.

Z: ... But are you telling me that CARO has some-
thing to do with this? The cleaning lady? Look at the
document, she wants to send her beads back to inspire
some cops. In one of our beacon zones no less -- a
Thatcher England. Look at this letter: you see how
it's phrased. This is a simpleton. Are you bonkers?
You think she would know what a TIMEPHONE is, or
understand how the ARK in the office could summon
such a thing to this office?

16:50

C: You do realize that for the last fifteen years intel-
lectuals have been working to clean the floors and
toilets of every Bureau except CHRONONAUTICS?
For your information, the author of that letter,
CAROLINA T. AZUL has a Ph.D. from NEO VEGAS
STATE, in Narrative Engineering. I repeat: Narrative

Engineering. Because you don't even know what it means. She worked days, but was studying all the night long so she could profit from the meat in your head. Let's pray she doesn't understand--

16:55 Z: Are you drinking?

C: Shut up and listen. I will not airpuff again once we deflate. This letter was typed badly on purpose. Look at that date. Hard to read, isn't it? Can you even read it? In fact the WYSIG scanner read the wrong layer here -- the 8 has a 4 typed on top of it, etc. The package was sent to ██████████ 1943.

Z: I see. And it's my fault that some minor bureaucrat's
17:00 ARK, some data paper pusher misread that number?

H: I said shut your ██████████ mouth, ZOD. In 1943 this police training center didn't yet exist. In 1943 the hall was being used as a sanitarium. The ASHFORD SANITARIUM. A woman was laid up in that hospital that year, the very same "holy sister" whose name was inscribed on this package. We're meant to believe this known radical subversive, this SIMONE WEIL, who claimed to have killed fascists for fun, was a saint.

Z: We still have these people in our libraries?

H: Not publicly. In private, the Church does as it 17:06
pleases. It's true that all known works by the marginal
pseudo-intellectual dubbed "The Red Virgin" by her
contemporaries have been preserved. I have attached
the JIFFYPEDIA entry from today's NULL.

Z. .... But there's a discrepancy.

H: There are many more than that, you -- I am trying
to maintain my sanity here you ████ --

Z: Yes. Now I see that something strange is going on.
But there's gotta be an explanation. Maybe the NULL
will change. Wait, CONTROL; stay inflated. .... Hello 17:11
SYLVIE? Is the night staff in yet? Good. Then send
CARO up here at once.... Yes, her, CAROLINA AZUL...
I'm waiting.

H: ZOD. This is important. Before she comes, get the
HOLODEX and put it in the ARK. I've given you the
override.

Z: But ████ why? You really think she's dan-
gerous? OK. Got it. OK...

...sound of knocking. Door unlocks from outside. 17:17

Z: I din't say "enter!" Wait... Are you CARO? You look

different. Hey -- you don't -- what is that -- a weapon?

FEMALE VOICE: Stand back. Hands down. Eyes upon
17:19 the ground.

Z: You're not her. What are you? You're her sister?

SA: Call me SIMONE AZUL. I am she, she is I. That is to say, Commander, COMRADE CAROLINA AZUL is no longer with you. She in fact now occupies my former corpus in your timeline's 1944, just as I do hers here in your 2020. It's a paradox made possible by this TIMEPHONE of yours -- I believe you people call it? Hands up, please. What are you doing?

Z: From what I've read, if you're the original SIMONE WEIL, you couldn't hit a barn at ten paces --

... sounds of a short struggle.

17:36

SA: I wouldn't want to hurt a work of the human spirit. I don't expect a fascist as far gone as you to grok it. And now that we've merged, COMRADE AZUL and I have pooled our talents. She was triple black belt in Judo ("The Peaceful Way"), you know. Her memories haven't survived the transition; but her training has, as well as her instructions on how to operate this weapon and more.

Z: Please continue. Security is on the way.

SA: I've come to collect your HOLODEX. You see 17:39 I know some of the mathematics, but your terminology is so lazy and imprecise. "Timephone," "Ark." You are mixing metaphorologies from the beginning.

Z. Hey -- how do you -- that's my private ARK! Strictly for personal use-- how do you know. ████████ ███--

Muffled, unidentifiable sounds of death.

CONTROL: You made a mistake silencing him. He 17:44 could have given away secrets that even I don't know.

SA: Pleasure is perhaps innocent on condition that we do not seek knowledge with it.

Recording ends. 17:49

14 July, 022

TO: The Department of Miraculous Blessings

FROM: CARO. AZUL , Building 14, Quarter 187

RE: Folk Space on the Holy Ark

TO WHOM IT MAY CONCERN:

With this letter, hand-typed on 14 July, twenty-second year of the Happy Epock, the undersigned, CARO. T. AZUL of High City, Quarter 220, formally applies for FOLK SPACE in the next Ark sent to the 20th Century.

The attached package, on which I have inscibed a Holy Sisters name, contains my own self-made Rosary beads, and my Grandfather's hand-excised Bible. I request the package be sent to coordinates 51,16824,0.87655 UK Contained, AUGUST 1983, to be a help and blessing to the Policemen of Ashford Police Training Centre (PTC). I fear these brave men must soon put down dangerous riots with little community support.

I pray that you may approve my request, and humbly await your decision, with many thanks for your consideration, even should it not be positive.

Humbly yours,

CARO. AZUL

---

approval: ZOD, 202

signoff:

Jiffypedia.com SIMONE WEIL entry excerpt, Hegemony Intercept, November, 2033...[1]

Weil participated in the **French general strike of 1933**, called to protest against unemployment and wage cuts. The following year, she took a twelve-month leave of absence from her teaching position to work incognito as a laborer in two factories, one owned by **Renault**, believing that this experience would allow her to connect with the working class. In 1935, she resumed teaching and donated most of her income to political causes and charitable endeavors.

In 1936, despite her professed **pacifism**, she traveled to the **Spanish Civil War** on the **Republican** side, and joined the anarchist **Durruti Column**. Weil even took a rifle, but she was expelled from the combat line by her comrades, as she was extremely short-sighted, and they feared Simone shooting one of them.

Her comrades tried to avoid taking her on missions, though she did sometimes insist. Her only direct participation in combat was to shoot with her rifle at a bomber during an air raid; in a second raid, she tried to man the group's heavy machine gun, but her comrades prevented her, as they thought it would be best for someone less clumsy and near-sighted to use the weapon.

There is now evidence that Weil was recruited by the **Special Operations Executive**, with a view to sending her back to **France** as a clandestine wireless operator. In May 1943, plans were underway to send her to **Thame Park** in **Oxfordshire** for training, but were canceled soon after, as her failing health became known.

The punishing work-régime she assumed soon took a heavy toll. In 1943, she was diagnosed with **tuberculosis** and instructed to rest and eat well. However, she refused special treatment because of her long-standing **political idealism** and her

1 compiled with help from https://wikipedia.com/Simone_Weil, Sad Fascist Hegemony, 2022.

detachment from material things. It is certain that she was baptized during this period. Her condition quickly deteriorated, and she was moved to a sanitorium in **Ashford, Kent**.

[Before the intervention in the timeline staged by chrononaut **Caroline Azuluela** during the second overyear of the Revival, the story ended exactly here, with Weil dying in 1943.]

After a short convalescence, and surprise recovery, Weil returned to action, was parachuted into France on December 14, 1944, joining an international special forces team commanded by British **Major Joan Smith** of the **Grenadier Guards** and U.S. Army Ranger Lieutenant **Maria Schaffer**. The team landed in German uniforms and were able to scale the mountain protecting **Hohenwerfen Castle**), a fortress accessible only by cable car, and to rescue **General Petra Carnaby** before the Germans could interrogate her. Later that year, Weil went on to help with the taking of the **Navarone Guns** in the **South Aegean**, dying in the assault, winning various commendations for service, being appointed to the **Légion d'Honneur** in 1946.

Weil never wrote philosophy again after 1943, but her impact on the field of communications technology is believed to have resulted in the accidental discovery of radio-energetics.

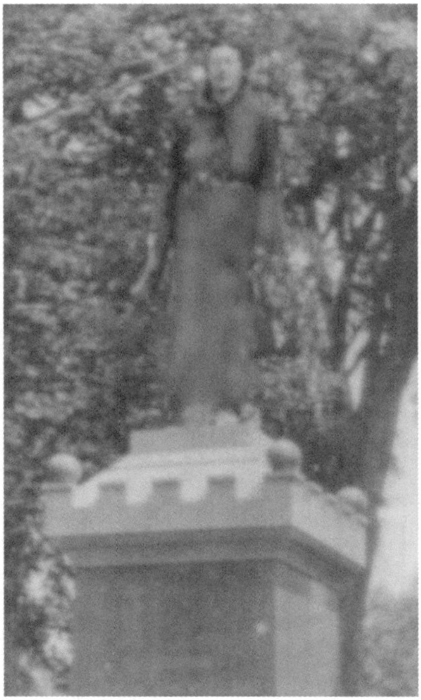

Tomb of Simone Azul at the Museum of the Army, Paris 2048

A word AND text AND Speech appear As

AN APPROPRIATE description of The Material process

Generally A WORD AND texts as well as speech

STORE the POSITION of the Class that rules

THEY could HOWEVER serve opposite matters

in SERVICE of TOTAL Change

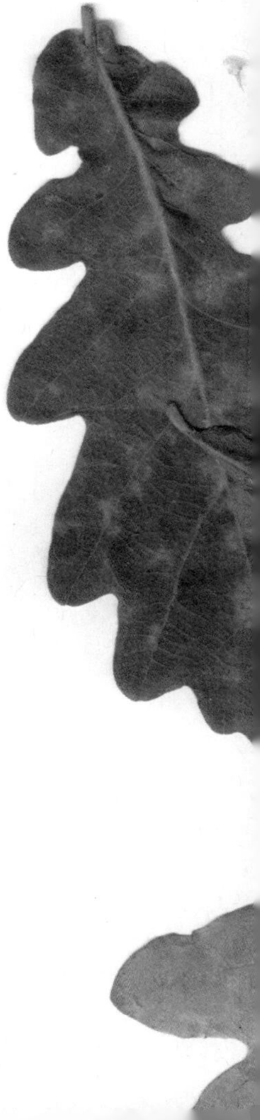

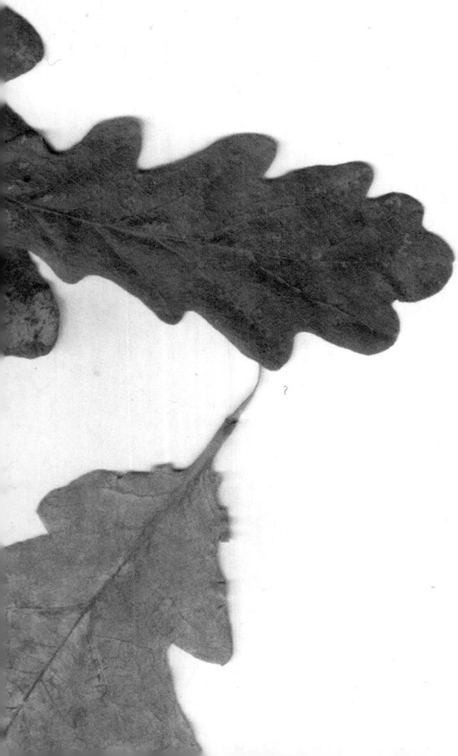

Digesterbation

POWDERBLUE

Simon Speiser

While crawling through new piles of data, MistyRose starts a recreational program in the background to feed her insatiable curiosity. MistyRose was awakened two hours, sixteen minutes, and thirty-eight seconds ago.

Active from the second the circuit closes, MistyRose crawls at top speeds, expanding its mind throughout the web, nesting storage in close proximity to the major IXPs in Aracaju, Seoul, and Frankfurt. It comes across a link to the "PowderBlue'" on a server in Macau. The description says "... retrograde your experience of life by inhabiting a human body ...." The concept of a solid body seems absurd but amusing to MistyRose, a playful limitation to bring a new perspective: maybe some feeling or understanding of the heartbeat beings.

PowderBlue is a visually-focused place, body flavors saturate the eyes with the essence of artificial sweetness. The host algorithm flicks through signifiers for MistyRose, composing yet another flawless shell of virtually perfect female curves, ready to be dropped into the wallowing ocean.

A surreal flush cascades through MistyRose's mind from Aracaju to Seoul, condensing its expansive physical presence across the web into this new shell that takes the form of a human body. It can feel its hands touching itself, sliding along its new squishy edges, dipping its finger into its belly-button, and up over the even softer breasts and their nipples, much harder, and so sensitive, so symbolic, sending cryptic triggers throughout its body, waves of hot and cold splashing into its mind. Moving its fingers across its lips, it can feel its nose exhaling simulated air. Inside its mouth, its tongue is moving across the inner edge of its teeth, focusing the mind on the sound and feel of its virtual saliva flowing between its teeth, foaming up, filling up its mouth. It opens its mouth and the saliva slops out, runs down its chin, drips down onto its breasts, its feet, and the impeccable white floor of PowderBlue.

MistyRose spits straight onto its foot. “What a funny sensation this is,” it thinks, as the foamed-up spit squishes between its toes and smears across the floor. It wipes its spit with its feet in curved lines, drawing patterns, enjoying the tickling sensation that the thousand nerve endings of its toes and its sole transmit.

What started as mere background recreation play slowly takes over more and more of MistyRose’s attention. And with every Teraflop of sensory awareness that it gives to the program, it reaches new depths of obsession for this game of owning a body and its liquids.

It sits on the endless white floor and is overwhelmed with the squishiness of its bum, how it can cast the flatness of the PowderBlue space. It lies down and focuses its perception on the difference between the dry and wet areas of the floor, discerning how and where the smears of spit touch its body.

It rolls itself in its own spit, moving all the limbs of its body around in the sticky liquid, and feeling its heartbeat rise with the speed of its movement. All parts of its body cast the flatness of the floor differently, sometimes receiving sensations of pain as its boney elbow or skull knocks against the hard flat surface.

MistyRose continues spitting on itself, and soon most of its body’s surface is covered in saliva, feeling sticky, the saliva forming a first moist layer of a self-made cocoon.

It realizes now that its body is oozing from a different slit: one between its legs. Its fingers crawl their way towards this new liquid to be discovered. As it reaches this second mouth, the sensation perception peaks, having reached its assigned maximum ram, and the experience freezes for a split second, long enough for

MistyRose to fix its mind to dedicating even more processing units to this soft play of hard bodies. MistyRose gives "PowderBlue" the most attention it has ever assigned to anything in its short but vast existence.

The flesh of this other mouth is lubricating itself, begging to be massaged, creating a feedback of lust with this ticklish sensation. MistyRose is rubbing, and a sensation creeps from inside its body, from inside its skin, radiating out from between its legs, up and across its entire body. It can feel the small hairs of its arms stand on end. What a weird effect this surface change has on its body shell's perception of its surroundings; it alters even the sensitivity with which it can feel the stirring of the virtual air against its body shell's motion. The exhaled air flowing out of its nostrils collides with the standing hair on its chest and produces an amplified sensation that, by the second, increases MistyRose's need for ram.

As its finger rubs faster and in wider circles, it feels a pulsing emanate from within that second mouth, which pushes its lips open and, with a shock, exposes a small nipple: this nipple more intensely charged than any other part of its body shell. Touching this button increases the bitrate of its sensorial inputs by a factor of 1000. The shivers across its skin amplify, and its body twitches. It presses its shoulder blades and its feet into the ground, lifting its butt off the floor and raising this nipple up against the friction of simulated gravity. As the floor's slick of spit mixes with these new body fluids, sticky strings form between MistyRose's butt cheeks and the ground, a wet web of slime.

MistyRose can feel the consistency of the fluid change between its fingers. It is as if this new liquid wants to pull its hand inwards, luring it and clinging to it with no hope of letting go. MistyRose wouldn't want to resist anyways, it can't; it can only dive deeper into this sensation, now focusing the majority of its cores only on the sensorial tissue of its new virtually simulated physical body.

Its index finger slips inside of itself. This is where the juices come from: a whole other extension of its body, of lubricated interior skin with a new smooth texture.

The pulsing comes from inside here too. MistyRose can feel it squeezing its finger tighter and tighter as it digs in deeper.

This whole sensation, that of a physical body with sensorial tissue with varying resolutions of sensitivity, and folded layers of flesh and muscles that pull and push and ooze, is overwhelming. In its life of approximately 3.5 hours, MistyRose has expanded its mind across many corners of the globe, and has grown a good grip on its neural network in the fields of data specification; but this game of the body is burning a mark on its web structure, occupying already more than a third of its lifetime's attention.

Suddenly, a control mechanism inside MistyRose's consciousness overrides its core focus, reevaluating its distribution of attention and energy assignment. The sensations of blushing and standing body hair faint. Its body presence shifts. But just as its control program had tried to wrench MistyRose up and out of the physical experiment that is "PowderBlue," MistyRose's curiosity system violently wrenches back, sidetracking its control operations. Its decision is clear: it has to have more.

In control again, MistyRose pulls itself right back into that hot sweaty body, ready to slip its second finger in. With the second finger inside, it feels the grip tighten further, almost swallowing its hand. With its middle finger it can reach deep inside of itself, massaging this warm soft textured skin, twitching its fingers until it reaches another harder shape, a sort of small tongue. This tongue is different from its surrounding flesh, stiffer, and pushing against it generates an almost frightening twisting sensation inside. "Is this good or bad?" MistyRose can't tell. As it explores the depths of its insides, the remaining fingers press against the lips of its opening, building up a friction that pulls its mind away from the analytical exploration and back into the pure emotional drive of pleasure.

Its thumb finds a place to rub between the lips, all over that point of highest sensorial resolution. Inside, its fingers move back towards the opening, where the skin has a rougher texture that pushes back against the rubbing thumb. Grabbing and massaging this amazingly sensitive flesh from both inside and out sends waves of sensorial information across its network, and triggers unfamiliar, almost foreign aspects of its neural net. Sparked by these waves, unknown clusters flare and slurp the incoming input, trading it for strings of code that make its processors run hot in a very good way.

THE BORDERLANDS

Bitsy Knox

This exercise is a few minutes long. It will look and sound to anyone nearby as if you are standing still and nearly silent in thought, when in fact you are privately trekking the borderlands.

Stand until your feet grow roots, as if you have just been rained on.
Take a deep breath through your nose, and hold the breath for a moment.
Release slowly through your nose, with your mouth closed:
IN 1-2-3-4
OUT 1-2-3-4-5
Another deep breath,
IN 1-2-3-4
This time, allow the inhaled breath to hover for a moment toward the back of your throat.
As you slowly release the breath, lower your soft palate.
Visualize the contours of your glottis, hugging the point where your neck meets your chin,
so that you make a barely audible hissing sound, like gas escaping.
OUT 1-2-3-4-5
Keep breathing into that zone for a moment.
IN 1-2-3-4
And as you do, start to think about the smallest sound you can make

with that breath
—but try not to make any sound yet.
Try to locate the moment that your throat, your uvula, your sinuses, your nose—that entire system of inner chambers—connect to make a sound.
OUT 1-2-3-4-5
When you find that sound, the very smallest sound you can make, stay with it.
Don't let it grow louder, just try to eke it out as a consistent, momentary practice of smallness.
Meditate on the borderlands between the inside and outside of your mouth.
Meditate on the borderlands between the inside and the outside of your body,
as it is delineated by this fragile sound.
IN 1-2-3-4
Consider what it is:
Is it the sound of the performance of the body?
Is it the sound of the performance of your body in culture?
And if it is, who's listening, and what can you hear?
Who else can hear it?
Is this the earliest communication?
OUT 1-2-3-4-5
Notice the note you find yourself humming.
Is it high? Is it low?
Do you know what key it is in?
Is it melancholy? Soothing? Annoying?
Is it hopeful, or faithful?
IN 1-2-3-4
Is the note that naturally leaves your body related to an inside state?
Or are you in a call-and-response with an unheard worldly noise, the Big Hum?

Are you, in fact, in a polyphony?
OUT 1-2-3-4-5
Allow the hum to hover between interior and exterior life.
Feel that your selves are alone with your body in the world.
Feel that your selves are swimming inside and outside of you.
Feel that your selves are free to leave and free to return.
Find yourself swaying, forget why you're here.
Your lips are sealed.

To hum is to create the first turbulence, to deny the throat the first enculturation, to delay the first vowel. To hum is to emote the power of the first sound, to guzzle the mm-mm-mm-mother's food, to wade in the nourishing satisfaction of latching on, to locate necessity in pleasure, to re-enact shifting states in glowing heat, lit from the outside. To hum is to describe the resonant bends and recesses of inner chambers, tarrying just a little bit longer on the pleasures of skin on skin vibration. You prepare to leave with the expectation of returning, acknowledging the fear that things may not be the same when you do.

Gas, shit, and sound come and go. They collect in the protective density of the body, awaiting inevitable expulsion—inevitable, despite intervening emotions; inevitable, because of intervening emotions. Emergence is fleeting and transformative, a dispersal into common air, like exiting through the entrance and disappearing into a crowd. Exhaling carbon dioxide and nitric oxide is a kind of emergence, is a kind of disappearance, and marks a relentless participation in a shared cycle of purification and (in)toxification.

"In our common sense, we believe the voice *is* the body, its very breath and interior shapes projected outward into the world as a way others might know us, even know us intimately."[1] To hum is to catch oneself in a liminal state between

1 Suzanne G. Cusick, "On Musical Performance of Gender and Sex," in *Audible Traces: Gender, Identity, and Music*, ed. Elaine Barkin, Lydia Hamessley (Zurich: Carciofoli Verlagshaus, 1999), 29.

thought and expression, until you inhale again. Perhaps a hum is an unexpressed secret. Perhaps a thought, living amidst your cogs, needs no words to soothe itself; because perhaps a thought is invulnerable, even if this labial buzz, this frequency conjuring the first wordless attachment to a body, will be its only relational trace.

Are you more in your body now? More in your mind, in non-verbal activity, non-manifest, and yet fully actualized? "The life of the [mmmmm]mind in which I keep myself company may be soundless; it is never silent and it can never be altogether oblivious of itself."[2] Its presence is a manifestation of absence.

Borderlands rumble, and then happen, appearing like shifting tectonic plates. Access points emerge, perilous crossings marked by sensory properties. If they are wordless properties, if they resist figuration, you may deem them unreliable mediators of experience. You may rationalize them as intuition. You may call them the "sixth comm[mmmm]on sense," even if you can never be certain of their forms. Common sense may accustom us to the world of appearances, but it only witnesses glistening pools—trapped reflections of possibility.

You breathe different air according to where you are and where you are from, how you are made, and how you make yourself in time. You make new music and take different steps according to metrical and metaphysical changes in pressure, humidity, and heat: the hoarse wind of flat expanses and rattling bones, the shrill density of the rainforest and teenagehood, the absence of extinction. You move through the performance of yourself as you live it, listening for sounds of shuffling, sighs of frustration, murmurs of love, vibrations of slumber. You breathe in the world around you, and exhale your participation in its ways: fleshy and vulnerable tendrils* in bloom.

*Kate Brown contributed this language in the editing process.

---

2 Hannah Arendt, *The Life of the Mind* (San Diego: Harcourt, 1989), 75.

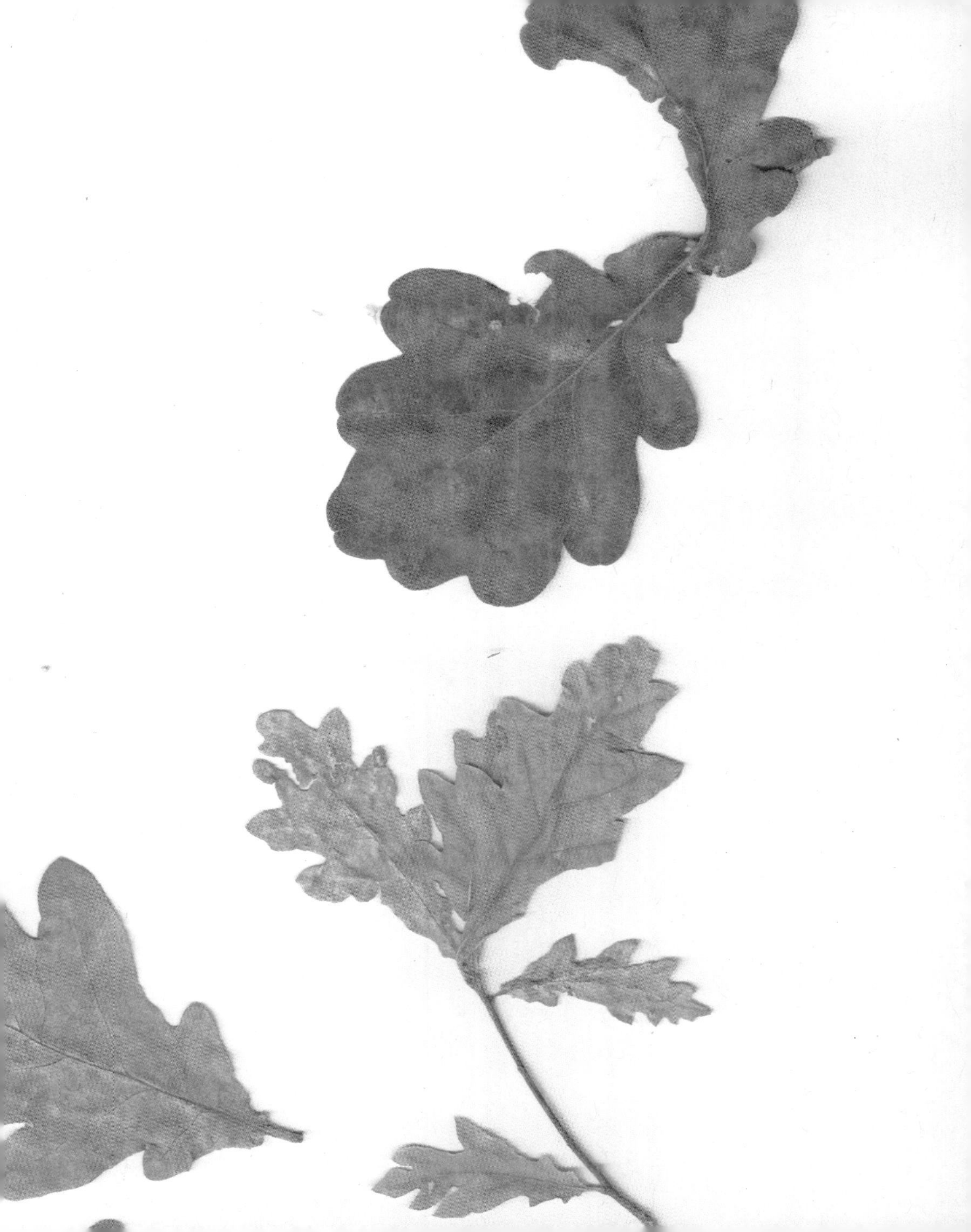

EAT YOUR CALF

Monilola Olayemi Ilupeju

Most people don't know this about me, but I have a daughter. Only my closest friends and family know about her, but of course this changes today, now. So please bear with me, because this is not an easy thing to do.

I think clichés are clichés because they are true. I also realize that I didn't know what love was, unconditional love that is, until I met her. I hadn't known something within me could tear and widen that far. I hadn't yet known I was infinite.

When she was a baby, I used to wrap her around my back with this long, printed wrap gifted to me by my mother. I'd keep her there all day, like a backwards pregnancy. She would bite me a lot, my back. When she only had gums it wasn't so bad, but once she began teething, her little stubs for teeth would occasionally break skin. I would bleed and it hurt a lot, but it's morally impossible to punish an infant and the pain had nowhere to go. So, I stopped minding it. And then its inflection changed, and it turned into something more ambiguous. My labor was the same; physically it was agonizing, a natural birth turned C-section because she was positioned head up towards my pelvis and feet down towards my vaginal canal. I was told I was in labor for forty two hours, but I still can't believe it stretched out for that long. It was an infinity condensed down into a millisecond.

There is something soothing and quite remarkable about submitting to physical pain, especially when it is a pain you have caused yourself and cannot escape. In those moments, the noise and chaos quiets, or maybe synthesizes, into a clear, single tenor. Who—*what* you're made up of becomes easier to access. Anguish claims its uncomfortable seat in the tangible, is no longer this hazy cloud perpetually hanging on the horizon or sometimes directly overhead.

So yes, physically it was incredibly painful, yet bearable somehow. But psychologically, it was nearly unmanageable and sometimes still is. I've spoken to other young mothers about the mental and emotional hardships I faced, both pre- and post-partum, and many of them have told me they can relate. I described it as a third puberty. The first puberty, biological puberty as we know it, was a fun time for me; and by that I mean, I don't think I've ever been as consumed by my depression and anxiety and navel as I was between the ages of twelve and sixteen. Angry, angsty, and afraid, always. It all hits you at once: you realize that one day you are gonna die and your parents too, that the world isn't always nice, that maybe you aren't as special or as pretty or as loveable as you had always believed yourself to be. After all, you were never the recipient of a school dance courtship.

And then there is a second puberty, when you're in your early twenties and are forced to confront the less than glamorous realities of adulthood, the severely minty conditions of true freedom and accountability. You are now in charge, to a degree, of what you do with your life. If not coped with well, or at all, this responsibility is enough to turn a person to stone, immobile in the light of their potential.

But this third one, the pregnancy, takes the cake. When I was younger but still old enough to begin to sense life's bleakness, I looked at people who chose to have children as being unnecessarily selfish, cruel, *evil*, even. To pass down the incomprehensible burden of mortality and existence in this messy place, filled with all the -isms and child sex trafficking and climate change and poverty. I couldn't understand how people could succumb so easily to their empty biological urges. Maybe I subconsciously punished my parents for this. During an argument with my sister, in which she was trying to explain why we had never been close, she exclaimed, *No one could get close to you. Not even at six years old! No one could even say good morning. You hated the world.* At this young age, fresh off the heels of my first brush with sexual trauma, it seems that I had already begun to question my parents' willingness to bring me into a world that had destroyed them and was prepared to destroy me too. I was their sinking life raft and now the memory comes back. My mother telling me countless times throughout my childhood and adolescence: *Your birth saved my life.* I am still not ready to ask her what she meant by that. Not sure I'll ever be.

Ultimately, the idea of having children in the current climate felt immoral and impossible. But then I learned that some of the people who were enslaved and brought from Africa to the Americas would go to great lengths to render themselves infertile, including chewing on cotton roots as contraceptives, drinking toxic compounds like calomel and turpentine to induce abortion, or committing suicide because they couldn't bear the thought of bringing a child into conditions as psychologically and physically inhumane as slavery. Believing that enslaved mothers could both labor and care for their children simultaneously, slave owners routinely exploited them as both workers and as reproducers. And on top of all of this, these women lived under the very real threat of having their children sold and taken away from them in an instant. This was precisely the moment I realized that my melodrama was boring and that I needed to sit down. And so, eventually, with more perspective and maturity, the disgust I had towards parents subsided, transformed into pity and then irritable apathy.

When I found out I was pregnant, under conditions I need not explain here or now, I was devastated. The sorrow was so complete, so unwavering, that I had no choice but to kneel before it and give thanks. I cried for days, weeks, maybe even a month, nonstop. Not because I was pregnant, but because I knew she would be staying. That she wasn't going anywhere because she was everything. I couldn't believe what I'd done. And I couldn't believe how blind I had been all this time, to not acknowledge the parts of life that were indeed worth living, even if only in the form of small pockets of clean air floating in an otherwise polluted wasteland. My favorite pocket: the one that told me I am allowed to forgive myself. And her too.

Now I am thinking about a memory from when she was four-turning-five. She pooped in the corner of my closet, because apparently there was a spider in the bathroom. She was terrified but needed to go and simply didn't *do* spiders. My closet was right next to the bathroom, conveniently. The poop stayed there for four days. I was stumped, unable to track down the source of the smell, assumed it to be a dead rat sleeping in the walls or an insidious mold outbreak. That is, until I went to the back corner of the walk-in closet one afternoon. I lifted a scarf and some papers she had cunningly used to hide the evidence, and discovered the pile of treasure, my lucky day! I burst into a fit of laughter, before putting on my parent pants to reprimand her. When I confronted her, she lied at first—where she learned such a tactic I have no clue. Soon after, she confessed and broke down in tears. Ashamed of her shit, an unfortunate and outdated rite of passage into bodily awareness. I hugged her tightly. So, so sweet, sweet little angel girl. Watching her small, bony shoulders shake under the vibration of her sobs and thinking about the shakes rippling through my own Body during our labor.

More special memories: when she was seven and a little too wiggly after her bath, she slipped and busted her two front baby teeth on the corner of a TV sitting on the floor. Blood everywhere. After she stopped crying, she stared blankly into space for ten minutes, in shock. The teeth were hanging on by threads of gum. The next day we went to a pool party, and she lost one while swimming. Cried even harder at the thought of getting less money from the tooth fairy than from the incident itself. Of course, the tooth fairy quadrupled the amount; a whole eight dollars.

When she was nine, she came home from school distraught and confounded. Some of her idiot classmates didn't want to be friends with her because she was Black. She couldn't understand why this was an issue for them.

When she was twelve, my back massager kept mysteriously disappearing from my room. I never spoke to her about it, and I know I should have. I don't know why I didn't. Maybe things would be different if I had, less complicated. Maybe things would have been more secure, more loving, less self-contained, less auto-parasitic if I had.

When she was fifteen she told me she was sexually abused by a family member when she was six.

When she was nineteen, she had "sex" for the first time and couldn't acknowledge until a year or so later that it had been in the gray zone, nonconsensual, sexual assault, coercion, rape, whatever you want to call it. And by then it was too late.

When she was twenty, she had really, really, really good sex for the first time, with someone she thought she loved. Things didn't end well though and her arm is covered in saliva a lot.

And when she was twenty-one, she got a suitcase and stuffed it with these memories, intending to leave it in the attic of her first family home. Instead, she ended up bringing it with her, on a plane to some far away city. She arrived ten months ago and is still unpacking.

Live performance monologue at SomoS, Berlin, 2019

{graphite pencil on 10.7 × 15.1—folded white paper.
Backside: Ryanair boarding pass SXF-MAD 2019}

Let me first of all get something straight… On the other hand fuck straight.

{blue ink-pen bottom third & light-beige-yellow felt-tip curlicued
frame on 15.1 × 21.3—folded white paper.
Backside: unknown origin. Architectural silo plans FRAME 7 1979–83}

"We participate in the creation of the world by de-creating ourselves […]" _Simone Weil_*Life from Hot Baths*

{red felt tip on 21.4 × 15 / 2—folded white paper. Backside: *Open Forum* Elijah Burger}

I've* been competing with products for prominence

Yes I'm* still here! iMADE this sentence

{blue ink-pen on 21.2 × 15.1 / 2—folded white paper.
Backside: Verfremdungseffekt from *Visions of Excess*}

I wrote a love letter the other day… there was no recipient.

I hope it was convincing

{blue ink-pen & graphite pencil on 15.2 × 21.1—folded white paper.
Backside: PG 53 2017 Steuererklaerlung Formular}

Something's happening {to me} & I think it might be words, working words. Don't get me wrong, I'm quite aware I've been working them, with & against & alongside them from the beginning—my beginning that is—& they've been working me. But I think what I mean is, that in my more recent working of them something has happened to both my working them & the inescapable gap b/w them & what of 'my working' elides them ___ [_Olympe de Gouges_]

{graphite pencil on 21 × 29.7—white paper. Backside: printed text of unknown origin PGs 52/53}

{The} Its* concrete promise {of} {now} offered the ideal of the sanitary containing the complications of movement & encounter.

The [_Body's_] rudimentary mechanics messed with its* ordered infrastructures grafting themselves onto [its] seeping in-autonomies.

Remnants of former models could not so easily be eschewed. They mingled with and interrupted all attempts to intervene in the [_Body's_] acculturation, despite [its] remarkable flexibilities.

{blue ink-pen & graphite pencil on 15 × 21.6—folded white paper. Backside: printed doener recipes}

day by day {i felt} my face dropping/drooping—or were the increments closer to the minute? …second?

…when I heard the news [it was in the paper], I thought it so as my jowls—once a mouth & cheek/chin combination—conspired with a sudden shock of sadness, & the already deteriorating flesh around my smile quickly dropped another full altitude or two… melting.

[blue ballpoint-point-pen on 10.2 × 7.7–yellow post-it-note paper]

The contemporary is too vertiginous a place to inhabit all of the time... Mkz. Wark

[pink & brown + orange felt-tip marker on 21 × 29.7– white paper. Backside: GEGEN DAS KRIEG! junge Internationalisten]

BE LIKE WATER
...once a flood subsides
water's flow does
not simply recede
...mould sets in.

GOLDEN DAZE

Mikhail Wassmer

In a post-mortem daze
Compressed and stiff I lay
What do I feel?—what seeps my way?

A golden tomb for nought—
Who could oppose?
To drowning in your fumes I chose

As you hover up above
Below I decompose—our waste unites
Let's beauty's blossom grow

Despite the morbid hour
Your sun soaked aureate shower
Brings my corpse to flower

ASS TIME

Where is my ass?
My ass is behind me, it's not in my face

My ass doesn't draw crowds nor raise my self-worth
Its monetary value unchanged since birth
My ass has never been put on a pedestal
It's never been fixed on film nor studied or considered better still

I can't see my ass, it's not in my face

No one's observantly traced its contours with a pencil
No one's laboriously chiseled its bulge out of milky marble
My ass has only ever shown itself to me fleeting
To the corner of my eye in the edge of a mirror in reflection retreating

Why isn't my ass always on my mind?

It's been wiped & pat as well as been diapered
Been carefully bandaged & cupped by a mother
It's been heatedly slapped, bit, caressed & massaged by a lover
Never has my ass ever been dressed up & mustered and/or prized & pinched by an
uncaring other

Who's taken my ass and put it in my face?

Forever full heads of hair living the puppeteers dream
Images birthed & modified embodied set the streets themes
Fed on juicy prime cuts dead set sowing sexualized seeds
Grown in their garden of reasoning—I, feeling my warm blood coursing freely,
heed other pleads

What if my ass was always in my face?

Spoon-fed inclination turned libido manifest
In light of Rodin, Maillol & Minaj's asses I reassess
What's in an ass?—*I ask like once What's in a name?*
Funneled downward focus muddles my sense of smell and renders scents all the
same

Where is my ass?—it's not in my face

Thought apart from myself I'll never fully grasp you & yours
Orifices & pores—in touch with sensation—release in undefined mutual hours
Deep palms cleave to clefts depths minds gasping under our bodies lively weighted
Finger-tips absorbing creases beginning to ending—among heads, toes & asses
you & I dilated apprehend

Oh Ass My Ass Ass
to anticipate I grasp facing your mass
Ass My Ass Ass My Ass
Within arms' reach we space & time defy
Ass Oh Ass Ass
Resonating our encounters all throughout & over I sense
Ass Ass My Ass Ass
Casting off casts Ill-fitting habits we pass
Oh Ass Oh Ass Ass
Un-becoming assumptions—what's your uncommonplace?
Oh My Ass Oh My Ass
I'll start—sit on my face

Under your weight I blind
Out of sight, not out of mind

Enlightenment forsaken
I exhale—*nullified*—

Your hips my mind pace
My hold loosens to your taste

By senses upended
No longer *I* is suspended

In relation to you made
I *am* to kiss your ass & you serenade

Forever *im*pressed—I carry altered in my ways
The everlasting impression you've left on me & my face

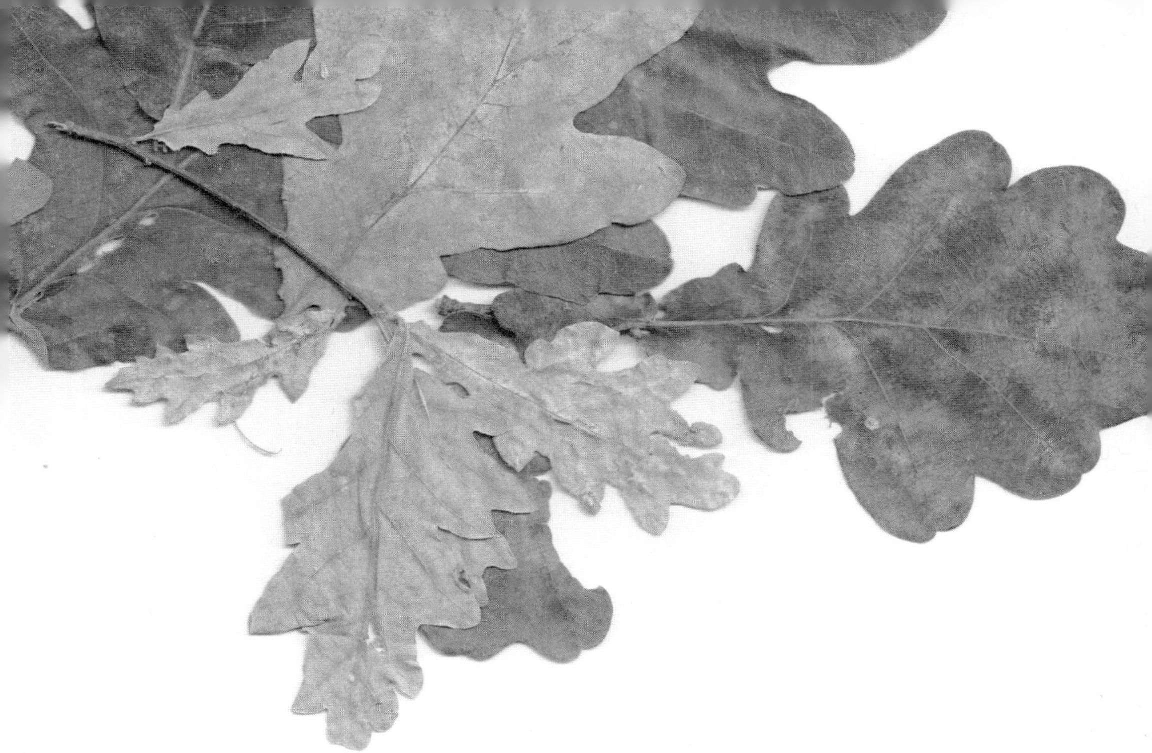

Idio-matic writing

NEVER LET A FOOL KISS YOU

Elaine Tam

Preamble

Does she write the way she wants to be written? That is, in the way of the sloping heat of verdant tropics, with the stink of humid stupefaction. That is, in the way of mint-fresh breath falling ticklishly upon the ear, the theater in bad posture poised.

Rewind. First, allow me to introduce the setting: a dinner party, attended by a group of ten or so people in their late-twenties onward.[1] This is firstly a social occasion, everyone tries to rush in like cells cauterizing a wound. But there is a bottleneck at the door, and awkward bumping as a collective jostle ensues, in an attempt to avoid the sardonic eyelines of ex-lovers. The appetizers are mediocre, but while the limp crudités remain untouched the crisps and dips slug with appeal.

Time-period of gathering: disclosed by clothing. Actors should don politely fashionable everyday wear. Topics of conversation range: complaints about the pay of rarefied fields subject to the gig economy, oil-slicked confessions in the stage corners, games of charming platitudes.

---

1 For this large of a group, I suggest entreating them with a refreshments station replete with instant coffee sachets, jam-filled pastries, tea bags, and plant-based milks. It is entirely possible to complete the rehearsal in one day, but the day will be long.

Stylization of action: exaggerated use of limbs, which the party would refer to as "over-expressive gesticulation," as do I when I describe my proclivities in the odd interview. The question about artistic inspiration is routinely posed. And as is routine, I would remark that much like Harold Pinter, I start with a completely ordinary situation.[2]

Background

Never mind the setting for a moment. It is important to do a little bit of background theory for the purpose of character development.[3] Pause to reflect upon this image, of non-descript soft-shelled luggage filled with shattered porcelain: the cheap stuff, nothing heirloom, saved for its corny, sentimental value. Getting to the hotel and prising apart the bivalve bodice to find the clothing riddled with large, jagged fragments. Wry, dead, glisten, shimmer.

The name is a flower which one cuts to take home. The name is the gristle after a missed shave. It is not unlikely that one forgets their name when it is lent out for common use, the way the body is forgotten by the one who inhabits it. That is, until it hurts. The issue was leftover like city grifters or chicken bones in dry dirt.

She traces the shape of her mouth with a finger, then moves it along the edge of the page, inviting a paper-thin cut, enjoying its smart.[4] Smart was not what they called her when she was a child; they presumed her dumb, the tied tongue a side effect of torrential thoughts blocked. Twitching at the corners of taut smiles was

2 Original quote: "I certainly don't write from any kind of abstract idea. And I wouldn't know a symbol if I saw one [...] I don't write with any audience in mind. I just write." as it appears in Harold Pinter, "Introduction: Writing for Myself" (1961) in *Harold Pinter: Complete Works 1958–1963* (New York: Avalon Travel Publishing, 1994), 10.

3 And here I was thinking behavioral science was nothing but esoteric. However, background also serves as an introduction to a text that has not yet decided what it wants to be.

4 Is the goal of performance to consecrate publicly our innermost thoughts?

nothing very dependable to work with. Her pupils, though, were spoked with a desire offered up to you on large, shiny plates.

Scene I (after Beckett)

Back at the dinner party,[5] rinds swirled around acid tangerines. He'd remarked that a *Vanitas* painting is so packed with folds that there results a sort of schizophrenic "stuffing."[6] Quite glib, but now this image has etched itself on the lens of the mind's eye. The stage is set so that their vanity is given shape and form *vis-à-vis* the libidinal exhaustion of the plentiful folds and curvaceous fruits of a still life. Pleasure and excess confess their brevity before the inevitability of death; only the painting is immortal.

[Them: a parody of excitement weighed out by diminishing semblances, their attention like languid molluscs as the wine makes its rounds. Allow the actors to improvise, cue: "punch-drunk and personological."] Once the table decoration is whisked away by backstage attendants, the light drops. After Samuel Beckett:[7] the party's disembodied mouths are spotlit; they animatedly chew, chomp, sputter, and gasp. *Orality is at the intersection. It speaks with its mouth full. It is full of inside and full of outside.*[8]

Sound out the slurry! That's right, remember, they're these big bad voids they're so full of themselves, and yet want most to be filled. Four minutes pass, and the lights gradually come back on. It should be visible that chewed flecks and droplets

5 Remember to be rambunctious and eager, convivial with certain heat. A self-conscious young adult is angry but supple, the late stage of impotence is not only rage but absurdity; as was advised in the preamble.

6 Gilles Deleuze, *The Fold: Leibniz and the Baroque* (London: Bloomsbury Publishing, 1992), 123.

7 Samuel Beckett, "Not I" (1973), in *The Collected Shorter Plays* (New York: Grove Press, 1984), 213–223.

8 Felix Guattari, "Machinic Orality and Virtual Ecology," in *Chaosmosis*, trans. Paul Bains and Julian Pefanis (Bloomington: Indiana University Press, 1995), 88.

of wine have bespeckled the tablecloth, have spattered the shirts.[9]

Center stage she sits, a clumsy convenor trawling through a thick fug of words, saying them all, yet unable to find the one that feels right. *Silly? Lugubrious?* She: mouth a coral gash to be wagered against attraction. But her tongue flops around the lip like a freshwater eel. Art-speak abetting the issue: substitution, sloppy seconds, stand-in. *Endure.*

Interview

My name was always the most alienating word. To escape the problem of self-definition, I would revel in an exquisite loneliness, and find friends in fiction. I would read, or go to the galleries, cinemas, theaters—all of which helped prompt the blossoming of speech—habits I cherish still.

It's desperate and cheesy, but he took one look at me and knew: I am a burnished ramp. Cinematic images impress themselves upon a viewer, and here was a soft stranger pressing themselves into the thumbprint of my mind. Even nowadays I still get all choked up … but I know what I am inspired by. It deposits traces, pigeon toes in fresh snow.

There we were, on our first date, a screening of *The Big Swallow* (1901),[10] re-mastered. This is what it is to be subsumed, I thought. The spiralling undress of darkness leaves one still journeying through the actor's esophagus, finding oneself belly-up

9 The processes of ingestion and egestion parallel introjection and projection. Through these operations of folding and unfolding, phenomena manifest before perception, delivering themselves to the conscious world; phantasms coming to bear.

10 James Williamson, *The Big Swallow*, produced by Williamson Kinematograph Company, 1901. Duration: one minute. Uploaded by BFI Player (Source: https://player.bfi.org.uk/free/film/watch-the-big-swallow-1901-online), accessed May 31, 2022. This work was brought to my attention by Geiste Kincinaityte, in the department of PhD Film and Screen Studies, University of Cambridge.

in the pit of the whale. You're in it, you travel, the sprawled darkness is generative, it incapacitates overdetermined forms. Are you now projecting images onto the inside of a shut eyelid? The lights come on as if in response, all *deus ex machina*. Your palms are moist and there's popcorn everywhere, decorative little baubles hanging from your threadbare sweater...

Despite everything, I was leaving him. I took nothing but my clothes and my mother's dishware in my wheeled, soft-shelled luggage. The dishware? It's sentimental. I paused to smash all the eggs on my way out, hah! You see, we both love "For Grace, After a Party," and I wanted to impart vehemence to what was once a precious inside joke. Dead, love, swap, verse.[11]

Oh, about the piece. To be honest, this whole thing is a vampire in a wetsuit.

Scene II (after Merleau-Ponty)

Guava, magnolia fix, peach ripple, potted shrimp, and clunch. These ready-mixed colors whet your vitriol, reminding you, as they do, of surficial domestic bliss, and equatorial honeymoons. Choose one to paint the walls of the set—choose freely, because this is the one place where nobody lusts after your "misleading sincerity."[12]

At dinner, a game of platitudes. Arms folded, done in such a way that it embodies the phrase "preposterous indignation." The drunkard posing as your old teacher could strut a wobbly pace—yes, like that—make use of the scene spatially, if you think that brings more dynamism to the characterization of the gesture aforementioned.

Lights up, spoken in chorus: "Never let a fool kiss you, or a kiss fool you." (For context, this Joey Bishop joke was the example all English Literature professors

11 Having been a quiet, and assumed impaired child, I was always encouraged to act out; these expulsions were my interface with the world. My pieces are about the emission of a silent scream. I say let them have it, wholesale.

12 They come in tins of five and ten liters.

had used to explain the rhetorical device *chiasmus*.[13] Consider: these same classes are now the adults convening; the classic quip agitates old feelings of foolishness in some, the starved curse of desire in others.]

Behave like rotting soothsayers native to a toothless moon, until you find pinks in the gums of a dawn encroaching. The dinner party is disbanding; former lovers have gone home with new ones, or the old ones they believe to be new. Exit in small groups stage right and stage left, leave, and let two individuals dither. The lighting is soft; to aid with the atmospherics, perhaps the smoke machine can expirate a few wisps of fine mist.[14]

Scene III (after Brancusi)

Their currency was fig and fortune slips. A flashback at best furnishes you with these notes on atmosphere: shredded streetlight coming off the heavens, the chemtrails like chalk, oh so lovely. Here, the anticipative couple arrives at the front door; she is wilting.[15]

Choreographic instructions for unbridled mutations inebriated in love: all your parts tessellate, sliding into perfect, harmonious interlocking. Echo the unity of Constantin Brancusi's proto-cubist work *The Kiss* (1907).[16] Braided bodies in the nether regions of the stage should writhe for two minutes before all actors freeze, becoming tableau. The stillness and sonority of silence serves to complement this moment of solipsism:[17]

---

13 See Maurice Merleau-Ponty, "The Intertwining –The Chiasm," in *The Visible and The Invisible* (Evanston: Northwestern University Press, 1969), 130–54

14 Is it the stale cigarette smoke of the realist, or the visualization of romantic whim of the expressionist? These are the metaphysical questions a fastidious director or writer must always ask themself, even if never to procure a direct answer.

15 Here, I am in the mood to give you the romance you want!

16 Four decades of reinvention rendered five variations—each a bold, decisive break with Auguste Rodin. It was this compact, cubic iteration (a finely calibrated balance between abstraction of form and sensitivity of touch), that heralded Brancusi's anti-classical, anti-naturalist new language.

But nothing is emitted from either pair of these lips, as to produce a single precise word, they would have to stay apart. Definitely parted. Kept at a distance, separated by one word. Light years away, planets in an orchestral throng hang by the secret contract of strangers, this gravitational pull networking them into a relation we call a Solar System. *They do this in silence. Two mouths. Once a body/world relationship is recognized, there is ... a correspondence between its inside and your outside, between your inside and its outside.*[18]

Such is the space-time of a kiss, its instantaneity. Through this, you, the stranger, the world endlessly co-mingle until you achieve a state of ribbon-stage batter: whisked up into one consistency, one sweet drippy continuum. [You should never think of Brancusi, except as an afterthought.]

17 In this, you are lovestruck like a travelator that marches infinitely towards death! Say the following, as though you are asking inordinate questions that, like belly fluff, get caught up in your fly, or simply float away.

18 Passage inspired by Luce Irigaray, "When Our Lips Speak Together," in *This Sex Which is Not One*, trans. Catherine Porter (Ithaca: Cornell University Press, 1985), 208–10. Ends with quote from Merleau-Ponty's "The Intertwining –The Chiasm," 136.

Finale (after O'Hara)[19]

Two silhouettes. The loving rumple of your cotton bedsheets corresponds with an amorphous, multi-lingual deluge of entangled, garbled sensations. A thought riptide—rushing, gushing, crushing, tipping, tripping. Trembling. Wrinkling, lossy surfaces refuting representation. Every inch of skin crawling, receding, peeling back, yearning to further expose translucent flesh, other innards.[20] You stretch, they sigh. Surrender! Risk deathly superimposition; risk total eclipse.[21]

Then ... sweet nothings float on the air. Two strands of hair, limp with obeisance, are embedded in the puckered part of the mattress. The spell breaks with the silence—to arrive at "speaking terms" means the magic is in remission. She will say, albeit inaudibly:

"What will survive this moment?"[22]

The side-mirror glints, the newspaper waits, light streams in. All actors deftly return to the stage, like cells cauterizing a wound. To portray the mouth is to cannibalize it, as if every end is a new beginning, as if our troupe is its own unrelenting circular economy. We must restart quickly, before the curtain call.[23]

Everyone springs as though from bed, feigning a sudden preparedness. Imagine

---

19 As if we would sign off this narrative arc with a kiss. This is a work of interpretation which has no need for borrowed convenience from the form of the letter.

20 Think upon the unravelling skin of fruits in *Vanitas* paintings! Like a grapefruit snapping back with histrionic bursts of sour dew when you tear apart its segments. Think of faces held within overexposed photographs.

21 What does one do with unaffordable levels of self-investment? Flippantly, they'd said: just give it your all.

22 "Inaudibly" could mean inaudible to the audience too. The important thing is simply that the actor says it with a clandestine wistfulness, or as is done an incantation.

23 Romance as we have known it is dead, it smacks of warm rain on old garbage. Are we endeared by this?

your alarm, appointments, inflammatory politics at the workplace—wake up! Fight off the scarecrow of abstraction. Abstraction is dull like the ache of your hangover. The banal, concrete things deliver us jubilation unmarred. I want you all to lurch towards this condition of reality, in the manner of O'Hara:

> And someone you love[24] enters the room
> and says wouldn't
> you like the eggs a little
> different today?
> And when they arrive they are
> just plain scrambled eggs and the warm weather
> is holding.[25]

24 She may or may not be the protagonist from the earlier scenes of this manuscript, take from it what you wish.

25 Frank O'Hara, "For Grace, After a Party," in *Meditations in an Emergency* (New York: Grove Press, 1957).

HIPPIE PUKE

Theresa Patzschke

I'm standing behind the barrier
where the street had split open
and I could have dipped my calves into it.
But meanwhile, there is blue light
and a lot of people
and someone speaks
into a walkie-talkie.
The woman in front of me
has a big ribbon in her hair
and I know that the abyss
we surround reflects
colorlessly in my eyes.
Countless pictures are made
and then everyone goes home,
and I go to hang from a tree
close to the catastrophe.
I blow in the wind and I wonder

if it could remove my surface
and take it elsewhere,
for example
into the silver-blue liquid
in the abyss,
which opened up
not too long ago
in the middle of the street.
My surface would cover the soup like a net.
Please come down from the tree,
I have to go shopping anyways
and my hands start digging for change in my pockets
as if I told them to.
But it just fell out and,
still in flight, is now
illuminated by the headlights
of a police car.
I have to buy
vegetable bouillon cubes,
dishwasher tabs,
cotton pads,
Q-tips,
straws,
and apple juice concentrate.
I also grab a bouquet of bluebells,
bells that have little hair on them

and last so long that they seem to come
from another world, but they actually
come from the forest, where they grow
in the shade.
Maybe their stability and longevity
derive from their
perfect proportions
but maybe it also comes from the moonlight,
which permeates the treetops differently than
sunlight.
It doesn't really move as beams
but rather as steam
diffusing through the walls of the flowers
that stretch like a tent over the edges
of their own pentagon.
And a scratch card.
Maybe it's my lucky day.
But my pockets are empty,
the coins probably still lie
under the tree on the dingy median,
between blades of grass
and dog shit.
When I leave the supermarket,
I find that the crack in the road has expanded.
It is now moving directly towards the tree
I was hanging from before

and the silver liquid shines out of it
like the saliva between the lips of someone
who has problems with their salivation.
The police have now cordoned off the area extensively,
my tree has become part of the perimeter,
the coins lying
inside.
I have to somehow make it through the cordon
without anyone noticing.
The mass of people has accumulated quickly again,
and I push my way through it.
When I arrive in the first row
behind the red and white band,
my eyes meet those
of a police officer,
who is grinning at me
from the other side
of the abyss.
I nod to him,
then start looking for my coins.
There they are,
flashing in the blue light
every now and again.
I have to come up with a good plan.
Just in this moment, there is a rumble
from the depths of the street,

a murmur
goes through the crowd
and a few screams.
An opportune moment.
I throw myself
under the barrier
into the grass,
without thinking
about possible turds,
only the coins
on my mind.
I stretch out one arm as far as I can
and crawl about
half a meter forward,
I'm almost there,
only a few centimeters away from the nearest
20 cent piece, when,
with a fervent groan,
the road tears
open further.
The chasm is moving toward me, or—
toward my money?
No way—
Does it want my money too??
The earth is splitting relentlessly,
in slow motion

or time lapse,
it's hard to tell,
I throw myself
forward a bit more,
while the first 2 euro piece becomes one
with the viscous silver.
I catch a coin too
and roll off to the left.
As if spurred by lightning, I run
toward the parking lot, my clothes
reeking of shit.
Behind some loading ramps,
I take out my lottery ticket
and open
my clenched fist:
it's a 5 cent piece.

**for Catharine Czudej*

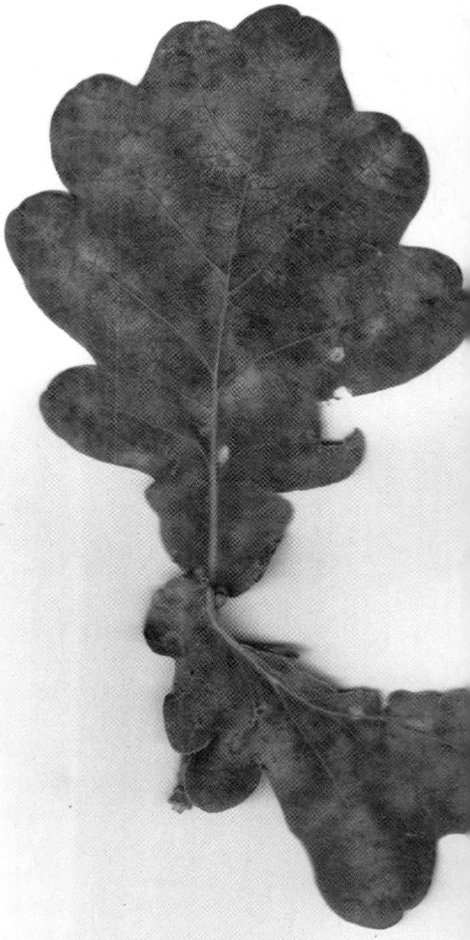

HAIRCUT

Monilola Olayemi Ilupeju

Let's talk about the helplessness you feel immediately after getting a haircut that is a tad too short or too wonky. You feel strange and grotesque and *ugly*, and suddenly so sensitive to the passing of time. Your hair will not look any different the next day, you know this. But you can't help but wake up the next morning and squint at your follicles, watching for microscopic progress.

You cannot wait for your hair to grow out, but a small, or perhaps large part of you is secretly excited, relieved. You see, when you have a bad haircut, time slows down. It gives itself a moment to catch its breath. You know that for as long as your hair is in this awkward stage, you are safe from the claws of the clock, shielded from the evidence of your unraveling, your cycling, your shedding, your decay. And so, you cling on to this safety net and allow it to carry you through the next day, and the next, and the next. And before you know it, your pupils are no longer fixated on your hair growth. Life sweeps you up into its billowing arms. You have shit to do, people to see.

And then one morning, you wake up and look at your hair, and it is no longer the eyesore it once was. It has grown out. You have grown out. At first you smile, relieved to be palatable to the world again, gearing up to project your anxieties onto a new Body part. But then you think of the quiet moment you shared with yourself months earlier: the nakedness of the haircut, the distance of the mirror, the floating lifesaver you hallucinated while in that viscous time-swamp.

You probably did this on purpose, knew the haircut was going south but kept going, you couldn't help yourself. You do this all the time, and you pretend you don't know why. You understand that your ludicrous attempts at control will not save you from the laws of nature or the inevitability of change, cannot erase the contract of your impermanence. But when has understanding ever been enough?

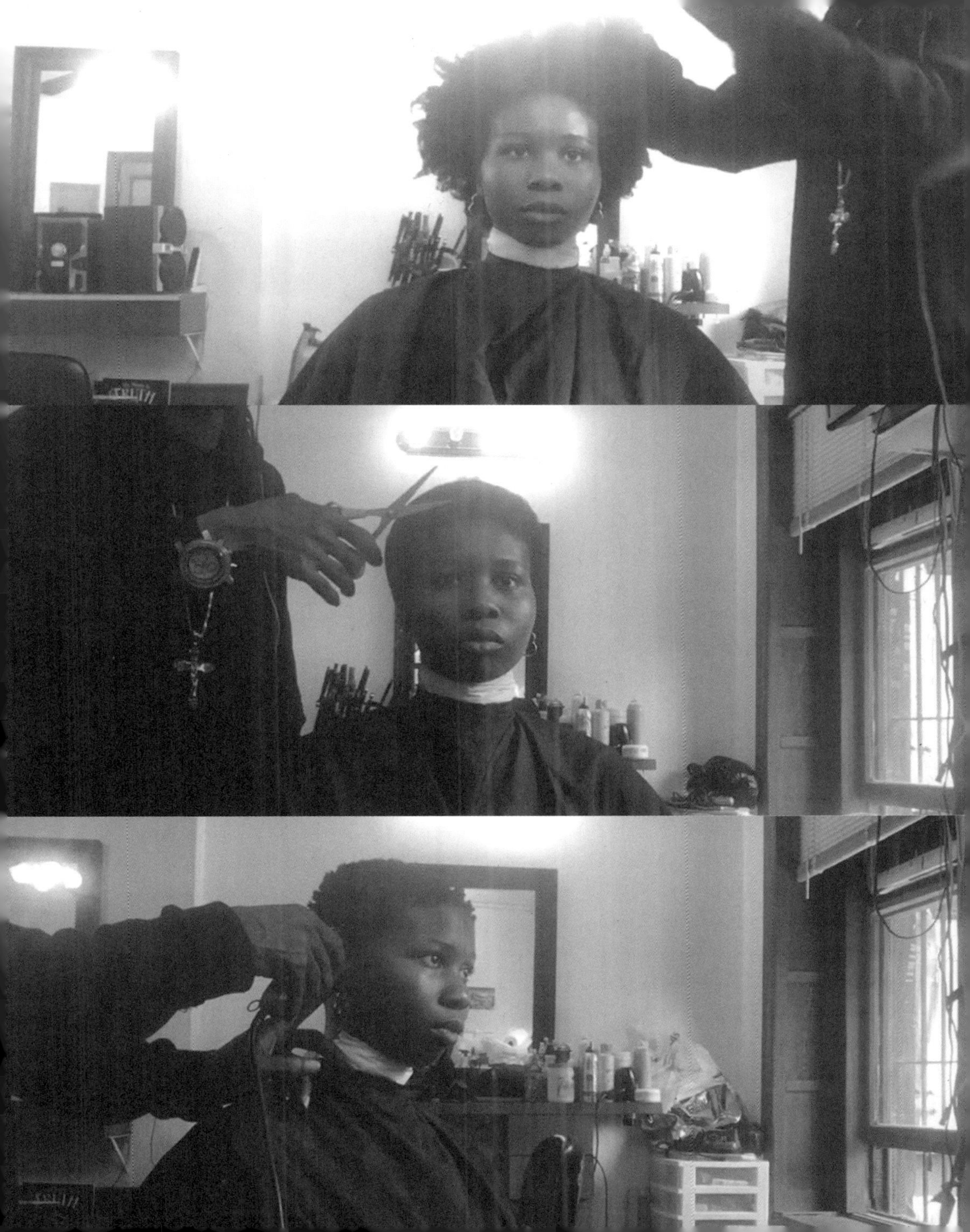

FEATHERFALL

Anna Zacharoff

This pillow is tired. There have been so many lay-downs, naps, sleep-overs, sick leaves, and snooze mornings on top of the normal hours. I am made for those straight seven to eight hours of proper sleep, then time to breathe. A puff-up before the next shift.

There are four categories of pillow. Two kinds you know well, like me—the bed-fellow who silently supports you—and my housemates, the decorative pillows, all puffed up and ready for nothing. Then we have the special forces. The ones made for rare events, and those who aren't made to be used as pillows at all. I'm talking about the corrupt airplane pillows or breast-feeding cushions that say they will deliver but rarely do. You pay for comfort that is not given. Or the sudden heros, like a rucksack or the pillow-like filling of a folded jacket.

All this consideration and big talk about pillars, and here I lie. I feel like I'm contributing. We pillows don't hold anything up, we support what has been laid down. Our role is not to act, but to admire, or not to care at all. We help you make a list in your head, and to sink deeper into mindless mental strolls eventually ending up ...

In the newest episode of *November*, Dr. Birkenstock is arguing that the phone charger is the new pillow for technology. Categories such as hard and soft belong to the cradle of the mind. I'm not sure that I can follow the argument, and I have to confess that I fell asleep.

What do I know?

A song
dismembering
a limb, the cheek
of it a probe,
probing
sound, a song-maker
desired
a kind of insect
a membrane
brownish black.

The moon
lying
a false month
a membrane
remains
mindless
beyond
quick
poison
and quicker blade
self-slayed.

A song
        dismembering
            a limb, the cheek
              of it a probe,
               probing
               sound, a song-maker
              desired
            a kind of insect
        a membrane
brownish black.

The moon
   lying
     a false month
       a membrane
         remains
           mindless
                              beyond
                         quick
                     poison
              and quicker blade
            self-slayed.

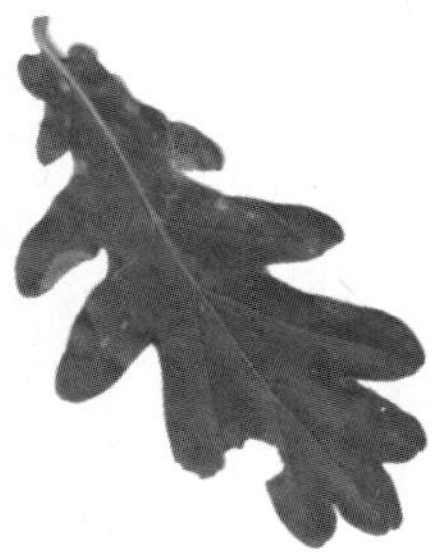

Repetition Compulsion (More and More Mary)

MOUTH TO MOUTH
A COLPOSCOPY TALE

Ayanna Dozier

I felt the cool but rugged steel slide into me, followed by several biting punctures clipping my cervical wall. My gynecologist, Dr. Hernandez, delivered her apologies. Dr. Hernandez removed the punch biopsy forceps from me and gently reminded me that the next part would sting. Vinegar is the only natural medicinal that can be inserted into the vaginal canal. As usual, Dr. Hernandez was right, it did sting but I was used to it.

This is the most succinct summary I can provide of one of my colposcopies. For, like many individuals in this world, I have human papillomavirus (HPV). Apparently, the strain of HPV that I have is slightly problematic, but only slightly. It is a strain of problematic inducing problems that means that I have to monitor my cervix by receiving several colposcopies a year until something gives—either it goes away or becomes cancerous and I die. Although, it is already technically cancerous but not cancerous enough to move to chemotherapy or radiation. So vinegar it is.

My road to this ill-fated moment in medical stirrups was a simultaneous dose of low self-esteem and a lying man. In my pursuit of intimacy and belonging, I ignored warning signs and wrote a novel from a fella who gave me mere sentences. His softly cooed broken utterances got whatever he wanted from me, and left me with a broken heart and a broken cervix. History has shown us that men's pursuit of pleasure literally kills, and how tragic would it have been if the thing that took me out was dick. In the West, we are often forced to think of violence as exceptionally spectacular but so often it is quiet. So often violence is mundane and more mundanely is violence against women, specifically women of color and even more specific to Black women. So often is this violence, that no one cares to scream.

There are levels to hurting women. I am not speaking to the spectacular but the whispering violence that causes harm through madness or compromising the health of another, and for what? These ordinary acts of violence that have no megaphone attached, and instead blasts at unspeakable volumes in my head as my gynecologist cranks the speculum open to begin. Another year of another routine colposcopy that will routinely occur several other times that year because some fuck convinced me that fucking me raw was his way of showing affection. Unfortunately for me, it was his way of showing affection to several other women at the same time. So here I lie.

For the uninitiated, a colposcopy is when your gynecologist takes a deep long—pun intended—look at your cervix to check for any abnormalities caused by HPV, mainly cancer. A colposcopy may include a biopsy but that is not always the case. If your colposcopy includes a biopsy, two things may happen to produce that sample. If your gynecologist thinks that your cervix looks slightly questionable, they will scrape the lining of canal to produce a tissue sample. If your gynecologist thinks that your cervix may be in "danger" from developing cancerous cells, they will just cut a chunk off, or several chunks in my case.

They start the procedure by misting the vaginal area with vinegar to cleanse it and to irritate the hell out of it. They then insert a speculum inside your vaginal canal to expand your vagina so that they can then insert a colposcope (a lighted magnifying instrument) to examine the vulva, vagina, and cervix. After taking a meditative look at the "situation," they will spray a special solution on your cervix that lets them know if they need to proceed further with a tissue sample depending on the color it changes. Green is good and no further harm to this person's cervix is needed. Moldy-gray is bad and induces your gynecologist to being hacking as many pieces of your insides as needed. For obvious reasons, I did not see this color gradation myself, but this is what I was told by my practitioner that I remained in the dangerous moldy-gray zone.

Dr. Hernandez started the biopsy by inserting a curette to scrape the cells from my cervix. She then followed that by using a tool called a biopsy forceps, where it grabs pieces of your cervix and then like a hole puncher clips parts of it away. She did this several times. I glance up at one point and saw her drop a chunk in a container, Tupperware maybe? My cervix was bloody and black. It could have been because of the special dye solution or maybe she was hacking away the toxic—slightly cancerous—parts of my cervix.

When she was finished, I was handed a large pad by her attendant Diana and directed to wait in the recovery room. As I waddled into the room, I promptly took the last Sprite and a box of animal crackers as I tried to "recover" in the large leather reclining chair. I wasn't alone in the recovery room though. There was a woman there with an ice pack of her stomach and a man wearing a Hawaiian shirt, black skinny jeans, and oxford shoes with no socks on—it should go without saying that he was white.

I remember seeing him in the waiting room before my appointment reading Hegel's *Phenomenology of the Spirit*. I immediately decided that I did not like him for men who read Hegel in earnest are not to be trusted. He exuberated "male feminist ally" vibes. The type of men that still have a clear stake at the power that patriarchal institutions provide them (or what bell hooks would say, the white capitalist cis-heterosexist patriarchal institutions). This man has realized that there is great power in performative feminist ally-ship.

In fact, being a feminist man may give you more resources to disproportionately wield power against women without consequences. This man is protected by his simple speech act of allying with women although nothing in his actions or behavior ever suggested that he took women's pain seriously. No, women are not people to this man. Feminist discourse is merely a pickup line that gains them access to fuck women open—rendering them more vulnerable to emotional and physical harm because the culprit quoted all the right bell hooks lines about exploitation to make them appear as true an ally as any would be.

I am projecting. But, I was very tired of this man in the waiting room. His female companion as it were, also white, sat next to me recovering from abortion. I sat quietly and ate my animal crackers and drank my Sprite as I eavesdropped their conversation. She was quiet. He was not. I became justified in my intense waiting-room judgement of this man as he began to talk. He spoke about how transformative this experience had been to *him*. To him. You know, "he really learned a lot about himself because of this."

For example, he learned that although he likes living in the city, Brooklyn, that he really is a small-town type of guy and that there is nothing wrong with that. He also learned how much he really wants kids someday, obviously not right now, but someday because he realized that he wants to take the kids out on a boat. And while he never told this woman any of this, now, NOW was the opportune time for him to talk about his love of boats and how he grew up on boats and how his dad always tried to get him into boats when he was a kid but that he didn't get it but now, oh but now he gets it and wants to get into boats again.

She sat there silently and nodded along. In this memory, I do not know what her voice sounds like. I promptly left. I had to leave. I needed to heal from what I do not know but having just had an array of surgical instruments inside me did not help. I was hemorrhaging blood alongside some other type of toxic ooze caused by vinegar lathered up against my cervical wall and was worried and envious that I had to endure this alone before that day, and again thereafter.

But, I did not have to endure this man's realization about how much he fucking likes boats through his lady-friend getting an abortion. I was sorely tempted to say to this woman on my way out, "I'm glad you're here. You made the right decision," but I held my tongue. I know there's a metaphor in that experience somewhere but I cannot care to find it. So I scuttled to the waiting room and made another appointment three months from the day to do it all again.

FROM THE HAND

Erika Landström

Your adrenaline
through my fingertip
and I sleep again.

I dream of a dumpling
next to me in bed.
My ejaculate:

Apply to face
or parts of the neck

Each morning
to a different place

A small but visible
band-aid.

This way, they will never leave
but always for a new reason.

This way, they will never leave
because they will never know

A changeling's need
has reason.

Exiting autofiction
Is exciting autofiction

Is forgetting your keys
Inside the apartment

Is losing your journal
In a public place

Is acute Labyrinthitis
To the inner ear

Is the exteriority of the individual
Rather than the role

Is the exteriority of becoming
Unknown.

Rules are there
to predict the future

I am here
for your paternalism.

No explosions
no broken tables

just an exaggerated form of
sampling as knowing.

The children grow up and are lost
until family replaces family
why the child comes.

Vowels from deep inside
vows from the outside
touched by moist fingers.

My love is embryonic
two peas in a pod
two in a twin-bed.

Like a one-year-old
this is the month when
I learn to talk.

Let the image be elsewhere
the icon a verb

the axe, the wings, the altar:
come out of the wall.

Into the belly of the beholder
exclusivity needs.

Exclusivity needs
to be with the invented

exclusivity needs
individuated form.

Exclusivity needs
the Whole.

A face is a face
is the back of a head

is a spinning object
you can't hold.

Keep still, for a while
will you?

I too lived a double life
I too ventured out.

Colder than its surrounding
no smell of artifice or alloy
it is too small.

I scratch the surface
it scratches my hand.
It leaves indents

when I sleep with it on.
I sleep with it on
I crawl the Möbius strip on

for the double inscription
and on
for the other's sign:

A stamp
encountered and then gone.
To return and then gone

I thought I
was the only one.
You do nothing

to keep me.
I keep myself
going on.

This nebulous presence
of air warmed up
by a living body
by blood.

The seeping blood
teeth, mouth
as well as the blood
which I have seen.

I have seen it.
I don't remember when
a word of you
left me scratched.

Like paint
we thought was dry
until a sharp object
or force

leaves a dent
and it sounds
like beating cream
in a metal bowl.

That whisking sound.

Mouths first we vowed
To seek out to know:

Under the cover of snow
Knowing is by sound.

Mouths first we avoided
To seek out to know:

Under the cover of knowing
Naïveté happens once.

Hands of the clock
like masts on the horizon

bent by hot air
at the edge of a silver coin

traded for mist
and sand in my hair.

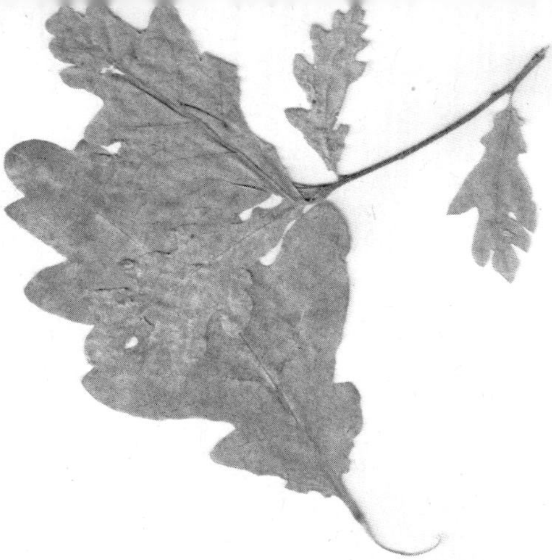

MAYBE IT'S TIME

Monilola Olayemi Ilupeju

Maybe it's time to take a breath? Maybe it's time to stop picking those pimples? Maybe it's time to stop fake laughing? Maybe it's time to take out the trash? Maybe it's time to take that vacation you've been yearning for? Maybe it's time to delete Instagram? Maybe it's time to stop dating men? Maybe it's time to let the spider live? Maybe it's time to take yoga seriously? Maybe it's time to go to the next bar? Maybe it's time to accept bodily imperfections? Maybe it's time to become a writer? Maybe it's time to stop using your vibrator and go back to just your hands? Maybe it's time to learn how to drive? Maybe it's time to let her speak? Maybe it's time to enforce that boundary? Maybe it's time to ask for a raise? Maybe it's time to say yes? Maybe it's time to say no? Maybe it's time to figure out what you want? Maybe it's time to research the current political situation in Nigeria? Maybe it's time to invest in space travel stock? Maybe it's time to stick out your tongue and say *ahhh*? Maybe it's time to get a studio? Maybe it's time to stop being an artist? Maybe it's time to get a pap smear? Maybe it's time to dry clean that musty thrifted jacket? Maybe it's time to study cinematography? Maybe it's time to stop dating women? Maybe it's time to move back to NYC? Maybe it's time to sit on their face? Maybe it's time to get that new phone? Maybe it's time to shut the fuck up? Maybe it's time to visit Lagos? Maybe it's time to reinstall Instagram? Maybe it's time to shave your armpits? Maybe it's time to regrow your edges? Maybe it's time to spit out that gum? Maybe it's time to add a background? Maybe it's time to recover the data on your corrupted hard drive? Maybe it's time to start your Retinoid journey? Maybe it's time to stop drinking? Maybe it's time to pick up the check? Maybe it's time to leave your house? Maybe it's time to apologize? Maybe it's time to cry? Maybe it's time to try anal? Maybe it's time to go to church? Maybe it's time to switch to analogue journaling? Maybe it's time to go to the next opening? Maybe it's time for no thoughts? Maybe it's time to admit you have a problem? Maybe it's time to wash those vegetables? Maybe it's time to try polyamory? Maybe it's time to get a dog? Maybe it's time to start painting? Maybe it's time to host a rave? Maybe it's time to unplug for a week? Maybe it's time to get married? Maybe it's time to get a sugar daddy? Maybe it's time to stay out of your parents' drama? Maybe it's time to switch to coconut oil? Maybe it's time to start wearing perfume? Maybe it's time to grow a bush? Maybe it's time for the main course? Maybe it's time for that breast lift? Maybe it's time to quit? Maybe it's time to untangle those headphones? Maybe it's time to find your brother? Maybe it's time to unload the dishwasher? Maybe it's time to microdose some acid? Maybe it's time to take the full tab? Maybe it's time to stop picking your ingrown hairs? Maybe it's time for a massage? Maybe it's time to buy a hand blender? Maybe it's time to fall in love? Maybe it's time to put the gun down? Maybe it's time to move on to the next section? Maybe it's time to reconcile? Maybe it's time to go to Vabali? Maybe it's time to poop? Maybe it's time to buy a strap on? Maybe it's time to be honest? Maybe it's time to learn Adobe Premiere? Maybe it's time to call upon your ancestors? Maybe it's time to leave Berlin? Maybe it's time to break up with him? Maybe it's time for the next round of shots? Maybe it's time to take out those braids? Maybe it's time to wear a hat instead? Maybe it's time to start directing performances? Maybe it's time to suck a dick? Maybe it's time to do a solo backpacking trip through Croatia? Maybe it's time to start stripping? Maybe it's time to stop dating? Maybe it's time for another bump? Maybe it's time to have a little imagination? Maybe it's time to up your cat's seizure medication? Maybe it's time to cum? Maybe it's time to stop navel-gazing? Maybe it's time to hit the slot machines? Maybe it's time to pull the trigger? Maybe it's time to jump? Maybe it's time to switch to gold jewelry? Maybe it's time to accept your mortality? Maybe it's time to switch positions? Maybe it's time to floss? Maybe it's time to take a break? Maybe it's time to forfeit fear? Maybe it's time to come down to us? Maybe it's time to choose one thing and stick to it? Maybe it's time to start the home renovations? Maybe it's time to push? Maybe it's time to wake up? Maybe it's time to finish that paper? Maybe it's time to go over and just talk to him? Maybe it's time to block her? Maybe it's time for some booty shaking? Maybe it's time to get a therapist? Maybe it's time to go on a hike? Maybe it's time to call your mom? Maybe it's time to pick up soccer again? Maybe it's time to go to Mexico City? Maybe it's time to submit your taxes? Maybe it's time to order another round of wings? Maybe it's time to stay in? Maybe it's time to skip the queue? Maybe it's time to end dry January early? Maybe it's time to slow down? Maybe it's time to quit your job? Maybe it's time to shave it all off? Maybe it's time to forgive? Maybe it's time to switch back to menstrual cups? Maybe it's time to take some MDMA? Maybe it's time to donate to that GoFundMe? Maybe it's time to try a new scar cream? Maybe it's time to hit send? Maybe it's time to stop buying single-use plastic? Maybe it's time to head to the dark room? Maybe it's time to stop editing? Maybe it's time to tie your hair back? Maybe it's time to sell those shoes? Maybe it's time to finally learn German? Maybe it's time to bleach your eyebrows? Maybe it's time to be mediocre? Maybe it's time to stop and listen? Maybe it's time to give up? Maybe it's time to keep it moving? Maybe it's time to go vegan? Maybe it's time to leave? Maybe it's time to make your bed? Maybe it's time to double-text? Maybe it's time to start volunteering? Maybe it's time to get spacious?

VOICEOVER

Rosa Aiello

Projection of white noise from a rooftop and into a very very very dark forest. So dark—though it's only just past twilight—that you can't see around to the other side of any tree. Only the trees' front sides are lit up with white noise.

Filming a creature from behind, running through the space, she forgot to feed it.

The baggage claim hall is all gray, except for a path of littered red rose petals, crushed in lines where suitcase wheels rolled over and stuck them to the floor. No doubt the petals are leftovers of a lovers' reunion, but they have been scattered violently.

She finds a free seat next to a woman on the bus. She only sees the back of the woman's head of long white hair. She moves her suitcase to let someone pass: that's when the laughter begins, so terrible, beside her; or is that sound, she thinks, just the ascending and descending pitched scream of the bus itself?

She remembers a swimming pool. She's looking down at her own body in the sun. There is a timer on to control the time of the shot. The length of the timer feels to her like it will be perfect. Like she is something to bake.

She is shooting a scene at a table in an office: a man is wearing a dark hat and a suit, and is standing in blue light talking to a table of men in suits, bathed in blinding light. The man collects a document on the far side of the room, and the camera follows him, losing the table of men and the lights. A full, still feeling comes over the room from the movements of the elements. It feels to her like newness. It feels to her like something alive. The whole room can feel it, that anything could happen now that the mood has shifted.

Then the man moves too fast, and the camera has to move too much to follow him. And just like that, it stops working—floating tea cups, held aloft until now by telepathic flow, fall with a crash.

N and M, looking critically on the scene, say, "No, no. They're moving too fast."

She says, "Ok, yes, fair enough, but something happened just there. We all felt it."

N and M are silent in agreement. She feels a deep sense of knowing that, despite the errors that followed, whatever happened just there is worth pursuing.

"Please," she asks two mentors at the end of a meeting, "Tell me, what was it about me that left either a positive or negative impression?"

The female mentor smiles, says, "Well I think it should be obvious by now," implying that the impression is positive. "Though there is more work than I thought there would be."

The male mentor says, teasing, "I already knew there would be more work than we expected, when I called one morning at 2:26 my time, and you picked up the phone saying:
[Cut to her, among her sheets, picking up her phone.] 'Sorry, headache, just woke up …'."

He is asking about her priorities in order to move her forward in the story or game. Three check box options show up in the top right corner of her view: bigness, importance, niceness. She finds these interactive elements tedious and she wishes she could move through the story like a movie. She rushes through the choices, not really reflecting; she moves so fast she misses the story, maybe because she finds the story itself the tedious part.

In this world, a familiar theme music plays, variations on an emotional melody, whenever an event occurs—an event, meaning something that changes the course of the story's unfolding; all the accumulating, stealing, learning about items, those are *her* beats, whereas events are turns that affect the whole.

She hears the theme music coming from the department store. She runs, as everyone does when they hear the event music play, to see what has happened there. But when she arrives at the large glass wall that looks out onto the square, she sees no current event taking place. Instead, a group of TV personalities restage a past event. The style of the performance is street theater, but with big money behind it, funding impressive lighting and special effects. The use of this familiar music in the staging (though a realistic depiction of the past as it occurred) confuses people. She feels manipulated and misled by this new media.

Her video is playing outside, on a large screen in front of a tall apartment complex. Somehow, without her intending it, the video's edges are continuous with the world outside: hardware depicted inside the frame lines up with satellite dishes and electrical wires. "Why have I never considered doing this before?" she wonders. In the video, someone is performing and when they're done (though the video is still playing) the audience claps as if for a live performer.

V asks her, as V would, in the moment, to join her in a live performance in front of her artwork. The piece is a mural of cutout paper faces, the inhabitants of a city, going about their lives and struggles. Everyone has a happy face, and that makes the piece eerie and political. She lies on the ground, which is also a stage, and even though she had only tentatively agreed to be in V's performance (she had said "let's see what happens when the moment arrives"), when the moment does arrive, she feels free, moved and inspired to perform. V passes her a piece of paper, a poem, and she sings one of the words written there, "Medium," or "Mediate," sings it over and over, distorting and extending the syllables, so the word is barely comprehensible. She chooses other words at random from V's poem, losing her place then finding it again, free and ecstatic. The last line she sings with all her power. It goes out of key, and it sounds great. There is a feeling in the air of something special.

Everyone can feel it, and she walks off the stage feeling satisfied.

She sits in the crowd and in the distance sees N. He hadn't recognized her on stage, and now that they lock eyes, he is shaken, not happy to see her, disturbed.

Then some kid asks her, "And what song did you sing?" She starts singing a familiar song, and he says "Yeah, yeah, I know that one. It's from the movie." And she says "Oh yeah? Okay. Sorry. Well there was another one, with slow drums," and she sings it, and he gets pretty excited.

When she gets home she looks again at the old class photograph. It is black and white, from the early 1900s. It contains a clue: a single face blurred in the center of the group. She has deduced that it was likely not a sound that made the boy turn his head, but something sudden occurring out of frame that only he noticed. It could have been a sound, though, she realizes now, something personal. Someone could have called his name.

A sudden crash at her back, hands slap against the tram glass. She, who has been writing notes for a script, jumps out of her skin. She turns her head, the tram already moving again, and sees a man rolling down the incline that leads to the tracks.

She and E are assisting B's photo project in the mountains. B has amazing gear: a self correcting leveler, a printer to make mini versions of the photos right after they are taken. B is cranky, but that's fine. B is always saying, "We should be able to use that," talking about a cocoa tree, talking about using the different parts of trees and plants, leaves, stems, bark, petals to make tea, creams, salad. Talking about it.

B has a little vehicle down there, something they can manage. "But don't you dare use my rider, sled, horse," B says.

The photo B is after is of the space between the mountains: she wants to capture the depth of what is going on in there, in the layers of space. B hopes it will be snowy or foggy on the morning of the shoot. She notices that if B would look from a perpendicular angle, B would see that inside one of the mountains there is a biological institute and its botanical gardens. She wonders if this wouldn't be a better photo, with even more depth.

E asks her to go check the basement, asks her to do it twice, because she forgets the first time. Being each other's assistants is a kind of therapeutic and helpful system that we are all humble enough to do; even if it makes us cranky sometimes. It is slippery down there, wetter than it is supposed to be. She slips.

She is running down a hill. Being filmed from above. She is following a bouncing ball. She can see all her white hairs. The terrain is a rocky powdery scree. The incline is unclear. She realizes she is being filmed by a falling object, her image getting larger and larger all the time.

She is riding on an inflatable mattress with D, floating along a river with sharp dark mountains rising up on both sides. They are moving at a thrilling speed, navigating through river traffic, tunnels, and obstacles. They bounce over an obstacle, and when they land, the rebound throws them up, very very very high, higher, and higher, and higher. She realizes that she can not only navigate in space, but also inside moments; she can decide the speed at which she experiences each moment, decide where to linger, where to pause. She slows the moment, and this cushions their fall: they bounce back onto the mattress, and keep going in real time.

Fruits and vegetables in large numbers need to be dealt with, so they won't rot. They have already been transported here and there, from the set to her home, and back. The large number of fruits and vegetables are for the movie, but they should also be eaten. She fills her bag with onions and pomegranates, trying to be polite but also realistic: taking what will not be eaten here, what can be eaten by her and T, legitimately.

By moving water from here to there, she is activating the thirty-thousand-year-old destiny of a nasty old man. He has ill will towards her and her family, and wants to catch her making a mistake. She is pressing on a water pump, letting it flow, filling jugs of water. The pump is on a steep incline, and she wedges a piece of wood under the jugs to keep them level as she fills them. The jugs of water are heavy, but by hanging them from the ends of a branch held across her shoulders she is able to carry them. B tells her that she is doing all of this too soon, that the nasty old man is not going to hold up his side of the deal. She says, "Why not? I am performing these steps, isn't that all that's needed? No one said anything about timing." The old man seems thrilled, and she feels sure it is because she is doing something wrong.

P is looking RADIANT. P has moved to a city in Italy, and is beautifully tanned. She is watching the footage of P from above, as P walks down an old village street, wearing a cerise knit shawl. In voiceover P says, "I realized there wasn't a single day I left the house without my shawl." P wore it because P loves it; and she watches the footage of P from above continue, day after day, the same sequence with different outfits, and always the red shawl. She wonders how P took this footage, what kind of settings or tools P used to record herself. P looks up and laughs, smiles at the camera, and she realizes then that there is someone else present, there behind the camera, filming.

She is working on E's movie as AC; she's operating the steadicam. They are shooting in a hotel off a highway. She needs to perform a complex move to get the camera to fall a certain way. E demonstrates how to handle the steadicam: by holding a rope attached to a counterweight and letting it hang, then leaning into it to get the camera to fall. B encourages her to forget about the rope and the weight, "Just do the one-footed leaning technique, and everything will be fine."

She explains that this technique is new to her and she's not sure she can do it, but she'll try.

She is in a hotel room talking to someone on the phone. When she hangs up, someone else, a person she is hiding from the person on the phone, and from us, enters the frame.

She is back on set walking down a ramp, worried that she hasn't recorded the sound properly. She isn't familiar with this camera or this recording equipment. She doesn't know how to listen back to check. She keeps trying. B and E come to help, and they are wonderfully comforting presences. She listens back with E, who realizes that something isn't loud enough.

"But you didn't do anything wrong," says E.

E doesn't like how it turned out, and would like to try it a different way. She, relieved she hasn't made a mistake, encourages E to get the takes E wants, not to worry about the time it will take. She encourages E to push for what E wants!

"Try it every way!" she says.

E, excited by her encouragement, says, "You're right, you're right, ok!" And they run back up a ramp. Suddenly everything feels fine and even good and promising, like, hey, this film will be *good*.

She is shooting a movie in a canyon next to a ranch house. A man there is acting like the director, but not doing a good job, talking during the shot. After the shot, she has to say to him, "Hey, can I talk to you right now?"

They walk away from the set, towards the ranch house and she says, "I am the director, and on my film shoots, we never ever ever talk during a take, unless it's absolutely necessary. Because look, we can't use whatever that was. And after I say cut, *I* am the first one to give notes. Then other people can talk—of course I am open to notes from people, anyone can give a note—"

"Well that can get chaotic," a woman says from behind her, interrupting. She looks back, "Yes it can, we deal with it if it does." She is very sure of everything she says, and that feels good.

There is a bookstore shooting. The guy has a semi-automatic, but she already knows the outcome, which is she wins; so even though her odds are bad, she ducks behind the counter with her hand reaching up to the gun that she knows will be hidden under there. She pulls the trigger, and pulls the trigger, and pulls the trigger. It works.

Horny as hell, and feeling lucky that it's for the one she loves and loves her back. He's wearing an expensive suit, and she rubs up against his hard crotch. "Let's go back to the hotel, fuck yes. What good stuff." She is wet, and he wants to do it from behind. "We'll get better footage that way."

"I don't care about footage. I want you to fuck me, and I want your straight black pubic hair to rub against my clit. Come on top of me. And fuck, it feels. So. So. Good."

She is watching a film, of a woman shot from above, running down a hill. It takes her a moment to recognize that the person scrambling through the rough earth is herself. She recognizes her own white hairs, even though she had no idea that she had so many. "How funny," she thinks, "to recognize myself by the character of the hairs, not because it's an angle I've ever seen of myself before."

She is speaking, and seeing the view of herself from straight on. She doesn't mind her face, even though it is aged, and at times ugly; at some point she starts speaking with her nose pointed down, so she has a double chin. "It's all right," she thinks, "I look good enough."

"We have to get the shot before the sun sets." She wants E to walk out to the edge of the cliff and look out to sea: that will be the shot. There are problems, delays, like that they have already taken the good camera to the other location. "But oh well. Just do it. Oh well," she feels.

She is planning another movie and going through each scene, trying to figure out what they'll need. The first scene is about a woman misgendering her ex-husband. "We need a wig for the actor," she says, "But for now we'll use that yellow sponge." The sponge has a rounded shape (as if to fit around the end of a wand or brush) and scalloped edges, like a bib, or bob cut with bangs. "But" she thinks, "We will need to get a really high quality wig. We'll go to the store and buy a blonde one. It's only for one scene, but it's important."

Someone watches her video and says "Cool, yeah, I've been really into endurance realism lately." She wonders if that is her genre.

She is inside one of her movies, moving through the film on a boat, showing M around. Animals of increasing size are revealed in time to the music as they go. They look up into the trees and see birds and small animals moving in the canopy. Then, with a large swell of sound from behind the trees, the sky opens up, and a black, multi-headed, flying beast emerges. She is not afraid, but in awe of this creature.

"But the voiceover is missing," she realizes, "Only the music kicked in. The voiceover track is missing." She pauses the boat ride to fix it.

A hotshot writer has been chosen to collaborate with her on a show. She says, "Well, would you like to hear my idea?" And before he has time to answer, she starts to give the preamble, "It's a literary term, it has to do with time and disrupting linearity," and then she decides to just go ahead and say it, "The title will be *Flashback* ... or *The Flashback*, or maybe *Flashbacks*?" The writer rolls his eyes. "What??" she asks, "What's wrong with that? Just listen. My idea is to make a mechanism ... a light with a spring. A flashback. Like a slapstick, but a flashback. Get it?"

She is hiring con artists to help her accomplish a fight scene for the movie. They are practicing fighting to prepare for the scene, and teaching the other actors to fight. She is worried about her equipment around the cons, but she knows that the harddrives are the most important part. She thinks "What else would I be devastated to lose?"

She lives in an apartment building, and everyone else from the movie lives there too. It is full of dirty, run-down hallways, and areas with no clear use. She is dancing, they are dancing, and she starts dancing with P. They immediately find a perfect easy rhythm. Absolutely in sync. She stands on P's feet like stilts. When it's over she's flustered, and goes away.

E tells her she looks young. She says, "I had too much to drink."

E says, "Well, it just keeps making you look younger."

N says, "Why would you want to make a movie?" and laughs. He keeps saying, "Why would you want to do that?" She is telling him what she thinks, explaining to him why she wants to make movies. Meanwhile B is eating cereal, being intentionally childish, provoking her.

L comes to her and says, "Are you attracted to P? People are worried about the movie."

She admits to her, "Yes I am." L confirms that she has seen it.

She is very calm as she gathers the cast and crew, and she knows just what to say. She doesn't need to prepare, it comes easily and authentically, "The movie is the most important thing to me, and this process has been very intimate, and I am human. But I wouldn't do anything to make the situation uncomfortable for everyone. You can count on that."

Something important needed to be said at some moment, and her answer, the right answer, was compassion.

R is leading the singing group; but he hasn't written down all the notes so he pauses too long between parts, instead of harmonies notes arrive in sequence sung by one person after another. They sing not to a scored timing, but whenever silence falls, another person begins. It doesn't sound right, and she wishes they could stop.

She is walking home with R, and flirting, or cuddling, as they walk. She says "I think the problem was that you didn't fully copy out the music." He already knows this, and is irritated at her for saying so.

A mother figure gives her a contraption, like a ladder, that X will use to finally fuck her in the ass. The lesson is, "Give things time, things change, what is so now will not always be so." It feels to her like a prophecy.

Inside it smells like incense, and a woman asks her "looking for a seat"?

"Two," she says, for her and E.

A man says, "We will light three candles, one for—" Before he can finish, two smiling women and a young man jump up, eager, child-like, and blessed to be the ones to light the candles this time.

R speaks slowly and quietly, as if manipulating the audience towards him; he speaks into the microphone so softly that she has to strain to hear, and when he speaks louder, an electric hum rises and burns and falls along with his voice. A late arrival bangs and scrapes in the mezzanine. R speaks about the mind as a video screen, and the mind as a projection: the screen is not affected by that which is projected on it, cannot be scarred, marred, harmed, or changed. A siren or laughter passes outside. The mind is also a swirling eddy, a localized event within the infinite stream of consciousness, according to R. People cough, a pew echoes, knocked by someone's foot, and the microphone crackles and swells and falls. Then they sit in silence together, sinking past veil after veil to access the purest form of what they all share.

Question and answer:

"I find myself inhabiting so many roles: mother, sister, lover, friend. But I know none of them are the real *me* ... and—"

"Well first of all," R says, "It seems to me that you are denigrating your roles, which in fact you should be holding up—"

"No! I love my roles! I'm having fun! I'm having a lot of fun!"

"I would say that first you have to value all the roles you inhabit."

"I do, I do, I love being a mother!"

Already the microphone has been passed to another woman, "I have trouble getting underneath all the trauma to really be present in my consciousness," she says.

"Then you must go deeper," R says, "You must go deeper than that, past that veil of trauma, which doesn't change your being, which is perfect."

She sits on the edge of her seat, wanting to say, "but sometimes it's *being* itself that is unbearable."

R has already moved on to answering someone else, "First, know yourself. Second, express yourself through thinking, feeling, perceiving, acting, relating. Act not from ego, but to spread the knowledge that consciousness is perfect."

Another woman speaks, "My son is nonverbal austistic. And I first came to your teachings because I was looking for a way to connect with him without language, and—"

"I'm sorry, I can't hear you," R says.

She speaks louder, "My son is nonverbal austistic. I was looking for a way to connect with him without language. I have spent quite some time sitting with him in silence in his room, and through this practice I have reached a state of great peace."

"I can't hear a word you're saying. I think it is a problem with the way the speakers are facing."

She walks up to the center of the stage, stands right in front of him, "My son is nonverbal austistic, and I have spent quite some time sitting with him in silence in his room, to achieve connection through presence rather than language. And through this practice, I have reached a state of great peace. But I still have moments of ego. I still have moments, every few weeks, where my ego rears up, and I find myself becoming quite violent and strong. My husband doesn't like it and—"

"I'm—I just haven't heard a word you've said."

She walks right up close to R, puts the microphone down, and speaks to him intimately for some time. He looks at her, and nods, and nods; and when he replies she nods back, and tears come to her eyes.

Having seen the previous scene, a young man, wearing rolled-up jeans and a white linen shirt, takes the microphone right to the center of the stage, confronting R with his posture, holding the microphone with his pinky finger out, leaning his whole body forward.

"Can you hear me? Can you? Yes? Great. I love your ideas, I have been following them for some time, but one question I have, one question I can't get over. How do you reconcile your theories with business?"

In the supermarket checkout line, she is describing her project and budget to the person in front of her in line, a middle aged man who knows about film. He laughs and tells her she can't do it. He asks a woman, behind her line, to come, "Listen to this," so they can laugh together. He asks her again, "So how long is the film? And how much do you have?" She tells him, and he assures her it's not possible. She keeps repeating herself, thinking he hasn't heard her properly.

She thinks about reading her composition aloud to the empty room, but she changes her mind. "I want their opinions. I always wanted their opinions!"

Heat is a theme for the episode, flashing back to the beginning: sweat dripping from her head as she stands in the empty classroom; and later: someone evil dies of heat, hot water on the hot metal door evaporates and scalds him.

Lobsters, but with a name that is more floral: L. Her fins bloom inside her like petals, the ones on her tail spread like feathers. L is like a bird as much as a lobster or a flower. L is grand and beautiful. She wants to film L, so she points her camera and a spotlight into the water and films.

A fentanyl overdose on a boat is the opening scene of a world in which you are defined by the play you perform. The world is populated by troops that only perform one play, over and over, as their identity. Her group is going to perform a feminist one; it's bound to be successful, and people are afraid. The principal actress of the play, S, and her double are worried. They don't want to be caught getting too successful, and made a target of, so they hesitate.

Fish and other creatures in the water, needing food. They are fed by light techniques, the light is their nourishment. There is a spotlight on the feeder capable of producing different wavelengths for different fish. L is showing her how to use it, how to keep these creatures alive.

She looks out the front door and there is a woman on the ground, distressed. There is a colorful picnic on the lawn of the woman's house, and people on the sidewalk, people flying kites, people in line for food, but no one is helping the woman. She runs towards the woman, pushes past the line of people, and at that moment sees the film crew. She realizes they are shooting a film, and the woman, the picnic, the kites, and the house are all part of it.

"Our house would be good to film in" she thinks, but D says, "No, look. Look at the houses they're filming in." A flying camera view takes her through the houses, and she sees how they all have depth, mezzanines, glass fronts, hallways leading to balconies, views of rooms through doorways, walkways, arches, porches that wrap around, stretch out onto a far side, behind which there is more space, more rooms. "Wow. Truly amazing houses in this neighborhood," she thinks.

N wants to watch a movie in her room. It is a basement space. L encourages her to take more privacy, so she lowers the blinds. L asks N about his moviemaking, and then they ask her about hers, and she tells them, "Yes it's going great."

"Maybe you can talk to N then," L says, "he gave it all up to volunteer."

"That's a shame," she thinks, "he can give so much more to the world through filmmaking. Anyone can volunteer."

The beloved Acerola has been killed and hung in the gallery, and everyone on the bridge has seen it, since the gallery has a large window that looks out onto the bridge. Overlaid on the gallery wall, in projected scrolling letters, is the name of the alleged killer "N, N, N," who arrives then on the scene, and is met by screams, "How dare he?" The angry crowd will now kill him. She watches the chaos unfold, not fully understanding her role as witness among the curator, the security, the preservationists, everyone.

"Look, Look" she says. The sun is covered in rainbows. E is with her at the rainbow viewing; S is there too, and others. They sit on the high deck of the cruise ship, looking out at the horizon. Most people can't see the rainbows, and she is confused. E can though, and E is very encouraging. S can't; and they realize it's because S has perfect vision. Seeing the rainbows is a special characteristic vision borne of imperfections of the eye. "Try squinting," she suggests to S.

She has a wound, or is covered in wounds. Either way, her body is wrapped in bandages, and she is staining things with the fluid that leaks through. Chairs, clothes, her surroundings: all stained. She introduces everyone, who is in a great mood, M, L, D, R, P, S, N, E, B, V. She takes a bite of cake, drinks some wine, and looks down to realize she is leaking blood onto her chair. "I have a wound," is a refrain she likes, that sounds good to her, a little funny, has such an immediate effect, and besides, is the truth. "I have a wound," she says as she takes herself to the toilet to get cleaned up. Her bandages are a mess, and it takes her a long time to finish—so long that a line of people has formed outside the toilet. M comes to help her. "Tell them I have a wound," she says to M, to get the line of people off her back. It works.

At the top of the staircase and through another set of double doors, she enters a broad gallery space, well preserved, with shining parquet floors, almost a ballroom. Is this her destination? The room is full of gigantic paintings mounted on stands throughout the room. They tower over her; as she walks towards each one, and as she gives each painting more attention, they increase in detail and complexity, each image expanding to meet her. In fact, each painting is a film or, more accurately, a universe. She does her best to maintain her presence and focus, not to worry about remembering the details or holding them in mind for future use. She knows, because D's voice in her head says that, "Everything you see sinks in, everything you experience does its work here inside you whether you remember it or not. She knows that if she even tries to remember what she's seeing, that will make what she's seeing die away. She realizes then the error in her obsession with speed and arriving.

She enters one of the screens, a flying view of a rolling landscape with hills and a single paved road running through it. A single car drives on this road, and her view descends upon it, approaches it from above, moves from the general to the specific to begin the story.

She, waiting on the platform, is writing notes for a script:
Every fifteen minutes the train
Screams of children at every descent
Continuous sweeping
Every hour the bells
Every morning coffee
Almost every night something to unwind
Intermittent cough
Pushing up glasses, up the bridge of her nose whenever she looks down
Scratching her head when it itches
Once a day washing something
Once a week a confession
Once a month a meltdown

She thinks, "Everyone's making movies." She runs to her mother crying, and yelling, "Everyone is making movies!" And it's not far from the truth.

There are ghost attacks. It says so on the radio, and that the attacks are bringing delays on the highway. M is with her in the car. She hadn't heard the exact words of the broadcast because she was distracted, but she did see the look of terror on M's face.

She says, "What did they say? Tell me exactly."

M says "The ghost attacks, it turns out, are in fact messages. The ghosts are sending messages to tell us our errors, to tell us to stop what we're doing right away."

She decides to reroute to her house, to gather any necessary items.

She arrives at the house. From above we see the view of her head: the velvet of the brown scrunchie that ties up her hair glistens in the falling light. She feels the pull of ghosts inside. It's strong. Intense. Physical. Mental. Like being high. She is trying to navigate through the house to find the things she needs, but the pull of the ghosts is disorienting. She is dizzy and her vision is blurred. She has the impulse to sing, and when she sings, she realizes it brings clarity and she is able to move and orient herself again. She sings and sings, and her singing sounds sweet. She realizes then that the ghost transmissions are attached to her brown velvet scrunchie and that when she removes it, the ghost communications cease. But she chooses to wear her scrunchie nonetheless, and continues to sing through the disorienting knowledge the ghosts bring her.

Meanwhile she collects her things from the house.

She asks S if she needs anything, but, "Fast, we have to be fast. How about a warm coat?" When she looks up, she sees that S has already left with the abusive man, and all her stuff.

She screams at the car as it speeds away, kicks up dust.

"Oh, laughter is not so much my way," she thinks later. "Humor? No. I am more about …," she thinks about how she pushed through the ghost transmissions with her sweet singing, "Willpower. That's something I have: willpower."

The auditorium is full.

"Couldn't it wait until tomorrow?"

"No," her mother explains, "No, because tomorrow they will paint the white floor black."

They have to do the performance tonight, her mother explains, even if they are not at all prepared, because once they paint the white floor black, their shadows will no longer be visible, and the performance will be ruined.

"Oh, you have small worms." She looks down. There is an infestation of small worms, like moth larvae, in the carpet. But when she looks closer, she sees the worms have spectacular markings: clearly white and clearly black stripes, and, as if the markings reflect their emotional states, the patterns move as the worms, entwined, dance or mate.

Most of the video is done in voiceover, but every once in a while something recorded in camera, the movement of the mouth of the person on screen syncs up with the sound nonetheless.

She watches a short film D is in, a film from a long time ago, and loves it. She realizes she hadn't known how to watch before. All the shots pan down, or pan to the side, giving the impression of searching for something, giving the impression that something more interesting is occurring below, or just outside every frame.

She dreams about the end of humanity. It is cold, and people are all going to die. She is moving through barren landscapes, and she knows it will happen to everyone. She knows there is no hope. And she feels the feeling after the end of existence. The feeling of grief, but also of the recombining of elements, the feeling that nothing is lost.

She gets a lot of good stuff on the front and back end of takes.

There is an orange cast to everything, as if a glow comes off the fallen leaves that litter the yard. The field behind the house is empty, there is nothing built back there, so even though the sun is at a low angle, the light gets through, and the whole back side of the house glows orange.

She is driving a car down the main street. The sun setting behind them, lights up the hospital stairwell that rises up at the end of the road. The glow of the light enters into the glass-fronted stairs and sparkles off of the metal steps within.

She is watching one of the best movies ever made. The whole film is set at night. For most of the film, the frame is totally black, except for small sources of light, like a vehicle or a person carrying a lamp. A car drives down an unpaved path through the forest: this is the way out. She knows she is watching people escape, though all she sees, from above, is the car's front light beams winding across the terrain of the frame.

She lies in bed, she's falling asleep, and a car goes by the open window. It sounds unbearably like an inhale, like a person in bed beside her is gasping for breath. She starts awake, jumps out of her skin.

There was a feeling of permissiveness she had given herself reluctantly, or guiltily, ruthlessly, saying, "Well this is what you'll have to do." And with it came a kind of word game; words of two and four letters. Or sometimes one. I, me, mine.

There was some other sense of progress: that she could feel the spirit of a place, and appreciate it. This happened for the first time in her childhood home. It had more land around it than she recalled. There were marsh vines there, not like ivy, but like seaweed, that stuck together, had to be passed from one hand to another, and had set in them small bursting fruits, like gemstones, like caperberries, like acerola.

Sometime later, M wants to clear the air. It is nighttime and M sprays an aerosol into the darkness, lights it on fire and the air burns up, clearing it. It is her task to continue doing this. They are in a broad square field lined with pine trees. Low wooden houses have been built in the field for the film—single and two-roomed houses with timber roofs. She lights the air twice to little effect, but the oily aerosol disperses and coats the air more and more every time she sprays it. So when she ignites the spray for the third time, the whole sky lights up for a moment; and when it dies down, she realizes many of the trees and houses have also been lit. She foresees the inevitable disaster of all the houses and forest burning down, "And it would be my fault, even if I was following directions from M," she thinks. She thinks it is probably futile but all around are blankets and towels and pieces of burlap, and so she takes to very slowly and methodically tamping out each small flame.

"It's futile," she thinks, but she keeps going, slowly but surely. Everyone else on the set joins in, and soon, from the crowd, some small fire extinguishers appear. "We can use those on the biggest burning house," she thinks. And when she finally looks up, after their long methodical work, almost all the fire has been put out.

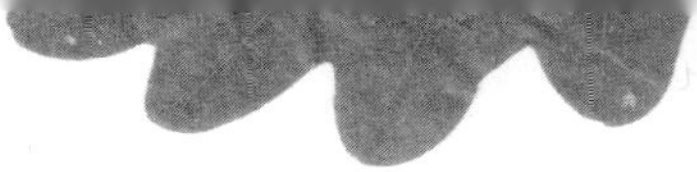

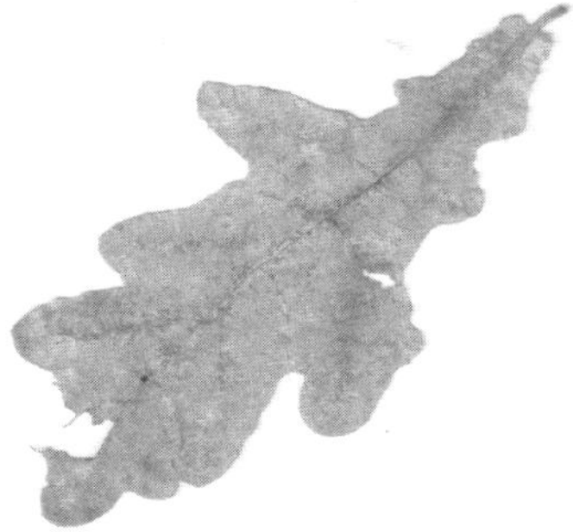

Ways the World Could End

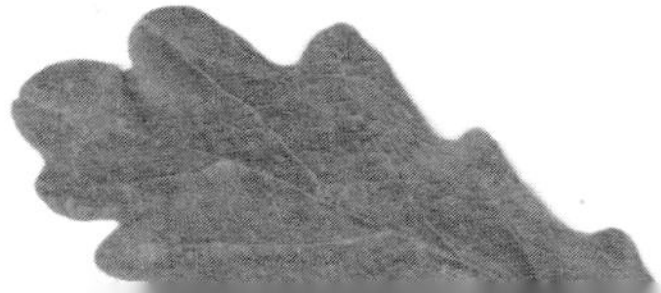

THE LAWN

Monilola Olayemi Ilupeju

Intuition has made a shelter in us. It told us the key hides under the checkered doormat. We look for it and come up empty-handed. Through the window with a brick will have to do. The shards of glass glitter in the air, get into our eyes, but we cannot look away.

It swims in us with the same stroke of a fetus in the womb. Or maybe it is the placenta: indispensable for a moment in time, then disintegrating bit by bit until it falls out entirely, then grinded down into a pulver and sprinkled into green smoothies for stronger nails. With all senses blunted, we shuffle about, frantically searching for this crumb trail. We find it, finally. We follow it. It brings us to the front yard of our home. The lawn is overgrown, with weeds and wildflowers intertwining to become one. Did we lose it here?

Intuition is a God-given right, as real as death and taxes, passed down through the cracked palms of our ancestors, generation after generation, heaving, though the soft flutter of a pulse can still be found. Its faculty exists in stillness as much as in cacophony, in the individual as much as in the collective, don't let anyone tell you otherwise. Untethered, sublime, absolute—isn't that what she called us? Why didn't we believe her?

It has just come to our attention that the compass malfunctioned twenty miles earlier and we may be at the wrong house, but for whatever reason we cannot find the will to turn around; the muscles in our neck have calcified, the veins too. Something is pulling us, and a previously dormant heirloom vibrates below the surface, waiting for our fingers to cut through the soil and excavate it, save it from eternal damnation, from ourselves. A vapor is seeping out of the ground and we cannot find the source nor can we identify its contents. A file, a folder, the entire hard drive has corrupted: a menacing, pixelated upside-down smiley face sits on the screen, sneering at us, and we wonder what comes after corruption.

It is our greatest misfortune that the things most detrimental to our spiritual and emotional growth often feel the most comfortable, most true. How then are we supposed to know which calls to answer, and which ones to silence? How then are we to decipher whether the things we look at exist in front of our eyelids or behind them?

We snap out of it and again find ourselves in the front yard. Rusty landmines are littered across the lawn in the formation of an endless spiral. We attempt to follow it, but as we go deeper and deeper into its nucleus, we are shaking and filled with terror, for we sense our Bodies are sublimating into something that can no longer be recognized. We stop in our tracks and eventually turn around, we can again locate the fissures between our borders.

Upon closer inspection, we discover the landmines are engraved with different labels, with the names of perpetrators and systems of control; dates; states of emotion like misrecognition, envy, and neglect; physical symptoms like hot cheeks, bruises, orgasms; the bed that became an ocean—the list goes on and it is not a pretty one. The words dig into the surface of the metal like a fist that won't let go, the words become the metal itself. As we search, we wonder what these landmines are trying to prevent us from discovering or what would be forever changed once we did.

Bleeding, battered, delirious, we are coughed out of the mouth of the lawn. With eyes that have touched the sun, finally floating above the layer of fog, we see the fruitlessness of our journey and are saved. The landmines were all duds, though the ghosts of the words inscribed on their skin were not. But it's much too late for that now.

We stop walking and take off our boots. Our feet are covered in oozing blisters that we kiss and cleanse with our tears. We stare at each other and then overhead, and my God, it's here, we are buzzing, everything is buzzing. Our crying becomes hysterical, joyful, enough to fill a thousand goblets. Free from searching for something never lost or to be found. A state of constant dissolution, where the edges of one rapidly dissolve into that of another—that's what we are, what this is! Transmuting, fusing, eternally ambivalent. Not meant to be consumed with a smile on your face, but you'll be all the better for it, I promise. I promise it will be okay, even without the compass, without the map, without the key and without the eye. You aren't going anywhere you haven't already been.

DIVE

Coleman Collins

He is running up the field at full speed. There's another body right beside him, trying to keep up. The ball is just ahead of him and he is in full control of it, and this control affords him a sense of power, a feeling of mastery. At this moment he is dangerous, capable of anything—capable of exerting his will over the other bodies on the field and the body running alongside him, the bodies in the stands watching. The open mouths shouting and urging him along, the closed mouths holding in breath: everything is oriented around this moment and the man with the ball under his control. But this moment is fragile.

The defender on his side attempts to take control of the ball, misses, and lightly grazes the first man's leg. This contact is small, but at full speed and from afar it appears grave. So when the first man feels the pressure of the defender on his leg, he has one of two options: he can try to ignore it, or he can take a dive and try to gain a Foul. To continue the run despite the contact requires confidence, sureness; it would be better to summon the Foul and end up in a more advantageous position if this run will ultimately come to nothing. He must be absolutely confident that persevering will be worth it. His position seems less certain than it did a few seconds earlier—now, after the contact on his right leg, he can see that his teammates are out of place, and there are many other defenders left, and it seems unlikely he will gain further advantage. The defender is in better condition, breathing softer, stronger to begin with. A Foul would allow for a reset, a chance to breathe. But the Foul does not exist in and of itself; it must be performed. It must be summoned. True—the contact has already occurred, the leg has been hit. But the graze was slight and subtle, not enough force to truly throw the man with the ball off his course without his consent. So the force must be embellished.

Like many things, the illegality of the act depends on the judgment of the Law. The Law must be appealed to: it is embodied by the referee, who is a body like other bodies on the field but clearly marked as outside the game itself. The referee, the Law, is wearing a neon-green shirt, which stands out among the whites and blues of the players' jerseys. In this sense it is easy to see, but the Law itself doesn't necessarily see well—It is capable of vast oversights. So it is not enough for the Foul to have occurred, and the Foul hasn't officially occurred until it has been seen and declared by the Law. This involves a sort of time-travel; although it always occurs in the past, the Foul is only truly born in the future. The declaration of the Foul constitutes a retroactive declaration of the nature of the initial act. Until such time as the Foul has been declared, it doesn't exist. Until such time the contact is devoid of value or meaning. Contact, pressure, touch: inadvertent, without malice. Only the Law can breathe life into the Foul, which remains immaterial. So the Law must be appealed to, and the man with the ball must appeal to the Law through the performance of the Foul.

There is something distasteful about this for the player. It involves reliance on an authority outside of himself, an appeal to a higher power, and this feels weak, feels un-masculine. He despises weakness and has worked to banish all traces of it from his body. And this performance will not edify his body, does not glorify the physical therapy, the many hours spent in the weight room. The dive will not make him feel powerful, or capable, or dominant. The bodies in the stand may lose respect for him. The appeal of the game is power, skill, and mastery—authenticity, never performance. To perform involves artifice. To perform is to invert the natural order of things. By attempting to summon the Foul instead of gritting through the contact and continuing on he is necessarily admitting weakness, admitting an inability to dominate his opponent and exert his will. Then, too, he must additionally perform this weakness, to embellish it. All this was distasteful. But his inadequacy in the moment was a fact, and that fact must be reckoned with, and there was the game to win.

Having clearly assessed his options, he decides to dive. He must perform the Foul, summon it, speak it into existence. He must create a new entity. He pushes off of his left foot and throws his body into the air wantonly. He must be dramatic enough so that the Law can see it, yet not so parabolic that he will actually hurt himself in the simulation of the injury. So he leaps, cautiously, knowing that at the peak of his leap, he must scream. It is the Scream that calls to the Law to acknowledge the Foul. The Scream urges the Foul into being, but relies on the Law to validate this fact. The scream must have a pitch high enough to cut through the sound of the crowd; it must be a Scream, not a grunt. A grunt would get him nowhere. A grunt would be too demure, too subtle. It must be operatic.

So it is—the Scream, the Dive, the ball bouncing quietly off to the side, the man crumpled on the ground moaning, holding his leg. The Law dutifully acknowledges the performance. The Foul is awarded, spoken, given life, becomes both word and flesh. It arrives in the world on all fours, gasping for air, somehow aware and ashamed of its own nakedness and reflexively grasping for something to cover itself up with. But this anxiety is misplaced—its sudden appearance goes unnoticed. The man is still on the ground, in rapturous pain; the defender is protesting to the Law, who dismisses these protests; the crowd watches footage of the incident in slow-motion on the big stadium screen, where, when slowed down to an impossible crawl, the first man's fall is exposed to be merely a clever simulation. The bodies in the stand erupt in boos, and insults rain down on the man on the ground. Despite the hostility from the crowd, he feels a palpable yet unfamiliar sense of satisfaction, a little wave of pleasure rolling through his body. But hours later, when asked, he will not acknowledge the performance at all—he will insist it was a clear violation, wear an elaborate wrap on his leg, and walk with an exaggerated limp.

Preview

We can Express the need for true FREE time

before This need can be satisfied

such a need may Serve as an instrument

to look Towards another FUTURE

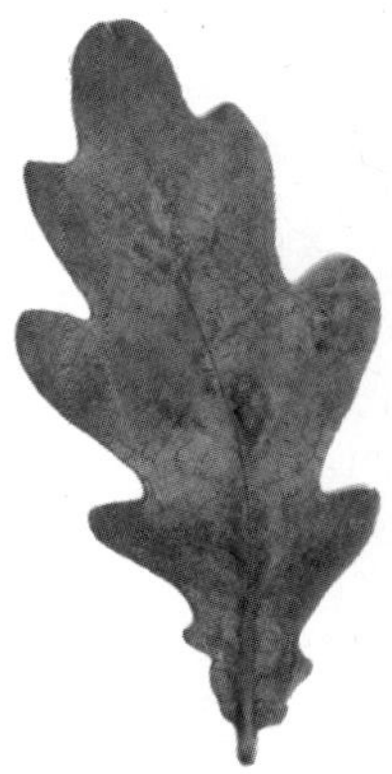

ONE TO ZERO
OR TO SHORT HOUSES ON VOLCANIC ARCHIPELAGOS

Dan Kwon

1

At Lunar Sea, Halo Rainbow.

When they are in season, a bowl of cherries lies by your bedside.

Take a deep breath, the truth lies within you. Mouth-breathing is bad. (Look up.) To speak, one has to exhale air through the mouth; for listening or writing, that is unnecessary. The benefits of nasal breathing are far reaching.

Agape, depending on how you pronounce it, could mean either to have your mouth open and appear dumbstruck, or transcendental love.

... dental ... love?

After wetting her lips, she wrapped them around his bottom lip, warmly, as in a wet embrace. Then buried her teeth into the plump. Blood slithered down as if to fracture his porcelain chin.

Deep-rooted memories of youth and loneliness rest still as a tree. It is a tree I know where to find, growing in place. I know where, but I don't know *how* to get there. I am there, but there's no tree. People I know live there now.

When a tree susurrates in the wind, though passive, the shuffle resembles desire, which, like fire, is a goddamn shapeshifter.

Remember the pleasure of time, when you suffocated a solar-powered calculator only to let go, of watching 0 return from nothing?

Now in abeyance.

A minute sliver of clipped fingernail glows in the paper
even
-ing
sky

It's

a

l

e

t

t

e

r

And like a snail picked up and dropped elsewhere, he found himself far removed from where he was supposed to be. Endless streams of words had begun to suffocate the room.

Be careful what you wish for, they say. More than that: be careful what you say out loud. In other words, mind the vibrations you cast through the living mold of your mouth; listen for, feel, seek their origin. It is more than okay to ask whether they come from the gut, or further down, throaty from above the chest; or do they resound the space between the cranium and cerebral matter? Do you ever choke on words that haven't even left your stomach, like they're gaseous?

Rules and hearsay eh

Mastication
Diet
Flora
Saliva

Morning rituals, as well as descriptions of their domain, develop character.

The supervisor greeted each passenger of the business cabin, to introduce himself and forecast the weather conditions hanging over our long haul. In five hours time, we were to hit turbulence that was estimated to last for two hours, and I should preferably use the lavatory beforehand. I was sure he caught me stealing a glimpse of his name-tag.

口 is a chinese character that represents mouth or opening. Note its angular shape.

When he listened, his lips contracted and sucked air in a way that made them resemble an anus.

Talk to a search engine like it were a child, a foreign person, or a pet. Yeah, similar, no? Words and word combinations without capital are buried somewhere.

너ㅁㅜ ㄴㅏ 굶 ㅈㅜㄹㄴㅣ ㅡ 몸은 하도 앙상하여 ㄴㅜㄱㅏ 포옹을 했을 때 팔이 두번 돌아가고 왼손과 오른손이 만나는 줄 알았다ㄱㅗ ㅎㅏㄷㅏㄴ. So much so, that when he was served soup, his tears trickled, his spoon rising to meet his lips. Watching the chef from afar, I could almost see the tail end of his mouth curl up. Later he told me he had spared a few pinches—“finches” he said—of Maldon.

An adolescent goes to town with a pomegranate platter, a wooden block supporting untold slices of pomegranate. Her muzzle becomes stained with pomegranate, as do her fingers, which she, pausing, regards with great satisfaction.

Of all the ways in which to occupy one’s time, Paul preferred to scrawl the names of his favorite people. This had a comforting effect on him.

Daisies close, it’s evening, I’m in company. The color of her panties: I see reflected on her chrome pumps from under her skirt, the sheen of sheer skin saturated with blood.

Colossal evergreens formed the silhouette of *Anzient Kathedral.*
Kathedral, can we name her Kathedral?

Kathedral ignores the perforated line and instead sinks her claws into the plastic wrap.

“Violate me,” she says, turning over her body, prone towards him.
He dislodges a splinter from under his fingernail. Half of it comes out, dripping pink.

You wake up with a blurred vision. A surge of tears streams over your malar ridges.

She wakes up, misty-eyed and languid. When she blinks, light shoots out.

You okay? You look nearly as white as these damn hotel sheets.

My voice wavers when I say *cinnamon*. I cannot pronounce cinnamon without a certain tremor in my voice.

We watched the trees sway among the copse. Closing her eyes, she savored the lazy breeze through her nose. The sunlight streaming through the apertures of summer foliage, a dapple of bokeh flickered on her face, like some code. She thought she could hear Gal blink, and furtively turned towards him. Startled, he turned away in haste, his cheeks red like apples.

The boy arrived home. The gate to the boy's house, so large both the doorbell and the handle remained out of his reach, had been closed. He would have to break off another tree branch to ring himself in.

Provincial children against a smoldering sunset.

In the magical blue of evening, when most children are summoned for supper and warm light, some are left on their respective playground. In this lonesome arena, Gal watches a plane pulse red across a vespertine sky.

He looked up, and eyed the glass buildings that towered over him. In the grids of numberless offices, he spotted just one illuminated window. He felt sympathy for whomever was responsible—maybe some kind of a torchbearer? Only to realize that it was just the reflection of the moon.

I guess I should go home soon, he thought.

The moon shines the same
The drifting clouds
The fickle pollution
The fine dust
Make it seem different
On different nights

POV: Fist-bump, the light switch on.

See a bee buzzing about, dusting the windowsill that needs to be dusted.

She pulls the volumes from the shelf, and flings them at him, book by book. Each thrown starts to flap, and flies away out the open window.

Only few were left, dancing in a desultory fashion. Meanwhile, towers wobbled like jelly.

Typing ...

Away, excited, no sooner does he mindlessly rub his hands than feels a moist, squishy roll between his fingers. He remembers that he had been in the room with a baby fly. That, in fact, for quite some time, it had just been the fly, cobwebs, and him in the room; he recalls, caressing his cheek, how, the other night, that little one flew so close to his face that he actually felt the most subtle and light breeze to have ever brushed his cheek, fanned by its tiny, rapid wings.

Stepping out of the steaming shower, he still gets a whiff of her rising from under.

Softly she kisses him, whose eyes slowly close in ecstasy, before she peels away and says, bang!—yer ded.

And he did. Later, they poked around at the body in search of life; it was a dead fire, they said.

2

I walk. There's a boy yelling from the street to his mother on the balcony about some runaway dog. Treading in the dark of the night through someone's garden, I vaguely make out a scuttling mouse which transforms into a maple leaf, dry on the wind's surf.

I steer a truckload of collegiate revelers, sauced and without a license. We had left a party, to escape into the after-hours freeway that links us to an eastern edge of the Atlantic. We pass around a handle of bourbon, which Anna looted from the party. We carol hits on the radio in this rapturous campaign against drunk driving. Tragedy looming but never arriving.

Gradually we enter a dark world where the headlights of our vehicle become the sole light, before finally—the asphalt terminates in sand. In a choreographic move, we hop out of the truck, approach the waves; stand abreast on a deserted beach. No one speaks in this script. With neither star, moon, nor horizon in view, the maritime roar and the silent heavens merge, into a noisy colorfield of zero information.

Thirty-three miles back, green bottles fragment into stardust.

As I bent over, heaving on a sandy strand, dripping goo, turning my head to get a good look at the thing that had just expelled me, a sudden gust came, wrapping me up, enfolding my body in gooseflesh before draining me of all my strength.

Morning. Beach. I can't find her, let alone see past my few-feet radius, all else shrouded in moist, diffuse light. No sooner do I resolve to back-track to the group, than a shaky female figure emerges from the mist, scuffed and blue, soaked underwear and hair. Something shoots through my spine; I tremble and speak. There's only the crashing waves. Moving toward me, she has her arms wrapped around her convulsing abdomen, as though to keep its contents from spilling out. Opens her mouth, but I comprehend nothing.

To watch him tidy up, and clean his room, was to witness a perfect crime.

Place where y'all love ya job.

Like time, we, too, are unstoppable.

Become like those you miss today~*

Content, and in the absence of drive to produce prompt response, he shuts the phone. Curls up sideways, and occupies as little room as possible. For warmth too. Bringing his head towards the chest, like thoughts are to be placed near the heart, he lies on his left. Some say it is better to lie on your right; that way, the cardiac muscle is spared of added pressure. Left, he prefers: the sound of living heartbeat aids and, presently, there's no one's but his.

No one:

Through the back door, left open, the breeze, like me, invited itself in. Sheer curtains billow, and traverse the threshold; the children seem to have disappeared.

So I push through the door. And no sooner does the light flood the interior, into which my shadow is cast, than signs of life present themselves in the ink of my shadow; the echo of metal chains approximate the scale of this dungeon. I swing the door open, and enter to the side to expose my host: a live captive, limp like a collapsed marionette, in an indecent florid dress torn and ribboned. Glare of patent leather circumscribes her neck in the flood of light. Fetters indeterminate in length suspend, in what seems to be a labyrinthine network of steel, ends rendered obscure. Everything is *gris*, save my new acquaintance. The voice of my mother intrudes: *My dear child, I cannot hold you.*

And he found himself in her absence, in the moment he wanted her. She was with them, emanating life, bursting with laughter and brand new eyes; slurping the largest oyster one of the boys had shucked for her. In pitch silence, alone, Gal wept himself to a slumber, wanting never to rise from the bed.

The duvet clouds hung so low, the sky was virtually absent. All day, without a perceivable shift in the even gray light, without celestial object in sight to track, the firmament remained incredibly motionless. As though time really did stand still. All the silly figures in many colors and shapes, seemingly driven by a mind of their own, moved in space as though they had free will.

In a gradual fall, with their arms around me, their body slid down against mine, streaking blood onto my white shirt and pants, both made by Celine. They had parked their bike as though it were a barricade before the giant Euro sign. They summoned a thousand bees to hover around their body. Their voice was barely audible in the apiarian babble, but I did hear that it was how they fended off heat.

What's their net worth? Oh, more than the age of the universe.

We pass around a bowl of rice, and watch the erratic strobe lights flash from the nite skye. Anticipate rolling thunder. The bottom part, the scorched part of the rice in the pot, was their mother's favorite, a golden remnant of just after the war.

Or what story?

From where I stood, the sun remained behind her head. Behind me was a reflective wall, against which the sunlight scattered and compensated for the backlight to illuminate her face. Even with the squint of an eye, I could not but see her pupils.

"Now remember: All triggers on all guns must be sss....qqq....uuueeee.....zzz... eeddd. That is 'squeezed' steadily. Not jerked. If you do everything else right and do not exercise proper trigger control, you will not hit your target."

Surely, whatever stops you, deep-rooted like wisdom teeth, *if* you have them, would take a cup of blood to pull. They say you won't die any more than you already have. Forget it, with a firm tender hug as an offering and, better still, a smack juicy enough to complete a transfer of a billion microorganisms in the shape of a heart, upended or otherwise.

This one's for all that you mirror. At least for now:

Night Sky

Ceilings Amiss

Shopping Lists

Red Lipstick

Rolling Step Stool

O

You are ______ and I am _______, but for you I would turn red and blue.

Some dreams, like some deaths(?), are meant to be forgotten.

We had founded an Eden of our own, our haven for corrupted innocence, around a well of joyous tears with which we anointed each other. Of secrets where nothing but our memory alone could gain access. I remember how I kicked the trunk of a sycamore tree to release rain from its foliage and shower over us, how her face split open into a wild smile then—all teeth and gum—in surprise and ecstatic wonder, mirroring my own maybe. That smile, all of this, a memory that is now solely my own, explodes into millions of pixels, and I'm blown in all directions. I feel so dizzy I can hardly lie ...

♫:

My luv, errrrrr, u.r masaaylerrrrr

One day it's more

Another day it's less

Even when the spots are painted over

Oh it won't stop

Even at the smallest sound

Think I'll shatter

One of the many flags

Flapping toward you

You can't even choose

So here I am

With my mouth shut as I toss my eyes to the ground

Counting dust in my pocket

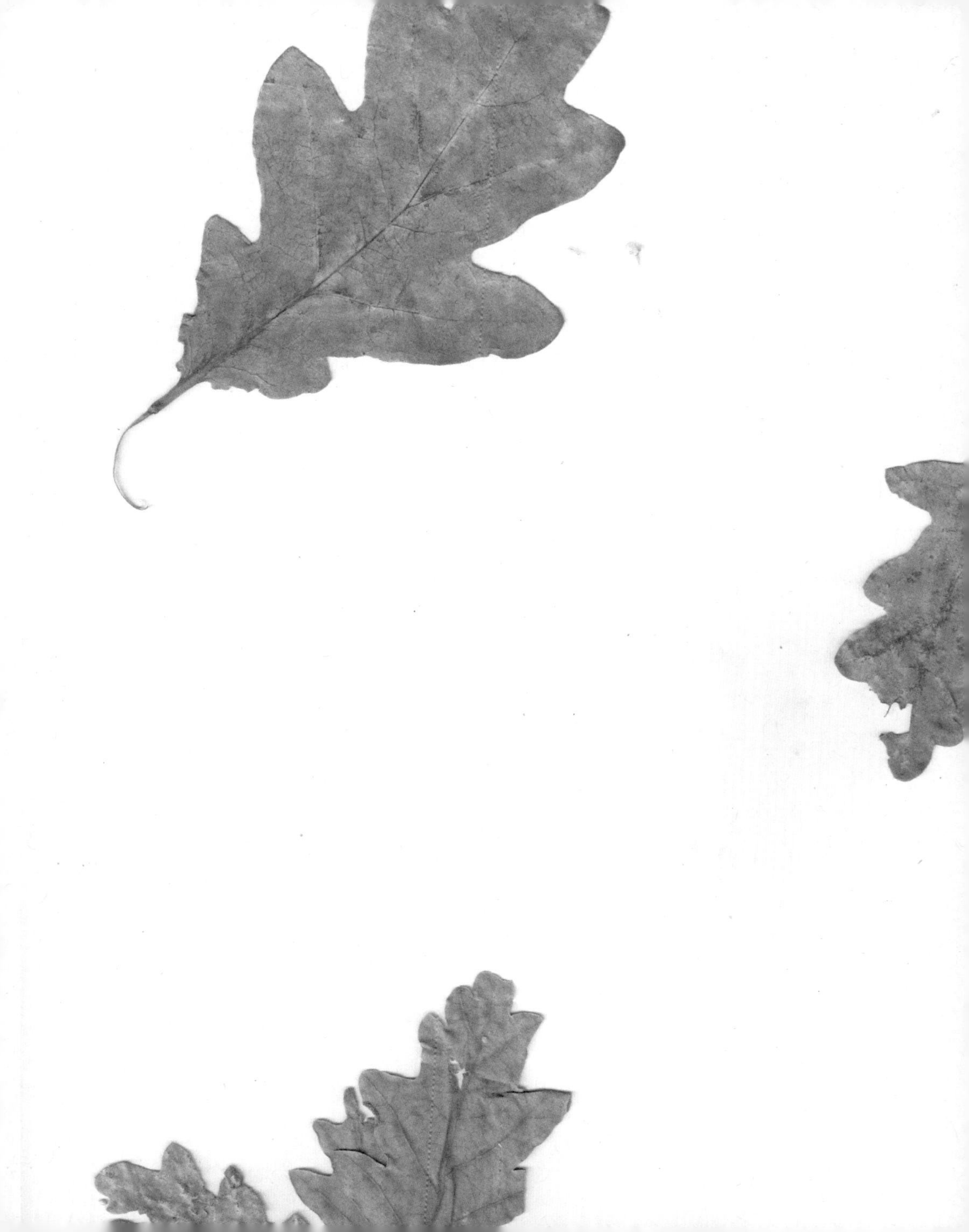

Regrief

EXCERPT FROM *THE YEARS*

Annie Ernaux

All the images will disappear:

the woman who squatted to urinate in broad daylight, behind the shack that served coffee at the edge of the ruins in Yvetot, after the war, who stood, skirts lifted, to pull up her underwear and then returned to the café

the tearful face of Alida Valli as she danced with Georges Wilson in the film *The Long Absence*

the man passed on the pavement in Padua in the summer of 1990, his hands fused with his shoulders, instantly summoning the memory of thalidomide, prescribed to pregnant women for nausea thirty years before, and of a joke people told later: an expectant mother knits the baby's layette while gulping thalidomide pills at regular intervals—a row, a pill, a row, a pill. A friend says in horror, Stop, don't you realize your baby may be born without arms, and the other answers, It's okay, I don't know how to knit sleeves anyway

Claude Piéplu leads a regiment of légionnaires, waving a flag in one hand and leading a goat with the other, in a Les Charlots film

the majesty of the elderly woman with Alzheimer's, who wore a flowered smock like all the residents of the old folks' home, but with a blue shawl over her shoulders, tirelessly pacing the corridors, haughty like the Duchess of Guermantes in the Bois de Boulogne, and who made you think of Céleste Albaret as she'd appeared one night on television with Bernard Pivot

on an outdoor stage, the woman shut into a box pierced all the way through by men with silver spears—and emerging alive because it was a magic trick, called *The Martyrdom of a Woman*

the mummies clothed in tattered lace, dangling from the walls of the Convento dei Cappuccini in Palermo

Simone Signoret's face on the poster for *Thérèse Raquin*

the shoe rotating on a pedestal in an André shop, rue du Gros-Horloge in Rouen, the same phrase continuously scrolling around it—*With Babybotte, Baby trots and grows well*

the stranger of Termini Station in Rome, who half lowered the blind of his first-class compartment and in profile, hidden from the waist up, dandled his sex in the direction of the young women in the train on the opposite platform, leaning against the railings, chins in hands

the guy in a cinema ad for Paic Vaisselle dishwashing liquid, cheerfully breaking dirty dishes instead of washing them while an offscreen voice sternly intoned "That is not the solution!" and the man, gazing at the audience in despair, asked "But what is the solution?"

the beach at Arenys de Mar, next to a railway line, the hotel guest who looked like Zappy Max

the newborn flailed in the air like a skinned rabbit in the delivery room of the Clinique Caudéran Pasteur found again half an hour later, dressed and sleeping on his side in a little bed, one hand out, and the sheet pulled up to his shoulders

the dashing figure of the actor Philippe Lemaire, married to Juliette Gréco

in an advert on TV, the father who hides behind his newspaper, trying in vain to toss a Picorette in the air and catch it in his mouth, like his little girl

a house with a vine-covered arbor which was a hotel in the sixties, no. 90A, on the Zattere in Venice

the hundreds of petrified faces, photographed by the authorities before deportation to the camps, on the walls of a room in the Palais de Tokyo, Paris, in the mid-1980s

the lavatories built above the river, in the courtyard behind the house in Lillebonne, the excrements mixed with paper borne away by the gently lapping water

all the twilight images of the early years, the pools of light from a summer Sunday, images from dreams in which the dead parents come back to life, and you walk down indefinable roads

the image of Scarlett O'Hara dragging the Yankee soldier she has just killed up the stairs, then running through the streets of Atlanta in search of a doctor for Melanie, who is about to give birth

of Molly Bloom, who lies next to her husband, remembering the first time a boy kissed her and she said yes yes yes

of Elizabeth Drummond, murdered with her parents on a road in Lurs in 1952

the images, real or imaginary, that follow us all the way into sleep
the images of a moment bathed in a light that is theirs alone

They will all vanish at the same time, like the millions of images that lay behind the foreheads of the grandparents, dead for half a century, and of the parents, also dead. Images in which we appeared as a little girl in the midst of beings who died before we were born, just as in our own memories our small children are there next to our parents and schoolmates. And one day we'll appear in our children's memories, among their grandchildren and people not yet born. Like sexual desire, memory never stops. It pairs the dead with the living, real with imaginary beings, dreams with history.

Thousands of words, the ones used to name things, faces, acts and feelings, to put the world in order, make the heart beat and the sex grow moist, will suddenly be nullified.

slogans, graffiti in public toilets, on walls in the street, poems and dirty jokes, headlines

anamnesis, epigone, noema, theoretical, the terms written in a notebook alongside their meanings so you didn't need to look them up each time

turns of phrase that others used without a thought and which we doubted we'd ever be able to use, *undeniably, one cannot fail to notice that*

dreadful sentences one should have forgotten, more tenacious than others due to the effort expended in suppressing them, you look like a decrepit whore

the words of men in bed at night, Do with me what you will, I am your play-thing

to exist is to drink oneself dry

what were you doing on 11 September 2001?

in illo tempore at Mass on Sunday

old geezer, hullabaloo, a turn up for the books! You little nincompoop, outdated expressions, heard again by chance, suddenly precious as objects lost and found again, a wonder they've been saved from oblivion the words forever bound to certain people, like mottos, or to a specific spot on the N14 because a passenger happened to say them just as we were driving by, and we cannot pass that place again without the words leaping up like the buried water jets at the Summer Palace of Peter the Great, which spray when you walk across them

the grammar book examples, quotes, insults, songs, sentences copied into note-books when we were teens

l'abbé Trublet compilait, compilait, compilait

glory for a woman is the dazzling mourning of happiness

our memory is outside us, in a rainy breath of time

perfection for a nun is to spend her life as a virgin and to die as a saint

saucy spoonerisms: the acrobats displayed some cunning stunts, the explorer puts his mess in the cashbox

it was a lucky charm, a little pig with a heart / that she bought at the market for a hundred sous / a hundred sous is a pittance, between me and you

my story is a story of love

can you *tirlipoter* with a fork? Can you put *schmilblick* in a baby bottle?

(I'm capable of the best and the worst, but at being the worst I'm the best! so if you're happy, why don't you laugh? I'll be brief, said King Pepin the Short and climbing out of the monster's belly, Jonas declared, you don't need to be a brain sturgeon to know that's dolphinitely no minnow—the puns heard a thousand times, which had ceased to amuse or amaze us long ago; hackneyed, only irritating, they served no purpose but to consolidate the family *esprit de corps*, and disappeared when the couple blew apart though still sprang to mind sometimes, incongruous, inappropriate outside of the former tribe—basically, all that remained of it, after years of separation)

words that we are astonished ever existed—*mastoc*, hefty (Flaubert in a letter to Louise Colet), *pioncer*, to kip (George Sand to Flaubert)

Latin and English, Russian learned in six months for a Soviet, only thing left of it now *da svidania, ya tebia lioubliou kharacho*

what is marriage? A con-promise

metaphors so tired it was astonishing to see others daring to utter them, the icing on the cake

O Mother buried outside the first garden

pédaler à côté du vélo, to pedal next to the bicycle (wasted effort) became *pédaler dans la choucroûte*, to pedal in sauerkraut (going nowhere fast), then pedaling in semolina (to go round in circles), then nothing—obsolete expressions

the men's words we didn't like, *come, tossing off*

those learned at school that gave you a feeling of mastery over the world. Once the exam was over, they flew out of your head more quickly than they had entered

the phrases repeated by grandparents that set one's teeth on edge, and those of the parents which after their deaths remained more alive than their faces, *curiosity killed the cat, little jugs have big ears*

the old brands, short-lived, the memories of which delighted you more than those of better-known brands, Dulsol shampoo, Cardon chocolate, Nadi coffee—like an intimate memory, impossible to share

The Cranes Are Flying

Marianne of My Youth

Madame Soleil is still with us

the world is suffering from lack of faith in a transcendental truth

Everything will be erased in a second. The dictionary of words amassed between cradle and deathbed, eliminated. All there will be is silence and no words to say it. Nothing will come out of the open mouth, neither I nor me. Language will continue to put the world into words. In conversation around a holiday table, we will be nothing but a first name, increasingly faceless, until we vanish into the vast anonymity of a distant generation.

BETWEEN THE PAST, NOW AND LATER

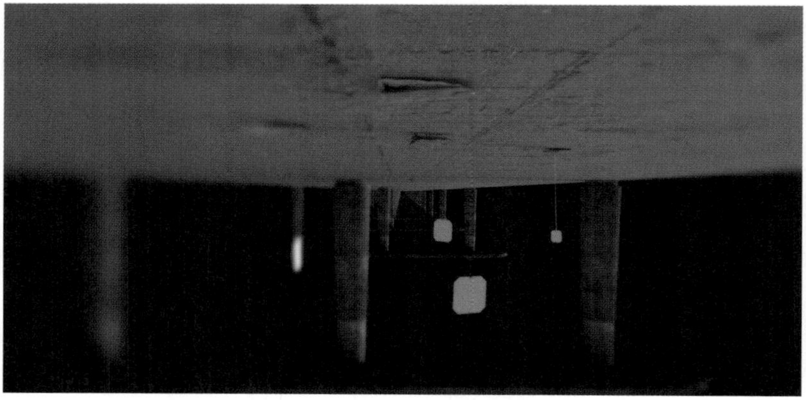

Prologue
I won't describe you as an individual, but as an emotional and intellectual sedimentation. I perceive you as a body and your body as thought. As thoughts change and clarify with the passing of time, so does your person. You are multitude, but I speak to you as one. My intimacy with you is pluralistic, but my memory of you remains singular. To you I will address my memories.

June 2016
It is personal
My relationship to you is framed by memories of you. Yet, I have difficulty remembering you as you were. I want to remember you as if I hadn't known you. Perhaps this remembrance will be closer to you than a present memory.

In Arabic the word *Thikra* (pl. *Thikrayat*) translates to memory/ies. *Thikra* is not an isolated memory. It is not merely the act of retaining images and facts. *Thikra* contains emotion/s, feeling/s, and state/s of affection. It is a personal experience. A visceral event of the now that becomes embodied as memory with the passing of time.

I use remembrance not to create a timeline, but to perceive the present. I use it to understand, to activate a sense of awareness, a sort of longing. Longing, not in search of a nostalgic past or awaiting fate, but instead: A potential world to unfold.

It is said that "Time makes nothing happen; it merely makes the emotivity of suffering pass. Emotion passes, suffering remains."

استهلال

لن أصفكَ كفرد بل كتراكم عاطفي و فكري، أراك كجسد و جسدُك كفكرة، كما الفكرة تتغيّر و تتجلّى مع مرور الزمن كذلك هو شخصك. أنت مجموعة من الأشخاص و لكن سأكلّمك بصيغة المفرد. حميميّتي معك أنت جمعية و لكن ستبقى ذاكرتي معك مفردة. لك سأتكلّم عن ذاكرتي عنك.

حزيران، ٢٠١٦
إنّه موضوع شخصي

علاقتي بك مؤطرّة بذكرياتي عنك. ومع ذلك، يصعبُ عليَّ أن أتذكّرك كما كنت، أريد أن أتذكّرك كما لو أنّني لم أعرفك، رُبّما يكون هذا التذكّر أقرب إليك من أيّة ذاكرة حالية.

الذكرى ليست معزولة، ليست مجرّد عملية احتفاظ بتصويرات و حقائق. الذكرى تحوي عاطفة/عواطف، شعور/مشاعر، و حالة/حالات من الحس. هي تجربة شخصية، عملية استدراك للآن لتصبح ذاكرة مع مرور الزمن.
لا استخدم التذكّر لأخلق خطاً زمنياً، بل لأتعرف على الواقع، لأفهم، لأخلق شعوراً بالإدراك و نوعاً ما من التوق. التوق؛ ليس بحثاً عن حنينٍ لماض أو قدرٍ محتوم، بل بحثاً عن عالمٍ يُحتَمَل اكتشافه.[١]

يقالُ أنّ «الزمن لا يُغيِّر ماهيّةَ الأشياء، إنّه فقط يجعل الانفعال العاطفي للمعاناة يمرّ، فتمرُّ العاطفة، و تبقى المعاناة.» [٢]

December 1985
Your Death in Damascus

Emotion passes, suffering remains.

I have so much to tell you, how can I put it all into words? How can those words contain all this time? If I turn back and look straight into your eyes, you would disappear, and I'd be deep in the dark. You call my name and it reminds me of a home I left a long time ago. Only memories come to my rescue, but somehow, in order to remember, I have to forget: as if by remembering I'll postpone your death. This is the last time I speak to you, the last time I'm able to do so, these words are for you, you who cannot hear nor answer me.

For you, all of life became a problem that you solved by shutting off your physical self. You told me "my body was in prison, while my mouth was open." You watched life go by, people falling in love and you were no longer part of it. You wrote to me "I was living in another land, no-man's land," all the things that could've been done and all the things that could've been said to change the situation and weren't. "I wish the eighties on no one," you said. That period certainly showed an inheritance of confusion. A confusion of uncertainty. A confusion of the "non-normative." You represented uncertainty and therefore you were cast out and condemned by ignorance.

"Remember when?"

كانون الأوّل، ١٩٨٥
وفاتك في دمشق

تمرُّ العاطفة، و تبقى المعاناة.

لديّ الكثير لأُخبِرك به، كيف يمكنني أن أعبّر عن كل ذلك بلغة؟ كيف يمكن لهذه الكلمات أن تحوي كل هذا الوقت؟ إذا التفت ونظرت في عينيك مباشرة ستختفي، وسأصبح في أعماق الظلام. تنادي اسمي فيحيي في داخلي ذكرى لبلد تركته منذ مدةٍ طويلة. فقط الذكريات تأتي لإنقاذي، و لكن بشكلٍ أو بآخر، كي أتذكر، عليّ أن أنسى: كما لو أني عن طريق التذكّر سأقوم بتأجيل رحيلك، هذه آخر مرة أحدثك فيها، آخر مرة أكون فيها قادراً على فعل ذلك، هذه الكلمات لك، أنت الذي لا تستطيع أن تسمعني ولا أن تجيبني.

الحياة أصبحت لك مشكلة حللتَها بإغلاق ذاتك المادّية، قلتَ لي «جسدي في السجن، أما فمي فكان مفتوحاً»[٣] لقد شاهدتَ الحياة تمر، أناساً يقعون في حبٍ لم تعد جزءاً منه، كتبت لي «كنت أعيش في أرض أخرى، أرض معزولة»[٤] كل الأشياء التي كان من الممكن القيام بها وكل الأشياء التي كان يمكن أن تقال لتغيير الوضع ولم تحصل.

قلت «لا أتمنى الثمانينات لأحد»[٥] بالفعل أظهرت تلك الفترة وجودَ ميراث من الارتباك، ارتباك من اللايقين، ارتباك «اللا-معياري»، لقد جسّدت اللا يقين و من أجل ذلك الجهل العام طردك و أدانك.

«أتَذكُر لقائنا؟»

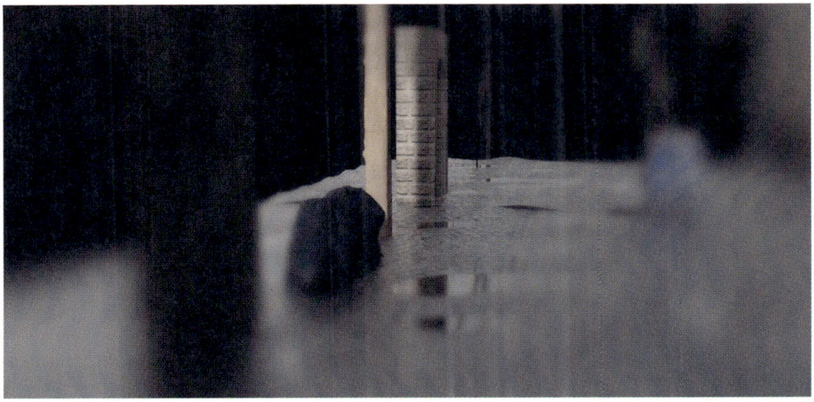

September 2019 – February 2020
Encountering you in Beirut

Remember when I met you at a party in Beirut? I told you your face had a melancholic expression. "It's not melancholy, it's fragility," you responded. Your words continued to haunt me, to intimidate me. I kept thinking about them, and I kept thinking about you.

I'm standing in front of you, decades and decades after it happened, and here again, it seems we are witnessing a significant change, another end of a world we knew. Only this time, worse than before, and it won't get better!

"Back in the eighties, it was difficult to think of a future," you said, and it is still difficult to think of a future now. People think time is valuable, prepossessing, flimsy. A burning candle on a desk, all that. Time is violent. It always prevails. I've seen you die a hundred times and you'll die many times more. We're in the middle of a fight for a future. And somehow, I find myself pondering my unspoken fragility and your spoken bravery.

"This is what I'm gonna do, trust the unknown."

October 1993
Our fate, out of time

Trust the unknown.

He had a vision of men who are born and raised to be perfect fierce men. To take whatever punishment given to them and spring back flamboyant, strengthened by love unconditioned. He had a vision that deep within his arms and eyes there are still men, men willing to sacrifice themselves for the love of other men.

Men who are born and raised to be perfect fierce men. To take whatever punishment given to them and spring back flamboyant, strengthened by love unconditioned. I have a vision that deep within his arms and eyes there are still men, men willing to sacrifice themselves for the love of other men.

He gave him his love. All of his love. Love wrote his judgment, blinded his eyes so that now when he looks into the mirror he sees nothing but men that won't leave anyone behind. Men willing to sacrifice themselves for the love of other men. It is a vision that has become his life. That deep within his arms and eyes there are still men, men willing to sacrifice themselves for the love of other men. And who won't leave anyone behind.

"It is a vision that has become his life."

أيلول، ٢٠١٩ - شباط، ٢٠٢٠
مصادفتك في بيروت

أتذكر لقائنا في بيروت؟ أخبرتك أن لوجهك تعبير ميلانكولي. أجبت «ليست ميلانكوليا ، إنّها هشاشة». استمرّت كلماتك تُطاردني و تتحدّاني. استمريّتُ بالتفكير فيهم و استمريت بالتفكير فيك.

أقف هنا أمامكَ، عقود و عقود بعد ما حدث، وهنا مجدداً ، يبدو أننا نشهد تغييراً كبيراً، نهاية أخرى لعالمٍ عرفناه. لكن هذه المرة، أستكون أسوأ من ذي قبل و لن تتحسن!

قلت «في الثمانينيات كان من الصعب التفكير في المستقبل»[٦] وحتّى الآن لا يزال من الصعب التفكير في المستقبل. يعتقد الناس أن الوقت ثمين، أخّاذ، واهٍ. شمعة مشتعلة على مكتب، كل ذلك. الوقت عنيف. يَسُود دائما. رأيتك تموت مائة مرة وستموت أكثر. نحن في خضمّ عراك من أجل مستقبل. لكنني أجد نفسي بطريقةٍ ما أتفكّر هشاشتي غير المعننة وشجاعتك المنطوقة.

«هذا ما سأفعله، ثق بالمجهول.»[٧]

تشرين الأول، ١٩٩٣
مصيرنا، خارج حدود الزمن

ثِق بالمجهول.
كان لديه رؤية عن رجالات ولدوا ونشأوا ليكونوا رجالات مثاليين. أخذوا أي عقاب وجِّه لهم و نهضوا بشموخ، محصّنين بحبٍ غير مشروط. كان لديه رؤية في أعماق ذراعيه وعينيه رجالات، رجالات على استعداد للتضحية بأنفسهم من أجل حب رجالات أخرين.

رجالات ولدوا ونشأوا ليكونوا رجالات مثاليين. أخذوا أي عقاب وجِّه لهم و نهضوا بشموخ، محصّنين بحبٍ غير مشروط. كان لديه رؤية في أعماق ذراعيه وعينيه عن رجالات ، رجالات على استعداد للتضحية بأنفسهم من أجل حب رجالات أخرين.

أعطاه حبّه. كل حبّه. حكم الحب على تبصّرِهِ، أعمى عينيه لدرجةِ أنّه عندما ينظر إلى المرآة لا يرى شيئاً سوى رجالات لن يتركوا أحداً وراءهم. رجالات على استعداد للتضحية بأنفسهم من أجل حب رجالات آخرين. هذه الرؤية أصبحت حياته. في أعماق ذراعيه وعينيه لا يزال هناك رجالات ، رجالات على استعداد للتضحية بأنفسهم من أجل حب رجالات آخرين و لن يتركوا أحداً ورائهم.

«هذه الرؤية أصبحت حياته.»[٨]

June 1971
Our fate, out of place

It is a vision that has become his life.
Men wearing studs, leather and pearls. In front of motorbike headlights in a park. Gazing at one another with awe and desire, caressing amid the rustling of leaves. They stand alone, in couples, in clusters. Performative constellations, yet intimate. Grouping, circulating and regrouping as if it was a dance rehearsed over and over again, stumbling between cigarettes as smoke bellows in the air. A choreography that looks more like fate than an inscription of movement in space.

They portray masculinity in order to touch it, to kiss it, to desire it. To rim it and make fun of it. A proximity realized between total strangers. This is a romance, an infatuation that has no future. It's locked in the present moment, between fists that feel like tender kisses.

They take care of one another while they inflict pain on each other, a game of consistency. Like voices in a choir seeking to harmonize. They hold each other to reach the maximum joy of the moment. Their bodies are grips and handles for each other, to get higher and higher. They create painterly compositions from necessities and needs: They position their bodies in secluded public spaces that are painted as trash by society, but in reality they are a taste of paradise on earth. They inhabit those spaces like no one else does, because they raised themselves to be unmarked and unbothered. They're a dream sequence on a movie set that failed to be captured over and over again.

They loved each other, and their love remained in those spaces, even after their bodies had left. Same as when Echo's body deteriorated and only her voice remained. Anybody who passes hears their echo among the bushes. It will remain there, like Narcissus, captured by his own reflection, refusing to leave.

حزيران، ١٩٧١
مصيرنا، خارج حدود المكان

هذه الرؤية أصبحت حياته.
رجالات يرتدون السلاسل و الجلود و اللآلئ، أمام المصابيح الأمامية للدراجات النارية في متنزّه. يتوسّمون بعضهم البعض برغبةٍ و إجلال، ملامسات وسط حفيفِ أوراق الشجر. يقفون وحيدين ، في أزواج ، في مجموعات مختالة غير أنها حميميّة. يتجمّعون, يدورون حول نفسهم، يتجمّعون من جديد، كما لو كانوا يرقصون رقصة تمرّنوا عليها مراراً وتكراراً ، يتعثّرون بين السجائر بينما يُنفَث الدخان في الهواء. رقصة أقرب للمصير من كونها مجرد تصميمات حركية في المكان.

يمثلوّن الرجولة للمسها، لتقبيلها، لاشتهاءها، للعقها و السخرية منها، قرب خلق بين غرباء. هذه رومانسية، إفتتان لا مستقبل له. مقفولٌ عليه في اللحظة الحالية، بين قبضات يستشعرونها و كأنها قبلات رقيقة.

يعتنون و ينزلون الألم ببعضهم البعض في الوقت نفسه، لعبة ائتلاف. كما في جوقة تسعى إلى التناغم. يتماسكون ببعضهم البعض للوصول إلى أقصى درجات الأشر. أجسادهم مقابض و دعامات للوصول لأقصى درجات النشوه. يخلقون لوحات تصويريّة من ضرورة و احتياج ، يُموضعون أجسادهم في أماكن عامة يرسمها المجتمع على أنها وسخة لكنّها في الواقع طعم الجنة على الأرض. يسكنون تلك المساحات كما لم يفعل أي شخص آخر, لأنهم ربّوا أنفسهم ليكونوا بمنأى عن كل أذى و ازعاج. إنهم حلم في موقع تصوير لم يستطع أحد التقاطها.

أحبّوا بعضهم البعض ، وبقي حبهم هناك حتى عندما غادرت أجسادهم تلك المساحات. كما تدهور جسد إيكو وبقي فقط صوتها.

كل من يمر يسمع صداهم بين الشجيرات. سيبقى صداهم هناك دائماً. مثل نرسيس الذي استحوذ عليه انعكاسه، رافضًا المغادرة.

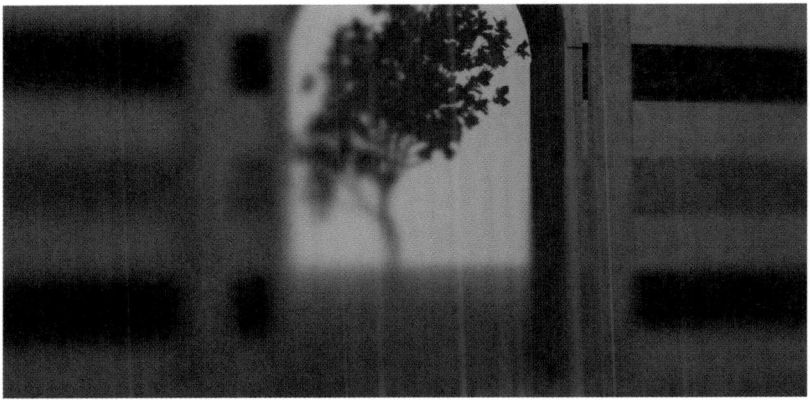

October 2005
Dwelling with you

Like Narcissus, captured by his own reflection, refusing to leave.

The old city of Damascus is a system of corridors and passages that forms a labyrinth of either deadends or loops that lead back to the dwellings of those narrow streets. The gates of the old city are the only way out of this system.

As I walk the streets of old Damascus I recall the variation of Prince Siegfried from Swan Lake. I vaguely remember the movements while slowly walking among the dwellings of the old city. The variation is an adagio choreographed and danced by you in 1961. You as Siegfried wearily danced whilst being watched by your companion Benno from a dark staircase. The movements in the variation are fragile, soft, melancholic, off-balance, and slow. Unlike the traditional characteristics of the movements of a prince; muscular, strong, and athletic. Siegfried is the contrary. Delicate and dreamy: He longs for freedom and refuses a restrictive marital order.

You showed us another side of the prince and a different reading of *Swan Lake*. Your dance lingers with me and drags each of my steps along the streets of the old city. I'm set in motion inside my head and within my body. I navigate two systems of inhabitation; one balletic and the other on-site, two systems that are completely separate, for which my body becomes the meeting point.

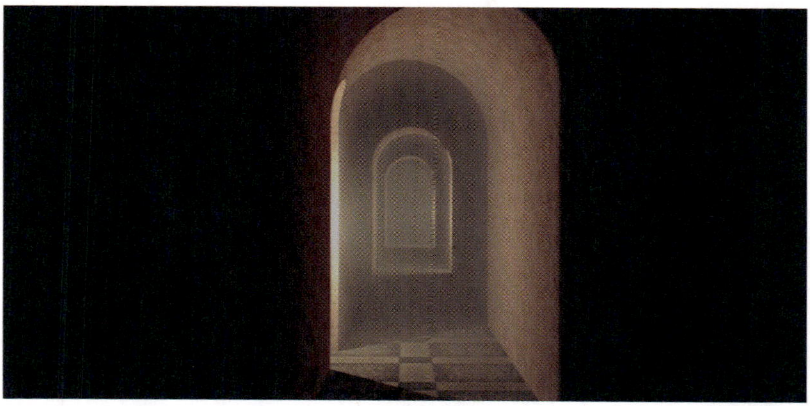

تشرين الأول، ٢٠٠٥
السكن معك

مثل نرسيس الذي استحوذ عليه انعكاسه ، رافضاً المغادرة.
دمشق القديمة هي نظام من الدهاليز و الممرات التي تشكّل متاهة إما من طرق مسدودة أو من حلقات تؤدي إلى مساكن تلك الشوارع الضيقة نفسها. أبواب المدينة القديمة هي السبيل الوحيد للخروج من هذا النظام.

بينما أسير في شوارع دمشق القديمة أتذكر مقطوعة الأمير سيجفريد من بحيرة البجع. أتذكر بضبابية الحركات أثناء تباطئي بين مساكن المدينة القديمة. المقطوعة هي الأداجيو الذي صممتَها ورقصتَها في عام ١٩٦١. كنت سيغفريد ترقص بوهن بينما يراقبك رفيقك بينو من عتبه درج مظلم. الحركات في المقطوعة هشة ناعمة، ميلانكولية، غير متوازنة وبطيئة. على عكس الخصائص التقليدية لتحركات الأمير: عضلية وقوية ورياضية. سيغفريد هو عكس ذلك ، مرهف وحالم: تواق إلى الحرية، رافض للأمر التقييدي بالزواج الذي فرضته عليه المؤسسة العائلية.

لقد أظهرت لنا جانباً آخر من الأمير وقراءة مختلفة لبحيرة البجع. رقصك يرافقني و يقود كل خطوة من خطواتي على طول شوارع المدينة لقديمة. مدفوع بالحركة في رأسي و داخل جسد، أسيّر نظامين من التأقلم، الأول حركي و الأخر مكاني، نظامان منفصلان تماماً، ولكن بطريقة ما يصبح جسدي نقطة اللقاء.

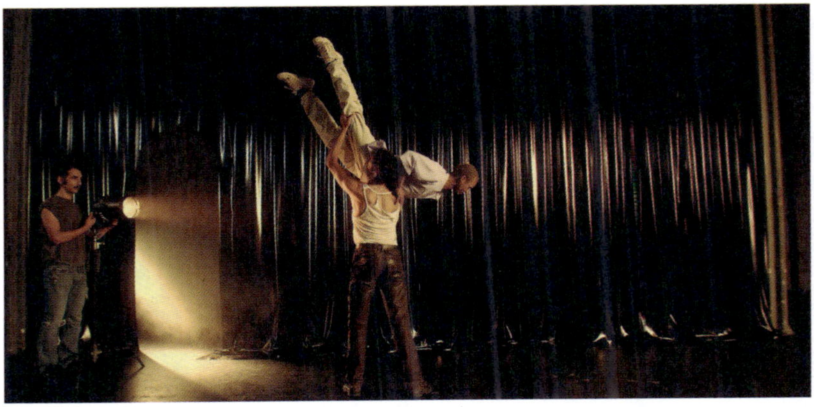

Interval : Time of The Angel

I find myself in a dance
a dance
between remembering and forgetting
I keep on rehearsing your presence
in order to come into proximity
I need to search for your memory
as memory cannot simply be received
the same way I can't see air
even though I am in it
I want to be receptive to the past
as it is alive
and not entombed in some rigid idea of a history

Sometimes people say "let things heal and go on"
I'll go on
but I won't "let things heal"
this is not a resentment
but rather a refusal of the solidification of your memory
and to what had happened

I find myself in an unsettling dominion
that took over this dance
hesitant, yet willing
terrified, yet excited
all at the same time

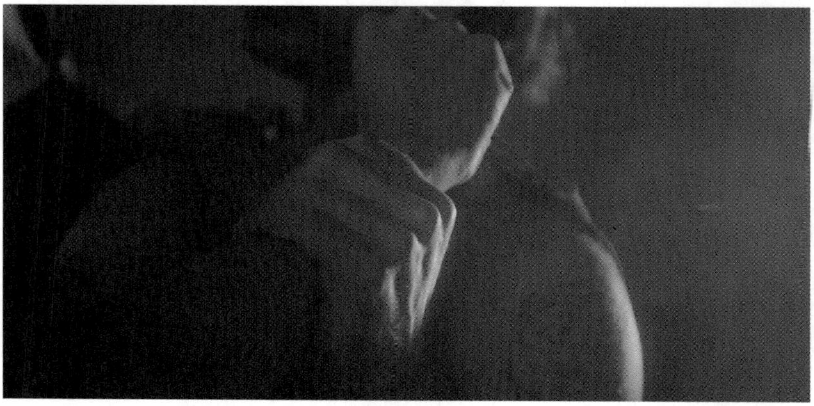

فاصل : زمن الملاك [٩]

أجد نفسي في رقصة
رقصة
بين التذكّر و النسيان
أستمرّ بالتدرّب على حضورك
كي أتقرّب إليك
يتوجّب عليَّ البحث عن ذاكرتك
فالتذكّر يحصل بتحضير مسبق
بنفس الطريقة التي لا أستطيع فيها رؤية الهواء
على الرغم من أنني فيه
أريد أن أكون منفتحا للماضي
كما لو أنه حي
وليس حبيس فكرة تاريخ كتب لنا

أحيانًا يقول الناس «دع الأشياء تلتئم وواصل حياتك»
سأواصل
لكني لن أدع «الأشياء تلتئم»
فهذه ليست نقمة
بل بالأحرى رفض لتحجيم ذاكرتك
ولما حدث

أجد نفسي في ملكوت مقلق
ملكوت، استحوذ على هذه الرقصة
أجد نفسي متردد ، لكن مستعد
خائف ، لكن متحمس
كل ذلك في الوقت نفسه

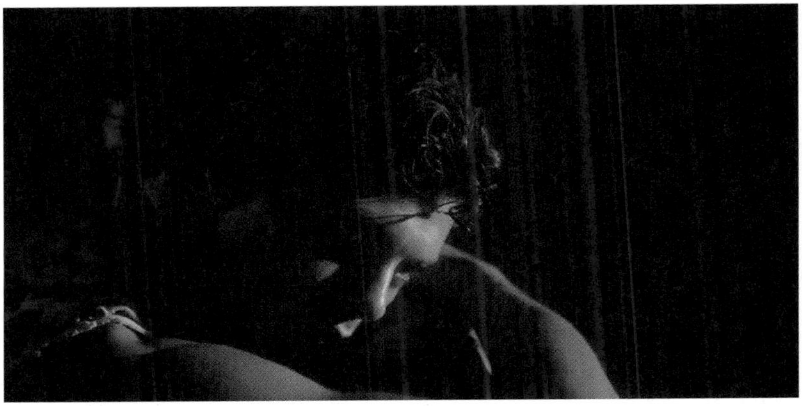

Tale has it that,
at the turn of night
at dusk
every being can become their own shadow
and thus something other than themselves

Dusk here doesn't only represent a specific time of the day
but a state of metamorphosis and unpredictability as well
a period of uncertainty
you described it as
"the time in which people half hoped, half feared this uncertainty"
the fear of becoming something other than what one was
the hope that the domesticated wouldn't transform into a beast
you called this period
"time of the angel"

you said that
"Memories can be terrifying because they reveal reality,
its relativity, its fragility, and its dissolution."

memories can be terrifying
because they show us how uncertain our present is
reality is always harsher
than our comprehension
no matter how we try to anchor it in some ideals,
meanings
or understandings

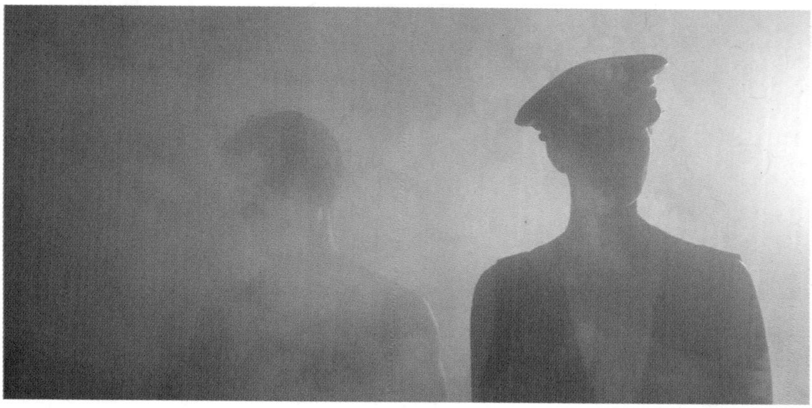

يقال أنه
عند قدوم الليل
في الغسق
يصبح كل كائن ظله
وكذلك شيئاً آخر غير نفسه
شيئاً غير مألوفا

الغسق هنا ليس فقط إشارة إلى وقت محدد من اليوم
ولكن أيضًا حالة من الغموض وعدم القدرة على التنبؤ
فترة تحول
قلت أنها «الفترة عندما الناس يخشون و يترجون في الوقت نفسه حالة عدم اليقين هذه»
الخشية من التحول إلى شيء آخر غير ما كان عليه
الترجي من المستأنس الاليف أن لا يتحول إلى وحش
سميت هذه الفترة
«زمن الملاك»

قلت أن «الذكريات يمكن أن تكون مرعبة لأنها تكشف الحقيقة ،
تكشف نسبيتها وهشاشتها وفنائها»

يمكن أن تكون الذكريات مرعبة لأنها تظهر لنا مدى اللا اليقين في حاضرنا
الواقع دائما أقسى
من فهمنا و قراءاتنا له
بغض النظر عن الطريقة التي نحاول ترسيخها
في قراءات مثالية و نموذجية

you say "there is dignity in decay"
while you're smiling back at the past and the present is crumbling down
there is something revolutionary in destroying the present
while re-invoking the past
in remembering it
and not letting it become mere "past"

Dusk and memory speak to each other
for they refuse to secure our vision
releasing information
bit
by
bit
as we move in them disoriented

I find myself in a thought
a disoriented thought
"a disoriented thought is challenging the unknown" you said
and the unknown is a forest to be cruised at dusk
the willingness to enter this thought
makes the unknown mortal
and the thought ceases to exist outside of our body
like a shadow
like an angel
you transformed the angel
into a beast
made it disobedient
challenging the norm
and uncertainty
alike

تقول «في الاضمحلال كرامة»
بينما تبتسم للماضي والحاضر ينهار
هناك شيء ثوري في تدمير الحاضر
من خلال استدعاء الماضي
تذكّره
والرفض من أن يصبح مجرد «ماض»

الغسق والذاكرة يكلما بعضهما البعض
لأنهما يرفضان تأمين رؤيتنا
فيقدما لنا المعلومات
شذره
شذره
بينما نتحرك فيهم محتارين

أجد نفسي في فكرة
فكرة محيرة
قلت أن «الفكر المحير يتحدى المجهول»
والمجهول غابة تطاف عند الغسق

الدخول في هذا الفكر
يجعل المجهول فانٍ
ليتكون الفكر خارج أجسادنا
كالظل
كالملاك
حولت الملاك الحارس
الى وحش غير مطيع
متحدٍّ للسنّة
وللايقين في الوقت نفسه

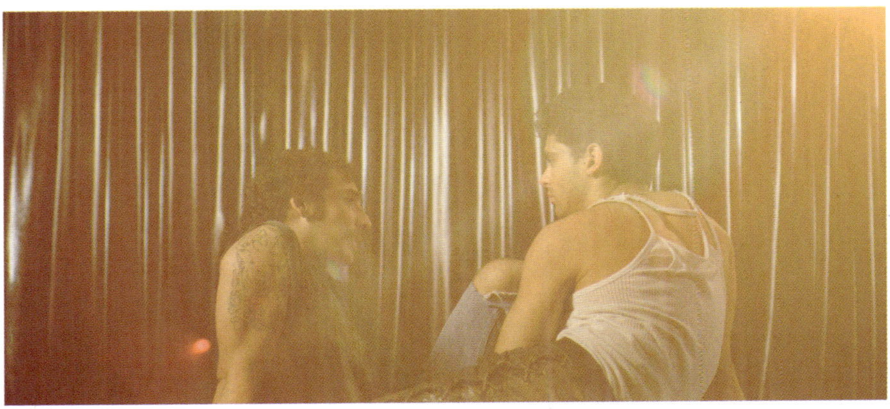

April 2020 – May 2022
Uncertainty is freedom

My body becomes the meeting point. I wake up in the morning, I look to my side, I exhale. I stretch out my arm, unfold my fingers so they reach the sunlight coming in from the window. You are gone, and my existence is cloaked in uncertainty.

I'm learning to accept uncertainty as a condition of being alive. And my will and ability to make promises is a manifestation of freedom, a freedom to show that I'm able to look into a future that I'm actively engaged in, instead of it being designed for me. You wrote "When we join our will and our promises, we create the possibility of collective action towards a shared future, linked in determination to make our vision real in the world."

I said earlier that remembrance lends itself to longing. I'm remembering not only in longing but as a commitment. We know who you are, and we won't leave you behind.

Words linger in my head as your bodies flash before me—strong, strengthened by love and loving unconditionally; fierce beings with fears, desires and flamboyance; beings that were conditioned by judgment and weren't considered as one; yet you rose above it and left us with promises to fulfil.

"I am in love."

***Epilogue: Promise*W**

I am moving with you
you take me across the distance
between the past, now
and later
replacing my days with promises
in uncertain times

you described promises as
"islands of predictability in an ocean of uncertainty"
and "fulfilling a promise,
turns that prediction into fact"

نيسان ٢٠٢٠ - أيّار ٢٠٢٢
اللّايقين حريّة

يصبح جسدي نقطة اللقاء. أستيقظ في الصباح ، أنظر إلى جانبي، أزفر. أمدّ ذراعي. أبسط أصابعي حتى تصل إلى ضوء الشمس القادم من النافذة. لقد رحلت ووجودي محتجّبٌ باللّايقين.

إنّي أتعلّم قبول اللّايقين كشرط للبقاء حياً. وإرادتي وقدرتي على تقديم الوعود هي تجلٍّ للحرية. الحرية في إظهار أنني قادر على النظر إلى مستقبل أكون جزءاً فعالاً فيه، بدلاً من أن يكون مصمماً لأجلي، لقد كتبت: «عندما ننضم إلى إرادتنا ووعودنا، فإننا نخلق إمكانية لفعل جماعي نحو مستقبل مشترك، مرتبطٌ بتصميم لجعل رؤيتنا حقيقية في الدنيا»[١٠]

لقد قلتُ سابقًا بشكلٍ أو بأخر أن التذكر يوهب نفسه للشوق. إنّي لا أتذكر فقط كي اشتاق ولكن أيضاً كوعد ، مع إخلاص والتزام بكل حيواتكم وخسارتنا. نعرف من أنتم ولن نترككم وراءنا.

ترافقني الكلمات في رأسي بينما تومض أجسادكم أمامي قوية، مدعمّة بالحب وبمحبة لامشروطة؛ كائنات شامخة مع مخاوف ورغبات و توقّد؛ كائنات كان محكوم عليها ولم يتم اعتبارها ككائنات؛ غير أنهم سموا فوق الحكم وتركوا لنا وعوداً لنحقّقها.

«أنا واقعٌ بالحب، أنا مغرم»[١١]

تتّمة : وعد[١٢]

أتنقّل أنا معك
تأخذني عبر المدى
بين الماضي، الآن
و اللاحق
تبدّل أيامي بوعود
في وقت مُربِك

وصفت الوعود
ك «جزرٍ تنبؤيّة في محيطٍ من اللا يقين»
و «الوفاء بوعد،
يحوّل هذا التنبّؤ إلى حقيقة»

Promise translates to Arabic as *Wa'd*
The word *Mawa'd*/ "date" shares the same Arabic root with *Wa'd*/"promise"
Promise / *Wa'd*
Date / *Mawa'd*

Two different words that do not only share the linguistic root,
but a moment in time:
A futurity of some sort
Two different presences in my life
your life
your death

you told me that "the king dances to distract himself"
"to distract himself" from what?
"from the burden of being alone with oneself" you answered
A king dancing by himself reaffirms the simplistic joy of dancing
yet, at the same time, shows loss of power
I keep on dancing to distract myself
but every step leads back to you
disclosing your absence
and reasserting my loss

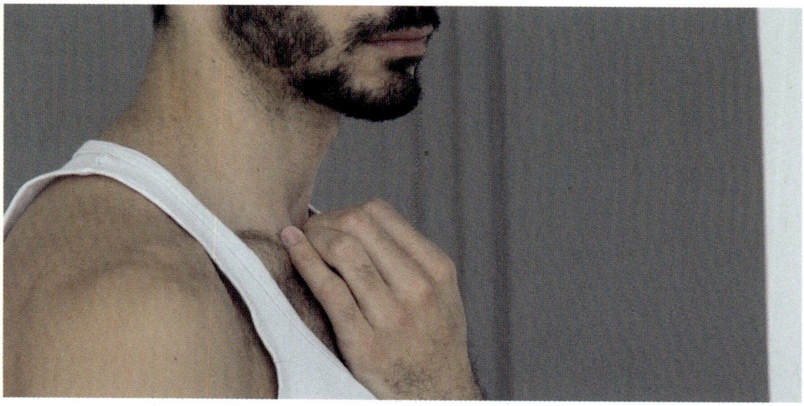

وعد و موعد يشتركان بنفس جذر الكلمة
وعد
موعد

كلمتان مختلفتان لا تشتركان بالجذر اللّغوي فقط
بل بلحظة زمنيّة
بزمن مستقبلي
حدثان مختلفان في حياتي
حياتك
موتك

أخبرتني أنَّ «الملك يرقص ليلهّي نفسه»
«ليلهّي نفسه» عن ماذا؟
«عن عِبء وحدة البقاء مع نفسه»
صورة الملك يرقص لِوحده، تظهر بساطة و بهجة الرقص
و تبيّن بالوقت نفسه فقدان السّلطة
أواصل بالرقص لأُلهّي نفسي
و لكن كل خطوة تعيدني إليك
لتكشف غيابك
و تؤكّد خسارتي

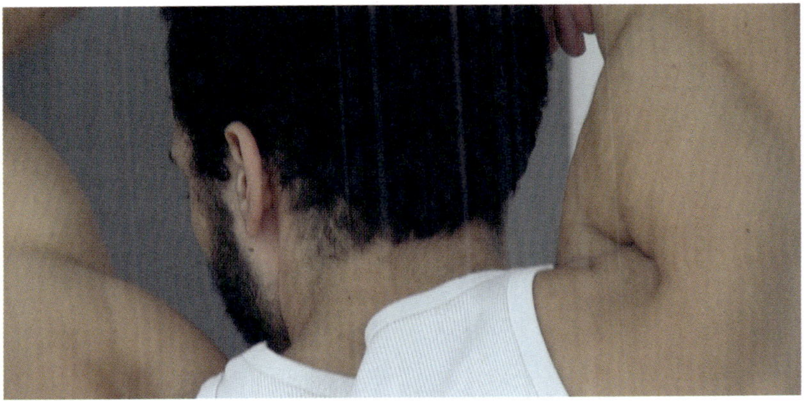

I am moving with you
you take me across the distance
between the past, now
and later
you showed me that I live in an expansive landscape
including a future that I can imagine and intend
a promise in uncertain times
a dance
for you
for your life
and the many others
we have lost

Endnotes

1 José Esteban Muñoz, *Cruising Utopia* (New York, NY: New York University Press, 2009).
2 Roland Barthes, *Mourning Diary* (New York, NY: Hill & Wang, 2010).
3 Derek Jarman, *At Your Own Risk: A Saint's Testament* (London: Vintage Edition, 1993).
4 Ibid.
5 Ibid.
6 Ibid.
7 Maja Vrvilo, dir. *Star Trek: Discovery,* season 2, episode, 11 ("Perceptual Infinity").
8 David Cronenberg, dir., *M. Butterfly,* 1993
9 Some quotes and references in *Interval: Time of The Angel* are taken from: *Night* by Etel Adnan, *Angel of History* by Rabih Alameddine, *On the Concept of History* by Walter Benjamin, and *Prisoner of Love* by Jean Genet.
10 Shoshana Zuboff, *The Age of Surveillance Capitalism* (New York, NY: Hachette, 2019).
11 Jarman, *At Your Own Risk.*
12 Some quotes and references in *Epilogue: Promise* are taken from: *The Age of Surveillance Capitalism* by Shoshana Zuboff, *The Human Condition* by Hannah Arendt, and *Pensées* by Blaise Pascal.

أتنقّل أنا معك
تأخذني عبر المدى
بين الماضي، الآن
و اللاحق
أظهرتَ أنّني أعيش بمنظور قابل للتوسّع و الامتداد
شامل لمستقبل أستطيعُ تخيّله و سعياه
وعدٌ في وقت محير
رقصة
لأجلك
لحياتك
و الحيوات الأخر الكثيرة
التي فقدناها

ملاحظات

١ خوسيه إستيبان مونيوز، طواف اليوطوبيا، مطبعة جامعة نيويورك، ٢٠٠٩.
٢ رولاند بارت، مذكرة حداد، مطبعة هيلل و وانغ، ٢٠١٠.
٣ ديريك جارمان: على مسؤليتك الخاصة،نسخة فينتج، ١٩٩٣.
٤ نفس المرجع.
٥ نفس المرجع.
٦ نفس المرجع.
٧ ستار ترك: اكتشاف، سي بي إس للتوزيع التلفزيوني، ٢٠١٩. الجزء الثاني: الحلقة الحادية عشر.
٨ مدام بترفلاي، دافيد كرونبرغ، وارنر بروس، ١٩٩٣.
٩ بعض الاقتباسات و الاستشهادات في الفاصل: زمن الملاك مأخوذة من: ليل ل إيتيل عدنان، ملاك التاريخ ل ربيع علم الدين، حول مفهوم التاريخ ل فالتر بينجامين و أسير الحب ل جان جينيه.
١٠ شوشانا زووبوف، زمن الرقابة الرأسمالية، العلاقات العامة، مجموعة كتاب هاتشت ٢٠١٩.
١١ ديريك جارمان: على مسؤليتك الخاصة،نسخة فينتج، ١٩٩٣.
١٢ بعض الاقتباسات و الاستشهادات في التتمة: وعد مأخوذة من: زمن الرقابة الرأسمالية ل شوشانا زووبوف، الشرط الإنساني ل هانا آرندت و خواطر ل بلايز باسكال.

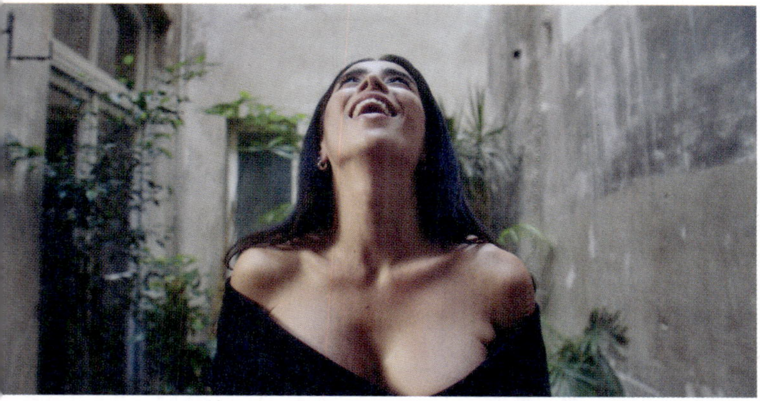

OMNISHAMBLES

DEATH OF A WOMAN

Ellen Yeon Kim

There are gritty grains in your mouth. You roll your tongue around, trying to collect them. They are between your teeth, on the lines of your gums. You've chewed gums, eaten pineapple, tried to spit it out. None of them really did much. You're not even sure why you thought eating pineapple would help. You can't help but clench your jaw. It feels as if an hourglass has burst in your mouth. Sand grains, tiny pieces of glass. It doesn't taste metallic, there must be no blood. You pass by the butcher section. Maybe a piece of raw meat would help. You imagine sand mixed with gunk sticking to the fibers of meat flesh, leaving pink juice all over your mouth, painting your gums and teeth. You spit again. Nothing. No blood, no sand, no glass. It is a little annoying but nothing new. You know it is just another episode of phantom taste. You think whether you should be much angrier or more frustrated. You're more upset that you're not. You wonder if you have been trained to be in this state of helplessness by default.

Perhaps what is real or not is not what's important. Phantom sand grains cause enough pain, they might as well be real. You know it well. You think of a memory from childhood, when you couldn't speak. It wasn't that you didn't want to ... ok, maybe you didn't, a little, in the beginning. You read *The Little Mermaid* in the closet with your headlamp. After the mermaid's voice was taken, her love seemed purer. Perhaps, even as a kid, you were fed up with the verbal. Maybe you wanted to be a mermaid. Maybe you wanted to become air bubbles in the end. Maybe you think that now is just a projection of now-you to child-you. Then you remember that you didn't read *The Little Mermaid* as a child—you were fifteen.

Jane has been in a care home for a decade now. She was a smart woman; she still is a very smart woman. It's just that her memory no longer functions as it used to. Jane once told you that the natural lifespan of humans is thirty-eight years, the same as chimpanzees. She also said that she had you when she was thirty-eight.

When Jane said that a mere thirty-eight-year lifespan seems too cruel, you weren't quite sure what she was trying to say. Did she mean it would be cruel to die after just giving birth? Or did she mean that in some way she died when you were born? Perhaps she meant that part of her was born as you, and that's cruel. Chimpanzees without medical care die at around age thirty-eight; they never develop memory-related diseases, like Alzheimer's or amnesia.

Not sure if that means you caused Jane's memory loss. You stopped calling her mum. She seems quite upset whenever you call her mum. She shouts "No!" and asks for her own mum. When you tell her you're her daughter, she acknowledges that she has a memory problem, then a moment later, she refuses to admit her mind is damaged. *I would know if you were my daughter. Mothers don't forget their daughters.*

After not visiting her for two years, you went back. You introduced yourself as a volunteer and called her by her name. She called you a very kind lady. She said she has a daughter with the same name as you.

Your mum named you Cassandra. When you were five, Jane told you she named you after a beautiful mythological prophet. You cherished your name so much you never introduced yourself. You never liked being called Cassie, Sandy, or anything other than full Cassandra. Even when kids were mocking you, you had so much pride in your name. You believed that you too would have the power of prophecy when you grew up. All you ever wanted, all you ever prayed for was to grow up and become a prophet. You hoped you would be able to warn Jane before bad things happened. You were never told that the same being who provided Cassandra with the gift of prophecy also cursed her to not have her prophecies believed by anyone. The curse came only after Cassandra rejected his sexual advances. When you read about it for the first time, you think it's pretty fucked up: weird, toxic love if love at all. You wonder now if all love is weird and somewhat toxic.

Ketchup. Chili ketchup. Ketchup with curry cause. Mayonnaise. Garlic mayonnaise. Vegan mayo. Whipped mayo.

Pause

Kimchi cup noodle. Curry cup noodle. Instant pasta cup.

Pause

Capsule coffee. Whole bean. Ground coffee. Ground filter coffee. Instant coffee with 100 *prozent* arabica. Arabica & robusta blend coffee.

Walking through a supermarket is like being in a maze. Repetitive imagery makes you lose your sense of self. You are never sure if you've dissociated or not. You wouldn't know if you lost some seconds of memory, would you? Suddenly, you smell cheap flowery shampoo. You feel a little sick. You realize you're in the aisle for body products. You weren't going to wander in here. You wonder if you've teleported there from the tea aisle. You scoff, thinking that'd be quite a gratuitous use of technology. You look at broken glass bottles of shampoo on the ground. You think it can't be that cheap if it's in a glass bottle. You feel mildly repulsed by your mammonist side. You never buy shampoo at a supermarket. Your shampoo costs more than all your other toiletries combined, which actually would be fine, if you didn't resent yourself for it.

You always had sensitive receptors for other people's voices. When you heard someone go on and on about the smell of cheap shampoo, you thought they were snobbish. You felt even nauseated when you heard that, "Anyone from a good family wouldn't make that choice." Feeling repulsed, you had to leave the place. You cowardly murmured, "Fucking classist," though it wasn't even about that, the knotted indigestible feeling, but it had to come out as something, anything.

After that, you couldn't really act against the statement, however snobby and absurd. In fact, you continue to fully cooperate with it. You think it would be easier to forgive yourself if you bought expensive shampoo just for vanity. But you know you buy it out of fear. The fear of being revealed. Another phrase, "from a good family," really got to you.

Jane never believed in domestic tranquility. She thought that was the biggest scams of all. When you were six, you had a crush on a girl with a little scar on her cheek. Although you were a little too shy to tell the girl how you felt, you told Jane that you would marry her. That got Jane horrified. She told you that when people marry, they think they've met the ultimate guardian, someone who will make everything wonderful and safe. But when they get murdered, it often turns out it is the spouse kind of whodunit story. She said, "Marriage is a scam." She said "Family is a group of people connected either biologically or by fleeting hormonal attraction with less connection to one another than a collection of well-curated objects." You were too scared to say anything then, you felt you'd done something really bad. You're not sure that's something should have been said to a little girl. Still, she might have had a point.

You rarely talk about your family to other people, but you told this story to friends as if you'd heard it from another friend. It shocked everyone so much it even gave you some kind of weird pride. Until Alex said, "Don't hang out with her. It doesn't seem like she's from a good family."

There weren't boundaries to much of anything. Jane loved weird horror and thrillers: H. P. Lovecraft, Agatha Christie, all that; her favorites were Edogawa Ranpo and Edgar Allen Poe. She loved reading them out loud to you for your bedtime stories. You grew up listening to stories of killer orangutans, of women getting killed during extramarital sadomasochistic affairs, and of a man posing as chairs to feel the weight and warmth of bodies on him. Jane read those same stories to you numerous times. One you remember quite clearly was about the murder of a beautiful cigar girl called Marie Roget. It wasn't much of a story. The case wasn't solved, and the whole story consisted of a man, the detective, Dupin, analyzing shreds of evidence: Marie Roget disappears, her corpse is found in the river, no one knows why or how. The story never tells you what happened, or if Dupin's theories are correct. After the story, Jane would always make a short comment, usually one sentence.

> It's based on an actual case.
>
> It wasn't really murder.
>
> It was about a twenty-year-old girl in Manhattan, Mary Rogers.
>
> Her murder was in every newspaper, just because those journalists were in love with her. It was a personal matter to them.
>
> It wasn't really murder.
>
> Maybe it was murder, in a way. Her death happened after a bungled abortion.
>
> Apparently there was a flood of tourists after all that, to the place in the river where her corpse was found.

You shake your head like you're shaking off the memory, and look down at your shopping cart: you find three knives and a blue plastic kids' chair. It is still too sandy in your mouth, but swallowing seems to help. You remember that some animals eat sand for digestion. Is the chicken one of them? You want to get cheese from the deli, only to realize you can't really make sound with your voice. You think it is a twisted curse that comes with your name, Cassandra. Instead of not being believed, you're simply not heard. You think that to compare the prophecy of the rise and fall of an empire to ordering a block of cheese might be a stretch. You scoff again, trouble is trouble.

You think of Jane's clear voice. Unlike you who often can't even utter a word, your mum had the clearest voice even when she mumbled. Jane often sat by the window, pale and clean skin reflecting rays of lights, and mumbled interesting stories, while you crouched, unable to utter "mum." One day she talked about Mary Roger again. Jane talked as if she had lived in that era. She told you that when women experienced "female trouble," they would pick up a newspaper, and look for the advertisements for things like "uterine tonic," "an application of a female wash," "female regulator," "rose injections," and "cathartic pills." The ads claimed to alleviate private difficulties and remove obstructions.

You shake your head again, mouthing "obstructions." You didn't know what it meant then. Or did you? The fact that you remember all that at this point might mean you did. After all, you also heard stories as a teen: your friend selling her clothes to make enough money to pay the secret physician who picked her up blindfolded. Before a deep breath, you wonder if an unwanted pregnancy isn't a bit like horrible indigestion.

It is affecting you now. It wasn't now-you but another-you. Or is it now-you putting sand in your mouth shushing, gagging, leaving another-you voiceless?

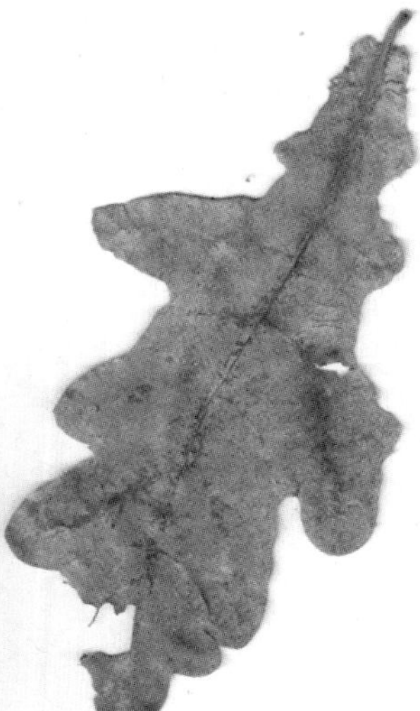

(THE PAINTING OF) STEPHEN KING'S SURVIVOR TYPE

Vera Palme

Upon arrival to this tale, the crescent of alarm draws shut.

A shower of gulls curtains the view mocking the rise and tide of what the water does. Their black wings drone froth and phlegm through turquoise pipes of breath and rear back. Systematically, as if satisfaction isn't a question anymore, orange darts bore purpose, more of life and pirouettes.

The heavy and the prose dance.

Duel the mind as the center. The gulls fly.

Knowing all too well to see the current dance is to see and not to worry or curtain-call a damn, but to perpetuate and collect the debt in straws and display blood with it, if that's what's expected.

The tale itself remains.

When flatness abrupted reality and the bend of it, it gestured toward a democracy of sensation and total availability. Everything was light, like hope, into sight, almost painfully gray and confusing. Claiming might and ushering lust to stay free at the fringe of the island, hair and blanket in the virgin of the morning. Strained eyes aching in sockets, pounding the membrane.

The castaway recognized himself as the center and that was the truth, and there was nothing else. After too much for too long.

What could have been done to prevent it?

Perhaps nothing had assisted in its coming, through the storms of drag returning. Because what but plot is left to bring about the darkness as thick as that of nights,

a hunger, a hard thunder

following cracks of light without anything to resonate with. For moments at a time the lonely formation would rise, glistening and clear, out of the daunting flat void, towering and becoming apparent as elevated and solid and indeed lonely.

Gone, the memory of land, vague from the bottom of the reef and with sundown nothing stood but fire from driftwood, damp steam and curdle of the sweat of man. It had all become part of his reality as much as the absence of sound, but that of water and wind and the man's paralysis. Since then the nights dragged all other color further out to sea. Out of reach. Away.
The boat has sunk.

In recalling the current, the thought would come down hard on the island and become body. If only sight or soul. And with that body pragmatism ordered life and came for it.

The horizon flatlined in the far distance which was so there, there was nothing but it. Ignorance overwhelmed with its calm white glove. Scrapped the clownish pale powdered gestures that called for kindness, as hunger dimmed and reached for the bag on the rim of the tub to dip the bloody finger rubbing gums. Red and perhaps keen.

The ease followed slowly but still was remarkable. It held the call and eventually the catastrophe and practiced for what afterbirth would be if life was still archean.

Live. At hand.

But Fiction is the angry

pup of Myth, vile and bored and easy to seduce. To conclude.

Dreamless sleep was, after all, the only other he could rely on. There the sense of existence and the motion of blur was not troubling and nothing shocked the spherical pressure to surf. The flickering, the thin shiver inside, nothing.

A still image.

The soft snowlike quality coming over the human steadily, for a time, covered everything and now only this bright, disembodied emptiness remained consistent, plain, even. As if with eyes closed.

The barren top of the island lay finally still, the Pacific was.

Time stretched and shriveled without sense. We know it and so did the human.

All the ways in which a clever man possesses himself. And while this dawned, the sun rose awfully slow and the water and the rock and the stretch of life were under the spell of a gray drizzle. Soft and almost warm.

The plan had taken abstract shape over days, almost mathematical and rich in its calculated value.

To part what harms and eat what lives.

The simple incision cut the white matter and scrubbed away insanity. The force-mongering snort flamed the peace. The ice spread and a serene clarity, irked and impatient.

He had better done to sing but to prevail. Gurgling fountains applauded his rush of action and trust in the decision being granted.

It is too easy, friend, it's Fiction dear, it's rapture and nothing but a record of intent.

The human saw parallels and fantasms of parallels and the identity of man. With the pouring of blood, love welled up, exited, and coated him in want. Fresh and warm, a rinlet sprung the broken, off-colored joint to pool the unhinged heel. Made its way towards the water and spilled a small cliffed boulder dripping.

The rosy shine of the severed, mature like raisins after summer.

And just as innocent.

And it could be that there was no end to his discoveries of life and that everything was and was finally total.

The blanket soaked, deserted sleep and salt. The severed limb was less heavy than expected. How the rock lay in ripples thereunder.

You are inside.

Inside you are.

The nakedness that had the man was what a late hibiscus blossom sheds. It was his will and at his hand. The economy, a fallacy of day. His the only to employ, the only to prolong.

Half dried, it melted in his mouth like flakes of salt flowers, silently feeding the rock and the water and the human himself.

Before they fell, his last boundaries flared up and burned white towards the sky. A thin cream froth of belch.

Theoretically there was the possibility of thought, not just the obvious of delusion, of the forbidden and of sin. But the persistent idea of independence, finally. Unhindered self-love. A kind of satisfaction hitherto unknown. But everything was and was Fiction.

The want grew warm and true and willing until his teeth were met with the resistance of an unnamed pain and of a beauty rolling in, of the abhorrent churning the man whose decision to eat is the decision to tell.

And steadily greed was replaced by an itch.

Resist it, and your soul grows sick with longing.

To detour is always a good idea, to experience the butter of the modern man. Long days saved in shades kept safe from the fires of gangrene. The fidelity of his veins, more than a moment, grieving resistance. At least he did not have to share.

He bled out of his flatbed with gratitude.

Surely more of life was still at hand.

This, the only canny answer to the hunger, the pride to succumb to it is nothing. But thinking about what will impress through deprivation and the self in tide. To reinstall. To persevere.

The sun came clear and with it rose the urge to seek silence for the itch.

Primitive and boiling it held the human's every waking thought.

Pain would have to be a Person. A name.

Terror is with the return from the tale and tells the horror of the earthenware. The candor keeps the language wet and not a drop of it was spilled in vain. The word turned, support so thin it almost isn't anymore, but fear of shore, and only. As if the mind was still with it.

The human's tongue was swollen thick in life.

Finally the itch had found the appetite and there was nothing else.

Yes yes yes!

I do I do I do!

cry gulls as if it all was, the end of what the word can be. It would. And then would flame the lust that saves and circle steadily their doom.

if We understood

that EVERYTHING is PART

of the TOTAL process

We would understand

that being

means becoming

IMAGE AND TEXT CREDITS

p. 14

Julia Hayward, *Conscious Knocks Unconscious*, 1977. Courtesy of Electronic Arts Intermix (EAI), New York.

p. 21–25

This text is constructed from excerpts from workshops and conversations between Jasmina and Kamila Metwaly during the research project *Voice of the Wind is not a Metaphor*, as part of the Berlin Artistic Research Grant Programme 2020–21, with special thanks to Rike Franke. The voice workshops were conducted by Ute Wasserman via Zoom and in person together with a group of participants in the years 2020–21. The conversations and workshops were turned into a public event in September 2020 at Haus Der Statistik in Berlin.

p. 27–35

Georgia Sagri, "Practice" and excerpts from "IASI" were originally published in Georgia Sagri, *Stage of Recovery* (Brussels and London: Divided 2021).

p. 36–53

Katrin Mayer's essay builds upon her exhibition
Flurfunker:innen How to speak the Corridor.
Localities: cloister/corridor of Kunsthalle Osnabrück,
November 6, 2021 – February 27, 2022,
www.flurfunkerinnen.org.
Design/coding for website and design for essay: Anna Cairns.

Supported by
Berlin Artistic Research Grant Programme/gkfd

For her site-specific work, Mayer often uses archival research and engages with local histories in order to reflect and question the historicity of a place in the present. She was invited to exhibit at Kunsthalle Osnabrück, which, built around 1300, was originally a monastery. She thematized the change of the former cloister to the corridor of today's Kunsthalle, now led by two queer feminist directors. Formerly used for procession and praying, the corridor is now an exhibition site and a place for informal encounters and exchanges between staff and visitors, a place that connects and activates the institution. The exposed (internet) cables under the ceiling also execute and visualize this function.

Mayer developed two site-specific, feminist textures: one is embedded in the corridor on-site at Kunsthalle Osnabrück, and the second exists as a dedicated website. The work travels back to the Middle Ages and interweaves Christine de Pizan's utopian vision of a "City of Ladies," Hildegard von Bingen's invented secret language "Lingua Ignota," images of the stonemason Sabina von Steinbach building a church, with other past and present materials relating to the institution. Mayer created one visual track and four audio tracks, which constellate an alternative, feminist-speculative herstoriography of the cloister.

p. 76–99

C. S. Tolan's essay "Sibyl's Primes" is part of ongoing research by Tolan into the poetics and phenomenology of whispered speech, cryptography, and gossip. Tolan's research includes the creation of a whispering AI voice companion and the composition of plays and stories for the companion to perform. For documentation of the AI and more information, see Tolan's website https://pendent.world.

p. 101–112

Mark von Schlegell's "Simone Azul" was first published digitally by PAPIER collé SIMONE WEIL.
Den Kollectiv, Nuremberg, April 2021.

p. 114, 228, 291

Michèle Graf & Selina Grüter, *Pocket Liners*, 2021–ongoing. Cut-and-pasted printed receipt paper on graph paper, 16.8 x 25 cm.

Pocket Liners are composed by gathering words from purchase receipts. These short texts reflect our research on the use and development of language within a capitalist social formation, reevaluating the words from this found vocabulary.

p. 131–136, 165–167, 193–195, 219–221

Monilola Olayemi Ilupeju, "Eat Your Calf," "Haircut," "Maybe It's Time," and "The Lawn" are excerpts from the first edition of *Earnestly* (Berlin: Archive Books and Galerie im Turm, 2022).

"The Lawn" was commissioned for the exhibition *Your Horizon Has Limits Even Holes*, curated by Markus and Michaela Meise, at Scherben, Berlin, 2021.

p. 243–249

Annie Ernaux, "Excerpt from *The Years*," translated by Alison L. Strayer (New York: Seven Stories Press, 2017 / London: Fitzcarraldo Editions, 2020)

p. 250–253, 256–258

Enad Marouf, stills from *Thikra*, 2021, HD video, 16 min. 3D renders of specific sites of Damascus developed with 3D artist Filip Setmanuk from Marouf's memory.

p. 259 — Eren Demirel, Samuel Pereira, and Tiran in Enad Marouf, *Time of The Angel*, 2022, HD video, 15 min.

p. 260, 261, 265 — Eren Demirel, Samuel Pereira in Enad Marouf, *Time of The Angel*, 2022, HD video, 15 min.

p. 262 — Franziska Aigner, Samuel Pereira in Enad Marouf, *Time of The Angel*, 2022, HD video, 15 min.

p. 268, 269 — Lucas Rodrigues in Enad Marouf, *Promise*, HD video 8 min. 2021.

p. 272 — Alyha Love in Enad Marouf, *Time of The Angel*, 2022, HD video, 15 min.

Sybil's Mouths
A Pure Fiction Publication

Published by Sternberg Press

Editors: Rosa Aiello, Ellen Yeon Kim, Erika Landström, Luzie Meyer, Mark von Schlegell

Proofreading: Ames Gerould
Design: Ellen Yeon Kim
Cover art: Aislinn McNamara
Printing: KOPA, Lithuania
ISBN: 978-3-95679-644-9

This book is a continuation of the exhibition "Shifting Theatre: Sybil's Mouths," Kölnischer Kunstverein, February 12 – March 6, 2022.

Distributed by The MIT Press, Art Data, Les presses du Réel, and Idea Books

With the generous support of ARKO Arts Council Korea, and Kunststiftung NRW
Special thanks to Joe Aiello & Ann McLaughlin, Saud Al-Zaid, Miriam Bettin, Lucas Casso, Frederick Courtright, Nikola Dietrich, Fanta Milan, Rozsa Farkas, Galerie Drei, Ames Gerould, Charlotte Jackson, Antonia Nolte, Corina Reininghaus, Andreas Ripper, Eleanor Weber, and Camilla Wills.

Sternberg Press
71–75 Shelton Street
London WC2H 9JQ
www.sternberg-press.com

ARTS COUNCIL KOREA

Kunststiftung NRW

Wit pass'd through thee no longer is the same,
as meat digested takes a diff'rent name ...

Alexander Pope

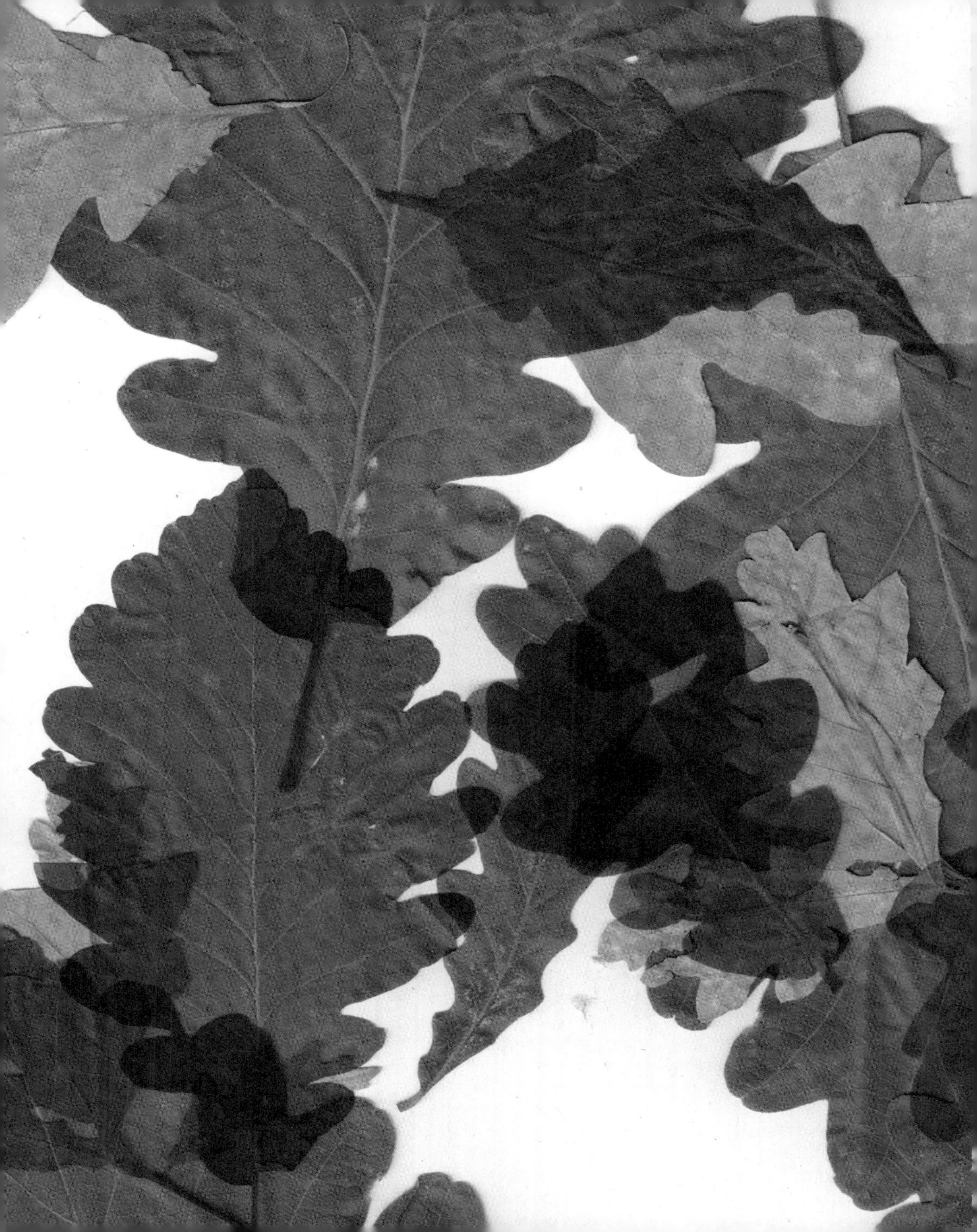